WHERE THE PAVEMENT ENDS

BARBARA SAVAGE
MEMORIAL
★ WINNER ★
AWARD
Miles from Nowhere

WHERE THE PAVEMENT ENDS

One Woman's
Bicycle Trip
Through
Mongolia,
China & Vietnam

Erika Warmbrunn

THE MOUNTAINEERS BOOKS

Published by
The Mountaineers Books
1001 SW Klickitat Way, Suite 201
Seattle, WA 98134

First edition: first printing 2001. second printing 2001, third printing 2001

Published simultaneously in Great Britain by Cordee, 3a DeMontfort Street, Leicester, England, LE1 7HD

Manufactured in the United States of America

Project Editor: Amy K. Allin
Developmental Editor: Mark Long
Copyeditor: Kris Fulsaas
Cover Design: Helen Cherullo
Book Design: Ani Rucki
Layout: Alice C. Merrill
Mapmaker: Michael Friel
All photographs by the author

Cover photographs: *The author's bicycle, leaving Irkutsk, Russia*
Frontispiece: *Horseman on the Mongolian steppe*

Cataloging-in-Publication Data is on record at the Library of Congress.

THANKS TO

Becky Barnett and Ann Bernheisel,
without whom I would not have made it to the plane.

Everyone who took the time to write letters.
They mean more than you know.

Greg Palmer and Renée Wayne Golden,
who believed that I could write a book.

Grace and Jim and Alice and Bob,
whose roofs gave me a place to start writing.

Ten Eyck and Leslie Swackhamer,
whose generosity and dining room table made it possible for me to finish,
and who are truly the patron saints of this book.

Frank Corrado,
who had time and wisdom when I needed it.

And now to Peter,
for putting up with me; for everything.

But above all, to the people I met along the way from Irkutsk to Saigon.
They are the life and landscape of this story,
and I hope that I have done justice to their hospitality
and overwhelming generosity.

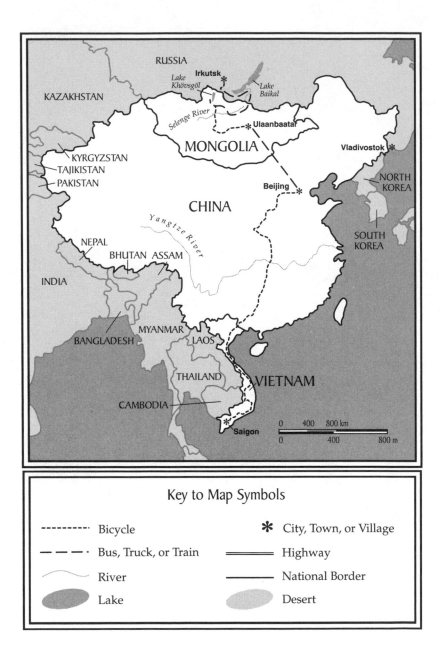

Key to Map Symbols

- - - - - - - -	Bicycle	✳	City, Town, or Village
– – – – ·	Bus, Truck, or Train	═══════	Highway
∼∼∼∼	River	────────	National Border
⬭	Lake	⬭	Desert

Contents

A Note to the Reader

Because the countries visited in this narrative use the metric system, all distances and other measurements herein are given in metric units. For conversion, see the Appendix at the back of the book.

In transliterating Russian, Mongolian, Chinese, and Vietnamese, I have attempted to adhere to consistent, standarized systems, but have made some concessions to conform to widespread usage, and some to reflect local pronunciation.

Prologue
Throwing Myself at an Idea

A circle in the center of the roof is open to the sky. The opaque winter dawn above it is impossibly devoid of color. I am lying on the floor, my sleeping bag covered by a thick quilt. Next to me, last night's dung fire is a pile of ashes in a cold stove, but the bottoms of my thick woolen socks are scorched where I held them too long against the hot metal when the flames were still alive. Behind me, a family of four is asleep in the home's only bed, a six-year-old boy and his infant brother cuddled between their young parents. I know nothing about them, not even their names. But last night, arriving out of the dark and cold, I asked—in the few words of their language that I have learned—if I could sleep in their home. I lie still, trying not to make any noise. The longer they sleep, the longer I can stay inside my warm cocoon. Without moving, I glance over to where my bicycle leans against the curved side of the tiny felt home. The snow and ice that were clumped in her wheels have melted into little puddles on the floor, but her thick tires are still clogged with mud. Her chainwheels are a mess. Her blue panniers are dingy brown. Spots of neon green peek through scratches in the gray automotive primer that I spray-painted on her back in another world, where my floor was carpeted, where there was electricity and running water.

The circle of light is growing brighter, and soon I hear the family stirring. Once the sun has risen, there is work to do. Outside in the crisp morning, we wash our hands and faces quickly in brutally cold water. All around us, desolate, glittering grassland stretches as far as the eye can see. Two other homes huddle close by, but beyond this tiny enclave of three nomadic felt dwellings, there are no powerlines, no fences, no signs of a road; there is nothing but untamed space. I have never been so in the middle of nowhere, the sensation of lostness made greater by the humans eking out an existence than if the wilderness were pure wildness. The other families rose even

Hauling hay, south of Xian, China

earlier than we did, and two women are already smoothly milking their cows, glancing up furtively at me. The woman in whose home I slept hands me a stool and a pail and points to her cow. "I am very bad," I warn her, but dutifully sit on the three-legged wooden stool, squeeze the cold metal pail between my knees, and reach for a teat. The animal sidesteps, and as I try to move with her, the pail slips. The three women are watching, trying not to giggle. I jam the pail back into place and try again, pulling hard and getting a skinny little squirt of white before the cow suddenly stomps a hoof. I jerk back, startled, and the pail clatters to the ground. We are all laughing now, as the young woman picks up the pail and shoos me off the stool so she can get the work done.

When the chores are finished and the mutton-noodle soup left over from dinner has been reheated and eaten for breakfast, it is time for me to go. I give the woman two candles. I give her little boy a pack of gum. She makes sure I understand that her family returns to the same place every year, so I can find them if I come back. I check my bicycle's tires and tighten the straps holding my sleeping bag to her rear rack. My bicycle is ugly, but she is tough, and in memory of what she is beneath the dull gray primer, I call her Greene. One of the other women steps out of her home. Her face is deeply wrinkled, her eyes narrow pools of vivid black. She holds a ladle full of fresh milk. She says something that I do not understand, but I say *"Bayarlalaa* ("Thank you")," and she nods, then with a flick of her hand she throws the milk into the air above me. The white drops splatter down onto my head, onto my shoulders, onto Greene's mud-spattered panniers, the milk mixing with the dirt. I do not duck or close my eyes. It is a good-luck wish for the traveler. The women point me in the direction of the road. I find a vague dirt track in the prairie and follow it straight east. It is warm now, almost hot in the sun reflecting off the snow. A hunter growls by on a motorcycle. Then, as he lies prone in the prairie, his rifle trained on a distant marmot hole, Greene and I pass him. We play leapfrog for hours, bumping over rocks, crunching through ice and snow, wading through freezing streams, until in the early afternoon a black snake of pavement wells up on the horizon. Like a deep gulp of oxygen after staying too long beneath the waves. Like a western plane from a Soviet airport. Like a language I know after one that I don't.

·

I wanted to run away. Far away. Drawn by its thriving theater community, I had moved to Seattle after college, ignoring my Russian major to pursue a life in the footlights. Five years later, I knew that I had failed. The only jobs I had had in the theater in two years had been as the interpreter for visiting Russian companies. I was working in a travel bookstore, hiking in the summer and skiing in the winter, but never setting foot inside a theater unless I had a ticket in my hand. I went to auditions and was not called back. I went to work and stared at maps and imagined getting so far away that it would be like starting over again. I had traveled a lot, by some people's standards; by others', I had barely begun. I had made beds in a nursing home in Berlin, tended bar on the French Riviera, and gone to Mass in Krakow because in 1984 the church was the only place open at 5:00 A.M. when the train pulled in. A friend and I had rented bicycles in Ireland, bungee-corded our backpacks to their rear racks, and spent a week tooling around the south coast, making tents out of our rain ponchos and sleeping on the cliffs. I had studied in Moscow, played the heroine in a little movie shot in the Caucasus, and walked out of Georgia into eastern Turkey. But I had never been to South America or Africa or Asia, and to make things new, you have to keep going farther and farther away from what you know.

The bookstore sold maps of Botswana, Delhi, and Antarctica. We sold phrasebooks for Arabic, Swahili, and Tagalog. We sold guides to traveling the French canals by barge, crossing Russia by train, and hiking the Andes. There are very few corners left on this planet where you are not following in everyone else's footsteps. I wanted, once, to trace my own path across a land as yet untrampled by hordes of tourist feet. I wanted to lose myself in unmapped landscapes and to meet the people who inhabited them. I wanted uncompromising, boundless space, and nature's reminders of how minute a human being is. I wanted the kind of empty, demanding landscape that some people call lifeless or inhospitable and that fills me with a visceral sense of freedom. Mongolia was one of the few countries not in the title of any guidebook we carried. I didn't know much about the vast north Asian land, but I imagined untamed expanses of steppe rolling to the horizon. I imagined puffy white yurts nestled in the middle of nowhere. I imagined hardy little horses running free across desolate stretches of grassland unmarked by the twentieth century. Mongolia sounded like freedom to me.

Four years earlier, in Munich, Germany, on my way to buy a train ticket to France, I had decided, on a whim, to buy a bicycle instead. When I started pedaling, I thought I knew where I was going. I thought I knew France and Germany pretty well, but over the next five weeks, my department-store bicycle's two wheels suddenly opened up the lands' remote corners—the farmhouses, the mountains, the villages where the trains don't stop. So now, as I stared at a map of Asia, I knew that where I wanted to go lay beyond Mongolia's dozen scattered towns and cities. I knew that I wanted to move freely, unconstrained by the routes and schedules of infrequent and unreliable public transportation. But I am not a hard-core cyclist. The charms of intense off-road travail are lost on me. I doubted that a bicycle was the optimal mode of travel in a country three times the size of France with fewer than a thousand kilometers of paved road and not one single bicycle shop. I moved on to a better idea: buy a horse—Mongolia's age-old form of transportation. But staring at that map of Asia, I could not help but see that there, not really so very far away from Mongolia, was Vietnam. White sand beaches, the inevitable mystique borne of war, and, in 1993, the attraction of an until recently inaccessible land. If I got to Mongolia, I might as well keep going. My finger traced a line across the paper, from Russia's Lake Baikal south to Saigon. I had no particular interest in China, never had had, but there it was, smack-dab between the other two, so across China I would go. I had no doubt that a horse was *not* the optimal mode of travel in China and Vietnam. A bicycle was.

So I had a plan. Or at least an idea, a fantasy floating around in the back of my mind. Then one day the phone rang and a man I had never met, a friend of a friend, offered me a job as interpreter for his theater's tour to Vladivostok, in Far Eastern Russia. Russia *east* of Siberia. They would be leaving in less than two months. Vladivostok, all things being relative, was just around the corner from Mongolia. This was as close as I was ever going to get for free, but a recent audition had gone well and it was a great part. If I got it, I would not say no, not even for Mongolia. A few evenings later, the phone rang again. They had cast the thin, beautiful blonde who could sing.

I started applying for visas. I started packing my apartment into cardboard boxes. I started bicycle shopping. I knew my trusty road bike was not up to the trip. I knew I needed fat, knobby tires. I knew I needed a frame that would withstand months of brutal abuse. That was all I knew. I tripped into cycle shops and asked, "If you were riding across Mongolia, what would you ride?" It was like a metaphor, "Mongolia." The middle of nowhere. The back of beyond. Someplace far, far away. Nobody thought that I actually meant Mongolia, the country. Almost nobody knew that there still *was* a country called Mongolia, that it was not part of China, that it was not part of Russia, that time and history had not wiped it off the map altogether. I rode bicycles up and down Seattle streets trying to imagine rocky, sandy, muddy grassland. With five weeks to go, I settled on a neon-green mountain bike with the fattest, knobbiest tires in the store and drop handlebars for my weak wrists. I strapped on an odometer and calibrated it to run in kilometers. For the next eight months, a mile would be an irrelevant measurement—all maps, road signs, and directions from passersby would be figured in kilometers, a distance equal to roughly ⅝ of a mile. I rode my new bicycle home, dubbed her "Greene," and drowned her in a can of automotive primer. Then I put her in a box and got on a plane to Russia.

After three weeks in Vladivostok, the American theater company flew back to California, and Greene and I aimed west toward Irkutsk. As the plane tilted over the vast stretches of southeastern Siberia, I could not believe where I was going. There had been heady days of anticipation and quaking days of terror. One minute, life was unalloyed exhilaration and I was pure courage. I could not wait to be on the road—just me and Greene and the weather and the wonderful, terrifying freedom of never having to be anywhere ever again. The next minute, there was a churning in my stomach. I wanted some really good reason to stop before I started. I wanted to burst into tears and flee home to an easy Seattle summer of baseball games and hiking trips. I knew nothing about Mongolia, and little more about self-sufficient bicycle travel. I was throwing myself at an idea, leaving everything behind and heading blindly into I knew not what. I was running away.

But I was also running toward something. Ahead of me lay the unknowns that are the soul and purpose of a journey. I was completely intimidated, and I was absolutely at peace. I was at the beginning of an adventure: Tomorrow was a mystery, and that mystery was terrifying. It was also the most enticing thing in the world.

The rich smell of earth filled the air, and the warmth of late summer evening hung in the twilight. It was August 15, 1993, in southern Siberia and I was on my way to Saigon. I had just pedaled the first fifty kilometers. Seven thousand nine hundred and fifty-some to go. I had left Irkutsk at noon, as wobbly on my overloaded bicycle as if my first set of training wheels had just been removed. Flowering green fields alternated with dark forest. People smiled and waved. People stared, Soviet, expressionless. I felt like I was five years old again, my new red bicycle barely under control, everybody watching me. Late in the afternoon, I turned down a dirt road toward a village. A woman leaned against a tractor talking to her neighbor. I stopped to ask where I could find a hotel. She said there was no hotel in her village. She said she didn't think there was a hotel in the next village, either. She said her name was Galya and that I was welcome to spend the night in her home. She made up a bed for me in her attic. She handed me a towel and sent me across the road to bathe in the river. She stuffed fresh peppers for our dinner. Then she wanted to know who I was.

I am not married and I have no kids, I told her, beginning with the Russian questions about husbands and children and parents. I live alone in a rented apartment thousands of kilometers away from my mother and father. I have one sister. She lives thousands of kilometers away in another direction. Then I moved on to the American questions, about work and school, because I am American and that is how I know to explain myself. I studied Russian at university. I tried to be an actress but ended up working in a bookstore. I have lived in Paris. I have driven a car straight across America. I have seen the Grand Canyon, the Mediterranean, and the Midnight Sun. And now I need to go farther, because Europe is not enough anymore.

To Galya, Europe was already a lot. She had dreamed of traveling when she was younger, but she got married, she had kids, her mother was in poor health, and besides, she shrugged, "You weren't allowed abroad in those days." We were sitting on the front steps now, sipping sweet, hot tea after dinner, and Galya's resigned sigh was still hanging in the air when a figure appeared out of the dusk. Decades of daily work on the land echoed in the old woman's still-powerful frame. She couldn't believe I was American. She didn't believe it at first, then it made her laugh, a deep, smoky laugh from a toothless mouth. She laughed hard and touched my arm with her callused hands, then looked hard into my eyes and explained that life in Russia used to be much better. "There was none of this inflation. People wanted to work."

Galya suggested quietly that freedom was important.

"Freedom to what?" barked her neighbor. "For women to wander around the streets drunk, for a few people to get really rich?"

"There was all of that before," Galya countered gently, almost to herself. "We just didn't see it. Drunken women and millionaires. It was all always there, we just didn't know."

"There used to be order," the woman retorted. I thought I felt a shudder run down Galya's back. But her neighbor's face was the face of many older people in Russia, people who had truly believed that they were building a glorious future, that they were part of the greatest system ever, only to wake up one day to the news that their lives' commitment had been a sham and a lie, and that the rest of the world was laughing at them. Everything that had been a given was gone. Their pensions no longer covered their rent. Their children were being fired from jobs they had thought were theirs for life. Their grandchildren were growing up in a world they could never understand, a world that was nothing like the one they had been promised.

A lithe, tan girl in cutoff blue jeans whose family lived somewhere down the road had come to sit on the steps with us too. Katya was fifteen, only three years younger than I had been the first time I had come to Russia, which had been the Soviet Union then, encased in the ice and snow of Communism, the Cold War, and the northern winter. It was a place where you learned quickly to think about the world in a way in which you never thought about it as a teenager in Southern California. There was danger there. Profound and dark and real. But I didn't understand that yet, not in any concrete way. Danger was theoretical and novel and romantic. So I took an exiled, dissident painter's book to his parents in Moscow, and I wasn't even nervous going through customs. I watched the old couple unwrap the book, unfold a page of newspaper with a photograph of their son, watched them struggle with the unfamiliar letters, unable myself, my Russian not yet nearly good enough, to translate for them. I saw the hunger in their eyes, because here was a little piece of him and he was inconceivably far away, and the distance was not about the kilometers.

And I began to understand.

And I was careful when I left, the artist's father walking me quickly down the damp stairwell—silent, because the neighbors were everywhere and I was a stranger with an accent—and out into the snowy Moscow night. Katya had been five years old then, and by the time she was ten, the world was a different place. I asked if she remembered not being able to say what she wanted to whom she wanted. "I can say what I want," she shrugged. "I mean, I wouldn't say certain things certain ways to my teachers or my parents, because I might get in trouble."

Galya looked at me. "She has no idea what you're talking about." There was a long, silent pause. Then she added, "I guess that's good."

The next afternoon I crossed the Trans-Siberian railroad tracks and stopped in front of a green picket fence to ask for water to fill my empty bottles. An hour later, Greene was locked up in the yard behind the picket fence and I was in the forest, searching for mushrooms with a white-haired hunter and his nine-year-old granddaughter. Sunlight filtered through the trees, and the dying leaves of early autumn crunched beneath our feet. He called the land the taiga and even though it was not the almost impenetrable forest that is the true Russian taiga, the word was enough to conjure strains of *Peter and the Wolf* in my head. That night, after a hearty dinner punctuated by the inevitable shots of vodka, his wife and I crossed the yard to the *banya,* where she hefted bucket after bucket of hot, steaming water over my head while the woodstove roared and candlelight flickered on the wooden walls. I could imagine nothing more quintessentially Russian.

The following morning, I dropped down out of the hills to the shores of Earth's largest lake. Home to more than 1,000 species of flora and fauna found nowhere else on the planet, Lake Baikal spread in an unrippled mirror to the horizon. The highway continued east around the water. I turned southwest, down a thin, asphalt ribbon meandering toward Mongolia.

That night I ate dinner in a tiny earthen-floored kitchen where a young woman boiled potatoes and reheated homemade noodles while countless flies buzzed above us in the hot, dim air, and her brother leaned against the door frame staring at me. He was drunk. I had not realized that when I had stopped at the village store to ask if there was somewhere to spend the night and he had invited me home. All the men were drunk, I realized now, but the women were in charge. His mother shooed him away from the kitchen and poured me a dish of fresh berry jam. Outside, two little boys with broad moon faces chased each other across the dusty yard. The whole family was dark-skinned and almond-eyed. I had passed into Buryatia. Like their Mongolian cousins to the south, the Buryats were traditionally a nomadic people who practiced shamanism and spoke a Mongolian language. In the late seventeenth century, the Russians annexed the Buryat lands from China, and by the 1990s, the Buryats constituted only a quarter of the region's population. But as the family's guttural language floated around me, I felt the nearness of Asia. There was nothing at all familiar about the sounds.

The road continued southwest, white birch trunks extrapolating their colonnades toward infinity until they were swallowed by the deep forest darkness. They were beautiful, they were something out of a woodcut fairy tale, and I didn't give a damn because I was tied heavily to the Earth, held down under the heat, trapped by the weight in my panniers, by my own inadequate body. I knew about the flying abandon of a bicycle, legs pumping, body and wheels skimming above the land, and this wasn't it. I had not trained for this expedition. It had been an idea, and now it was a reality for which my body had not been warned. I climbed hills 100 meters at a time, stopping every other minute to gulp down water and breathe hard until I could breathe easy again. A rhythmic clunking ground from the rear derailleur at every rotation of the pedals. I tried to ignore it. I willed it just to go away or to fix itself. I had no idea what to do.

The first time a tire had gone *pop-shhhhh* as I pedaled across southern France four years earlier, I had had no tools, no patching material, and no idea how to fix a flat tire. For five hours of a hot, sticky afternoon I sat in a retired judge's garden while he scrounged a long-since grown grandchild's repair kit from the depths of his garage and we attempted cluelessly to fix the tube. In the next town I found a bicycle shop and bought a patch kit, and quickly became proficient at using it, but that was all that had ever broken, so that was all I had ever learned to fix. Sitting in the middle of a dusty road in Siberia, I read my bicycle repair book. The chain was out of alignment with the derailleur. That much I could see. I read about set-stop screws. I moved one carefully half a turn. Nothing. Another half turn. Nothing. I moved it back. I tried the other direction. Nothing. I contemplated the difference between the chain being out of alignment with the derailleur and the derailleur being out of alignment with the chain. I opened the book again and read, "Derailleur adjustment is often a cable tension problem." I chose a seemingly logical cable and gave it an arbitrary twist— and watched the derailleur move right into alignment! I was all alone in Siberia with my bicycle and that was fine because I was Bicycle Repairwoman Extraordinaire.

I leaned back and glanced around. It looked like Switzerland, the deep-green valley, the river rumbling somewhere in the forest, the cowbells chiming on the wind. But I was worlds away from cuckoo clocks and nameless bank accounts.

A little old woman carrying a basket of freshly picked berries emerged from the trees. "Hi, where are you going?" she called out in Russian. "To Mongolia!" I called back, loving the exotic, impossible sound of the word. "From Irkutsk," I explained as she drew closer, and from America, and, yes, alone. And, yes, I know I won't get there today. And, yes, thank you, I do need a place to stay for the night. In her log-cabin home, with a fire dancing in the corner stove, we ate dinner—spearing marinated mushrooms from a communal bowl and dipping boiled potatoes into little piles of salt poured directly on the table. While her granddaughter wailed about the size of a mushroom she did or didn't get, her daughter asked questions about America. "Do you have cows? Do you have chickens? They probably sell meat in the stores where you live—how much does it cost? How much does bread cost? Do you have mushrooms? Wild berries? Do you use different money, or our Soviet money? Is where you live far from China?" Outside the walls of the cozy cabin, darkness was settling over the pungent ever-green forest, and the road running past their home toward Mongolia was no longer paved.

　　　　　　　　　　　　　▲•

The next afternoon, that road burst out of the forest into a barren alpine landscape and slammed straight into an impenetrable wall of Soviet bureau-cracy. Mondi, the final town before the border, looked like nineteenth-century Montana. Small wooden homes clustered beneath massive mountain ridges and fences of delimbed saplings surrounded carefully tended gardens. Directly in front of the tiny post office was an unsigned Y in the road. I went inside and asked the corpulent woman behind the counter which fork led to the border. Outside the window, children gathered around Greene, crouching and pointing, their curious, wary eyes darting back and forth between me and the bicycle. "Ten kilometers up the mountain," she said. "Have you been to customs yet? It's the green building across the bridge. They won't let you cross if you don't stop there first."

I believe in giving the fewest people the fewest opportunities to say "no." Don't stop until someone stops you. But the thought of ten kilometers up the mountain, then ten kilometers back down for some silly form sent me into the green building across the bridge.

"No," said the neatly uniformed woman. "Only local Russians and Mongolians can cross here."

I figured she had never encountered a non-Russian or non-Mongolian, and simply did not understand that I had a passport and visas that allowed me to exit Russia and enter Mongolia. I patiently explained that I had all the appropriate documents and would be allowed to cross the border, I just wanted to know if there were any additional customs forms I needed before continuing up the road. She walkie-talkied up to her boss at the border. "No," he said. "Only local Russians and Mongolians can cross here. This is not an internationally open border."

Annoyed with myself for having stopped, but not worried, I asked who could give me permission to cross. "Maybe the supervisor in the building up the hill," she offered with a friendly shrug and an ingrained Soviet readiness to let someone else take responsibility. In the compound up the hill, I was escorted to a bare-walled room where I showed my passport and visas to a polite, dark-haired lieutenant named Sergei. Twenty-one years old, Sergei had studied in Moscow for four years to earn the two proud stars on his shoulders. After graduating, he had been sent here to southern Siberia

for four years, but he hoped to work his way up to Irkutsk and then perhaps eventually back to Moscow. He sent someone to call headquarters in
Kiakhta, 800 kilometers to the east, where he claimed I should cross the
border. "If they say I can let you cross here, then no problem."

Devastating spring flooding in eastern Russia had knocked out power
and phone lines along with the year's unharvested crops, making a call to
Kiakhta even more complicated than usual on Russia's antiquated phone
system. After a half hour, Sergei decided to try the call himself. We went
upstairs to a comfortable office where another young officer, Pasha, told
me that four Czech journalists had also recently been denied transit.
"Mondi," he said, "is not an internationally open border—no third-coun-
try passports." I looked carefully at my visa, and for the first time read the
fine curlicue print—which allowed me passage via any *internationally open*
border. Apprehension skittered through my stomach, along with the hum-
bling realization that the woman in the green building down the hill had
met plenty of non-Russians and non-Mongolians before me.

While Sergei dialed the operator, I joked that they could let me hide in
the back of a delivery truck.

"No," he and Pasha both said, seriously.

I asked half-seriously if I couldn't circumvent the border through the
mountains.

"Sure," they answered half-seriously. "On foot, but not with a bicycle."

I offered to pay a fine. "Why should you pay a fine?" Sergei seemed honestly not to understand my offer of a bribe. "You haven't done anything
wrong." Where were the good old corrupt Soviets when you needed them?

The hours passed as Sergei tried to call. "I have two trucks leaving for
Kiakhta in the morning. You can catch a ride with them," he offered.

"Anything but go back," I insisted. I had arrived so confident that it was
all a silly formality. "There has to be a way. This is so stupid. I just want to
leave."

Around seven o'clock the call got through, and denial thundered back
across the line.

"Maybe," Sergei looked at me apologetically after hanging up, "if Mondi
were listed on your visa."

"So add it," I said with what I hoped was a disarming, perhaps even
flirtatious, smile, pointing to the typewriter in the corner. "Or give me
five minutes alone in the room."

"Only the so-and-so can do that," Sergei said gravely, not even considering my simple solution.

"And where is he?"

"In Kiakhta." Sergei played by the rules. A no from the top was a no from the top, and that was that. He and Pasha were already pondering what to do with me for the night. There was a hotel in town, but they thought it was "not very good." Theorizing that the greater a logistical nuisance I was, the better my chances of a miracle—"Just get rid of her, send her across the border"—I did not assure them that the local hotel would be fine. Eventually they decided that I could spend the night in Sergei's quarters and he would sleep next door at Pasha's. "Just don't," he grinned, "tell the commander in Kiakhta. I'm not sure we're supposed to let Americans sleep here."

Sergei and Pasha heated tinned army rations and opened a bottle of vodka, and the three of us settled in for dinner in his small bachelor's kitchen. I was still naively surprised by how negatively Russians viewed the changes of recent years. Sergei and Pasha, like most people, talked not about newfound freedoms, but about inflation. The first time I visited the Soviet Union, in 1983, the ruble was valued at more than a dollar and a half, the largest bill was a 10-ruble note, and it was dangerous for people to be seen talking with me on the street. Now I was sleeping in a lieutenant's apartment and the ruble traded for 1,200 to the dollar (within eighteen months it would hit 5,000). "Look at us," I laughed, "I'm American. You're Russian army officers. We're sitting in military housing sharing dinner. Don't you think things are better now?" But the freedom to consort with me had less impact on their lives than I arrogantly imagined. Less impact than the price of eggs. I had to acknowledge that what I experienced was the freedom to visit friends' homes without creeping wordlessly down stairwells, or to bicycle (almost) wherever my legs could take me. Decreasing job security and the cost of bread did not affect me. Several of the actors in Vladivostok had explained that they had adjusted to societal freedom immediately because it seemed so normal, something they had always thought they should have. Thousand-ruble notes they had never imagined.

⚓ •

It had taken me four days to pedal from the shores of Lake Baikal to Mondi. It took five hours to drive back. I rode with Sasha, a cheerful fellow with the floppy, angular body of a scarecrow, who was happy to have company for the long drive. Tolya drove the second truck, accepting my presence with a tolerant if not enchanted shake of his graying head. We picked up the highway where I had left it, and turned east. Beneath his sandy beret, Sasha's eyes danced with eager curiosity about America. We giggled, sharing delighted amazement at an American in the passenger seat of his military transport truck. When we stopped for gas, Tolya grouchily treated us to ice cream cones with the rough sweetness of a man uncomfortable with his own innate kindness. Long after dark, they pulled off the road and built a roaring campfire. We ate canned meat and drank tea from a kettle that Tolya heated with a blowtorch. Then we curled up in the cabs for the night. Huddled under his thin coat, Sasha fretted that I would be cold in my sleeping bag. The next morning in Kiakhta, indulging in the fantasy that I would convince some gruff officer to stamp "Mondi" on my visa, I told the drivers that if I could get permission, I would come back in a few hours and return west with them. Sasha artlessly believed this might happen. Tolya thought I was crazy and said good-bye.

The border was a patch of asphalt strewn with shards of glass and other trash. A dubious-looking crowd of Mongolian and Russian men lounged in the sun. I found the supervisor and told him that I wanted a visa to cross at Mondi. He responded that Kiakhta was not an internationally open border, and all foreigners must take the train at Naushki, forty kilometers to the west. I repeated that I didn't want to cross in Kiakhta, I wanted permission to cross at Mondi. That, he answered, could only be given by the police in Irkutsk.

Often the key to getting what you want is ignoring all the people telling you it cannot be done. Often blind persistence will result in someone suddenly, inexplicably allowing you to do precisely what they have spent the last hour telling you was impossible. I should have known that no border official would have the authority to alter a foreigner's visa, that the only person with the power to slap Mondi on my documents would be sitting in some shabbily grandiose office in Irkutsk. Maybe I had known, but had obstinately forged on in hopes of finding that unexpected chink in the bureaucratic wall. I had not found it. In Naushki the commander ignored my final weak appeal for a Mondi stamp and made it curtly clear that I could not cross the border on a bicycle. The train to Mongolia would leave at 4:30, and I should consider myself lucky—it didn't run every day.

Baby yaks licking Greene's panniers on the road to Khatgal

Part I

BICYCLING IN MONGOLIA

A Crazy Dream of a Faraway World

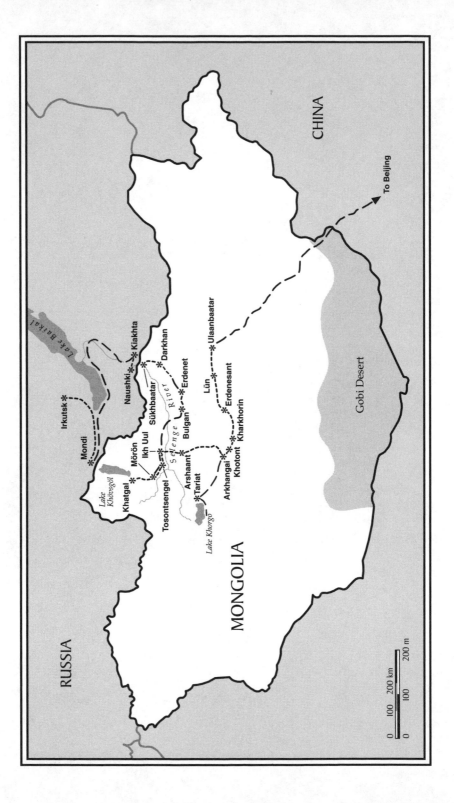

CHAPTER I

An Inexperienced Traveler in
a Land of No Road Signs

Sandwiched between Russia and China, Mongolia is a harsh, beautiful, wind-swept land of extremes. In the west, snow-covered mountains reach to more than 4,000 meters. In the southeast, the desert receives less than five centimeters of rain a year. In between are forests, tumbling rivers, salt lakes, and endless prairie. In the summer, these rolling plains turn green and nourish the sheep, goats, yaks, and horses that outnumber the human population by more than ten to one. But summer is brief. For more than seven months of the year, the country's average temperature does not climb above freezing, and only a tiny percentage of the soil is arable, so the vast herds of livestock remain Mongolia's primary source of sustenance, providing the meat and seemingly infinite dairy products that make up most Mongolians' daily diet.

Once the cradle of a vast empire, once home to an army that struck fear across a continent, Mongolia by the late twentieth century existed in world consciousness only as a pawn, a buffer, and a battleground between its massive neighbors. It was still on the map, a black outline around one of the most sparsely populated regions on Earth, but to most outside perception, Mongolia was a landlocked Atlantis, lying on the bottom of the ocean of history, submerged under the waves first of China and then of the Soviet Union. Yet as the regime to the north collapsed in the early 1990s and the strictures of Communist rule loosened, what emerged was a land whose spirit had not been drowned. Seven decades of Communism had inevitably brought massive changes, yet the core of an ancient way of life remained what it had always been. The Mongolian heartland was still a realm of hardy, nomadic herders living in felt tents beneath an infinite blue sky.

These were the people I wanted to meet; theirs, the land I wanted to know. I imagined myself, a tiny dot on a bicycle, pedaling intrepidly through glorious, sun-drenched grassland. I imagined myself, my odd foreignness notwithstanding, welcomed into a circle of rugged herdsmen gathered around a fire. Instead, I spent my first night in Mongolia in a damp, dingy hotel room staring moodily at maps. I was in Sükhbaatar, barely 20 kilometers south of Naushki, and I did not want to be there. I wanted to be 600 kilometers farther west, struggling down a rocky dirt road south of Mondi, camping along Lake Khövsgöl, arriving exhausted but triumphant in the village of Khatgal.

I like to plan things, and that had been the plan. I would spend a few days catching my breath in Khatgal, then continue south through a town called Mörön, across the Selenge River, and on to a town called Arkhangai before turning east toward the capital city of Ulaanbaatar. This curve would cover some 1,200 kilometers and take me right through the fertile center of the country. By my twenty-eighth birthday, in early October, I would have left Ulaanbaatar and struck out across the fringes of the Gobi Desert toward Beijing, racing south ahead of winter across the flat, barren landscape. The morning I woke up in Sükhbaatar was the morning I had expected to wake up in Khatgal, with a beautiful, uninterrupted squiggle on the map tracing my journey from Irkutsk. I like to make lists and organize things. I like things neat, and I was furious with every Soviet bureaucrat right back to Lenin for having ruined my neat, organized plan.

"So I'll just turn around and pedal right back to Mondi along this side of their stupid border," I muttered at the dank cement walls, my finger on the map tracing a route west across the prairie. But the previous week had taught me quickly that a mountain bike loaded with camping gear, spare parts, and winter clothes was not the same thing as a road bike, one spare tee shirt, and Western European pavement. Hundred-kilometer days belonged to another world. Or at least a more fit cyclist. It was already late August. The end of summer was just around the corner. I did not have time to pedal all the way back and pick up where I had left off. Besides, going back just because that had been the plan was not in the spirit of adventurous travel. No matter how much I wanted to draw a perfect, continuous line across my map, I had to learn to be flexible.

"So make a new plan," I told myself. "Accept where you are. Just pedal south to Ulaanbaatar and then on to Beijing, across those thousand deserted kilometers."

I threw out the new plan. I did not want to go back only because that had been the plan. I wanted to go back because "back" was the country I had come to see. Back was the Mongolian heartland, the vast, sun-drenched prairie ridden by rugged herdsmen. The compromise, I realized, was not in the *where*. It was in the *how:* I did not have to pedal the whole way. I did not have to take the northernmost route across untracked prairie. I could follow the main road south to the city of Darkhan, then turn west via Erdenet and Bulgan to Mörön and Khatgal. Some of that route would be paved, although my various maps disagreed heartily about exactly how much. I could accept any combination of conveyance—bus, Jeep, truck, train, or bicycle—that would get me quickly across the 800 kilometers. Then I could turn around, pretend I had pedaled in from Russia, and never get on another bus, truck, Jeep, or train. I had a *new* new plan.

And I had some exploring to do. I had run away to a land where I knew nothing of the language or customs, where past experience could provide few clues. I had removed myself from the knowns and givens of my world. Like a child, I had to start from scratch. I closed the door to my hotel room and stepped outside.

It was quiet. Cows wandered the dusty streets. Women with empty water buckets queued at a dark doorway. A gnarled old street vendor sold greasy piroshki out of a gym bag. The early afternoon sun pushed through high cloud cover and baked the air. The stillness was that of southern siesta hours or a dying frontier outpost, the quiet broken only by the occasional thud of a horse's hooves or a lone child's call. Bleak, quadrilateral Communist buildings loomed over the central plaza, but as the town drifted up into the surrounding hills, the Soviet cement gave way quickly to log and plaster homes behind high wooden fences. I climbed up past the homes and sat on the side of a hill and surveyed Sükhbaatar, Mongolia. Mongolia. I whispered the word to myself and grinned. I was in Mongolia. I felt as if I had clicked my heels three times, spoken the magic word, and woken up in a dream.

From somewhere above me came the sudden clatter of hooves on stone. I jumped, startled by the sound, and looked up to see three small children scrambling along the rock outcroppings behind a dozen cavorting goats. They waved, and I settled back onto my patch of short hillside grass. I was scared, because I had no idea what the next months of my life would bring, no idea what tomorrow would bring. Gazing down at Sükhbaatar and the empty prairie that began beyond the last home, I could just make out a skinny asphalt road streaming into the grassland. I grinned, then laughed out loud, shaken by a thrill unlike any other I know: I had no idea what tomorrow would bring.

Below me smoke had begun to rise from one chimney after another. I slipped back downtown and knocked tentatively on the locked door of the hotel restaurant. A woman cracked it open to peer at me. I had been to plenty of hotel restaurants in Russia. They were closed "for cleaning," or out of food, or just not in the mood. I waited for the familiar rude Soviet rebuff. The woman smiled and opened the door. Four men sat drinking Chinese beer at one of a half dozen tables. They were the only other customers. One of them fetched another warm bottle from the tiny bar and set it in front of me. They spoke enough Russian to ask where I had come from and where I was going. "Alone?! A woman alone?!" They shook their heads. "You are very brave."

"Or very stupid," I smiled.

I had asked the woman who had let me in if it was possible to eat. Phraseology learned in Russian restaurants—that they had let me in did not mean that there was food. She had nodded, but had not asked what I wanted. That there was food did not mean that there was a choice. Now from a cafeteria-style cubbyhole in the wall came a stir-fry of mutton, cabbage, and noodles, and a bowl of weak, stale bullion. The stir-fry was bland but good. I wasn't sure what to do with the bullion. The woman, who seemed to be waitress, manager, and, for all I knew, cook, had brought a fork along with the food, but no spoon. I decided it was probably all right to drink straight from the small bowl, as from a large teacup in a Chinese restaurant. Tea. Of course. It wasn't soup at all, it was tea. Salty Mongolian tea.

The door opened and two teenage girls slipped in. All across Asia, people appeared, my presence somehow mysteriously telegraphed: policemen to check my documents minutes after I set foot in a hotel room, teachers to act as interpreters in remote villages, students to practice their language skills. Zölöö and Dölgön were home for the summer from Ulaanbaatar's Foreign Language Institute. Did I speak English? Zölöö asked. Did I speak German? Dölgön asked. Her class was going to Germany in September. It would be her first trip abroad, and she had no hard currency. "What things can I take to sell?" she wanted to know. "Is it true that westerners like dinosaur eggs? I have three eggs from the Gobi Desert. Do you think I can sell them in Germany?"

Dölgön sat on my right, asking questions in German. Zölöö sat on my left, asking questions in English. Translations floated between them in Mongolian. Dölgön wore a sweater and black jeans. Zölöö wore a dark red *del*. A one-piece garment that reaches below the knees, the *del* has long, flared sleeves that roll down to cover the hands when winter temperatures plummet. Virtually identical in design for men and women, the *del* attaches to itself with loops of cloth over cloth buttons and is cinched at the waist with a sash or belt. There are dirty old *dels* for milking the cows, everyday *dels,* and beautiful new *dels* for festivals and formal occasions. There are lightweight *dels* for summer, and sheepskin-lined *dels* for winter. The *del* is neither old-fashioned nor the only available mode of dress. Zölöö wore a garment little changed in centuries. Dölgön was dressed like any Seattle college student. Tomorrow Dölgön might wear a *del,* and Zölöö a turtleneck and jeans.

As I sipped my beer and answered questions, I tried to picture Dölgön sitting on Berlin's Kurfürstendam selling her dinosaur eggs. It already seemed impossible that there could be a way from this quiet world into the hectic noise and light of that one. Eventually the beer was gone, my bowl was empty, and the girls were running out of questions. I asked how much I owed. I had not asked prices ahead of time. Now, I knew, the waitress/ manager could, and would, charge me any exorbitant sum she wanted. A guidebook with "Mongolia" in the title had been published just before I left, and it told me so.

"Nothing," she shook her head. "Welcome to Mongolia."

It was summer in Southern California. I was thirteen and wanted to hang out by the pool with my friends. My father wanted me to go to France and learn French. His niece had friends near Paris who had a daughter my age; I could live with them. My father spoke fluent French. He translated for me when we met Stephanie and her parents and her sixteen-year-old brother François. Then he left to do research in Belgium.

François was cool. He smoked, rode a moped, and didn't get good grades in school. I got As. I could recite long lists of French vocabulary and conjugate lots of verbs—and I could not understand a single word that François, Stephanie, or anyone else said. But at thirteen, you learn language quickly. You learn not to translate. You learn to relax, listen, watch, and put the pieces of the puzzle together. You learn that language is about communication, not about perfect grammar. Four weeks later, my father came back. His French was lousy. His vocabulary was minuscule, his accent ridiculous. I understood ten times more than he did, and had to translate for him. And that was it. The bug had bitten. A door had opened.

We traveled to Munich, where I had gone to kindergarten and learned to ride a bicycle while my family was there on a year's sabbatical; to Amsterdam because I wanted to see a real windmill; and to London, where

I ate a hot dog in Hyde Park and got sick to my stomach. And then I was back beside the pool, hanging out with my friends in the summer sun. But I was different now. My world had telescoped wide open and would never be the same again. I dove into the water, down and down until my fingertips grazed the bottom, then I pulled my feet in under me and shot back up through the surface, breaking into the air, laughing and gasping. It was wonderful. But it would never again be enough.

My father was glad to see his own wanderlust kindled in me. He was glad when, two summers later, I went to Germany to live with a family and learn German, his native language. He didn't even mind too much when I put off college for a year to go back to Paris. When I majored in Russian and spent a summer studying in Moscow in the mid-1980s, it made him nervous, but I was with a group, and Russia was still more or less Europe—and Europe was home.

Mongolia was different. Mongolia was an unfamiliar land full of unknown people. Mongolia was definitely not home. And I was going alone. A girl. On a bicycle! Horrified by the prospect of every inch of the trip, my father had given me $200 to spend on trans-Pacific reassurances that I was healthy and happy. I had warned him that international communication would be impossible from most of Mongolia, but I had also promised to be in touch whenever possible. So the morning after I reached Darkhan, a short (paved) 100 kilometers south of Sükhbaatar, I headed for the post office and asked if I could send a telegram to America. The clerk consulted another clerk, who led me upstairs to a third clerk, who handed me a pile of forms. None of the three women knew the Latin alphabet, so a year later, when I saw the scrap of rough yellowish paper my father had received, I was amazed at its accuracy: "DARKHAN ALL INE HEADING WEST NO COMMUNICATION EEW WEEKS DONT WORRY LOVE ERIKA." Still, it had not been enough. By the time I reached Ulaanbaatar in October, he would not have heard from me in six weeks and my name would be on the U.S. State Department Watch List.

Darkhan, population 80,000, is Mongolia's second-largest city. It lies 220 kilometers north of Ulaanbaatar and 180 kilometers east of Erdenet, the third and final urban area in Mongolia. According to two of my three maps, the road from Darkhan to Erdenet was paved. A short ride from downtown, the turnoff was announced in tall, faded blue letters. It was the last road sign I would see for more than a month. I swung west, and the pavement instantly disintegrated into hard-packed gravel. The fierce sun was hot and prickly on my arms. The next time I would see pavement, I would be pedaling in snow.

Five boys dashed their horses up the prairie for a closer look at Greene and me. Two of them wore *dels,* two wore baseball caps cocked backward on their heads. They sat their mounts as effortlessly and nonchalantly as their American counterparts would straddle a bicycle, and posed for my camera with the curious bravado of boys anywhere in the world. A cloud of tiny insects had enveloped me the minute I stopped, so I didn't stay still for long, pushing off west again to the sound of cantering hooves and the boys' whoops as they headed back in the opposite direction.

The previous day's ride south from Sükhbaatar had rolled through green prairie and intermittent stands of forest with only an occasional cluster of *gers* (yurt, I had learned, is a Russian word; the Mongolian name for the round, felt homes is *ger*) to remind me that I wasn't in Nebraska. This suddenly felt different. The road barreled straight ahead as far as the eye could see, cutting through a vast expanse of dry, ground-hugging scrub. In less than twenty-four hours, a road like this would be an inconceivable luxury, but for now it embodied only the stark uncertainty of not knowing what the day, let alone the night, would bring. I was still within the Darkhan-Ulaanbaatar-Erdenet triangle, still on one of the country's principal stretches of road, but squinting, searching the flat, sun-drenched land, the only sign of other humans I could now find was a distant pair of horsemen riding alongside a river of sheep.

Thirty-five kilometers from Darkhan I heard the rumble of a truck. It slowed as it reached me, then pulled to a stop. A small man with a sharp foreign face slipped down from the passenger side. "We saw you yesterday on the road from Sükhbaatar," he announced in Russian, "and we had an argument about whether you were a man or a woman. I said you were a woman. Süren"—he nodded at the driver—"thought you were a man. He said it was impossible for you to be a woman. My name is Abbas. We are on our way to Erdenet. Do you want a ride?"

No matter what I had told myself back in that hotel room in Sükhbaatar, accepting a ride still felt like cheating. I wrestled for a moment with my pride, with my self-imposed idea of what was "right" (if it's a bicycle trip, you bicycle the whole way), and with the simple draw, as I looked down the road, of feeling like my journey had finally really begun. Then I pictured Lake Khövsgöl, pictured the mountains and rivers beyond the urban triangle, pictured myself really, truly out there. We hoisted Greene into the back of the truck, and I climbed into the cab. It took five hours to cross 150 kilometers. All around us, endless unpopulated prairie stretched to the horizon. At every bump and pothole, Greene leapt and flopped beneath her ties like a trout gasping for air on a rowboat floor. From my seat between Süren and Abbas, I peered back through the window and winced at her every jump and crash.

The two men worked for a Russian company in Erdenet, Abbas as a supervisor of some sort, Süren as a driver. Abbas was a twenty-six-year-old Azerbaijani. Cheery and gregarious, he scarcely paused for breath all the way to Erdenet. He described his dreams of driving a blue Ferrari from Paris to Milan, of setting foot on each and every continent. He told jokes about Gorbachev and Shevernadze stealing golden spoons from a White House dinner. I never quite understood the punch lines, but laughed anyway. Süren was Mongolian. His face was broad and golden and serene, his body compact and muscled. He didn't say much, but whenever our eyes met, there was an amused, tolerant twinkle in his eyes. I glanced from one man to the other. Several years earlier, the leaders of the three Baltic nations had held a meeting as they prepared to break free of the Soviet Union. I had flipped from network to network watching the reports. Finally one of the commentators had made the observation I had been waiting to hear: "As the leaders of Latvia, Lithuania, and Estonia meet, they must converse in the only language they have in common." Likewise, Süren and Abbas would never learn each other's tongues. From two similarly dominated nations, they conversed in Russian.

Abbas was friendly toward Süren on the drive, but at dinner that night, alone with his Russian neighbors, they all talked about the savage Mongolians, the lazy Mongolians whom the Russians had had to teach to plant crops, the dirty Mongolians who don't let the blood run out of the animals they kill, who don't bury their dead in cemeteries. The ancient practice of taking bodies out into the steppe and leaving them there for the wolves and vultures had been outlawed in the late 1950s, but I would never see a cemetery. I noted what an odd custom of ours it is, really, to spend large sums of money on fancy boxes that we bury deep in a plot of earth to which we bring flowers for years to come. What is more superstitious, odd, "uncivilized"—that or taking a body out into the hills to become naturally again one with the earth?

⚊•

Abbas was worried about me. He gave me packets of dried soup. He gave me cans of condensed milk. He wanted to come with me. He wanted to find me a guide. I wanted him to get over it. My day was already creeping toward late morning and I was eager to be out there, on my own. I didn't need anybody to hold my hand. I said thank you. I said good-bye. I pedaled to the edge of town, and had no idea what to do next. Behind me lay Erdenet: a blinking traffic light and multistoried concrete apartment buildings. Ahead of me stretched Mongolia: empty golden-green prairie lifting into gentle hills. Muddy ruts crisscrossed into the grass, fanned out in various directions, and faded away. This was it—the reality of cycling in Mongolia: Sometimes there is no obvious road. Sometimes there seem to be three. For all my fantasies of untamed terrain, at this intersection of city and steppe a little ripple of panic screamed, "Where are the 7-Elevens, the traffic lights, the road signs, *the road?* Where at least is a charming old man on a horse to tell me which of these vague, mushy ruts to follow? How do I do this?!"

I pedaled tentatively several hundred yards to the left and stared out over the indecipherable, muddy green quilt. I remembered the road out of Darkhan and laughed at the neophyte traveler I had been only the day before, when that clear, broad swath had awed me. I turned around and pedaled back to the pavement. "Bulgan?" I asked the first passerby. The man smiled, nodded, and waved out across the prairie. "This is what you wanted," I reminded myself and, taking a deep breath, I aimed for the hills.

The ground climbed slowly into the folds of land. An hour passed. Then two. The mud dried into hard, rutted tracks. Greene's tires slipped heavily on half-buried stones. I was not very good at this. Then, across the valley, a charming old man appeared on a horse, cantering unhurriedly in my direction. "Bulgan?" I asked as he drew alongside, slowing to a trot. He nodded, moving in parallel with me, silent, watching, his horse's hooves thudding rhythmically on the earth. He stayed beside me for several minutes, then his body spoke imperceptibly to the horse, whose gait lifted fluidly back to a canter, and they disappeared across the grassland. My route climbed to a ridge. At a dip in the hills, it swung to the right and down into a broad valley. Cows, sheep, and goats roamed the unfenced expanse. Small clusters of *gers* dappled the lush grass.

Mongolia is a high, dry country. More than 250 days of the year, however cold, pass under clear skies. What little precipitation does fall comes during the brief summer. Streams and rivulets, seen and unseen, bubbling and silent, traversed the luxuriantly green valley floor, sucking Greene's tires suddenly into mud before releasing her again to a short dry stretch. I was no more adept at mud than I was at rocks. The weight of Greene's panniers pulled in every direction except forward. Progress was slow.

Across the valley I could see what appeared to be a steep but unambiguous swath of gravel climbing into the next string of hills. It looked like a road to me, and in my world, roads lead somewhere. I pushed Greene up the rocky, dusty incline. But instead of curving around the hill, the road simply stopped, like an unfinished roller-coaster track. Only a scanty footpath led on, disappearing sharply downhill into thick underbrush. Turning around was the logical solution, dropping the short half kilometer back into the valley and finding another route. But I compulsively hate to backtrack. Backtracking always feels like failure. Brambles scratched at my arms and legs, caught in my hair and at Greene's panniers as we dipped into the ravine. I was barely strong enough to hold her on the steep, uneven ground, or to drag her up the other side. At the top of the ravine, dripping sweat and gulping air, I sucked on my water bottle, squirted water onto the deeper scratches on my arms, and watched a pudgy white petrol truck climb out of the valley along the track my eyes had not been able to pick out of the hills, and disappear in the direction of Bulgan. As its trail of dust dissipated into the hot air, I swung back onto my bicycle and bumped after it.

A few curves in the road later, a pair of *gers* rose from the prairie. A small herd of horses milled nearby, and two young men emerged from their midst, watching me. One seemed to yell something back over his shoulder. Then a young woman appeared, heading straight for me across the dark, squishing grass. She wore light-blue jeans and white tennis shoes, and addressed me in Russian. Lkhamsüren was a student in Ulaanbaatar, and would return to the city at the end of the summer. She said she didn't think I could get to Bulgan before dark, which at the rate I had been going was certainly true. She asked where I usually slept in Mongolia. I said I had a tent. There was no "usually" yet, and "tent" sounded more self-sufficient than "hotel." She said I was welcome to stay for the night, and pointed to where I could set up my tent next to one of the *gers*. "Great, thanks," I said, crushed. I had already been hoping for my first night inside an exotic round felt home. Instead I unpacked my bright blue nylon triangle, an incongruous splash of modern color in the landscape of muted, harmonious hues.

We sat in the grass for a while watching her brothers, dressed in worn *dels* and muddy rubber boots, milk their horses. A half dozen foals were tethered separately from the herd. One by one they were led to their mothers, allowed to nurse just long enough to start the flow of milk, then dragged back to their ties while the mare was milked. The milk would be fermented into *airag*, a tangy, slightly alcoholic brew reminiscent of thin buttermilk. After the milking, the mares were turned loose to find their foals, which could finish whatever milk was left.

~• *My tent next to Lkhamsüren's ger*

Lkhamsüren wanted to show me her photo album. Ducking through a shoulder-high wooden doorway, we entered her *ger*. A latticework frame, rather like the accordion guards that American parents put at the tops of staircases to prevent small children from tumbling down, formed the circular wall. From the top of the frame, dozens of slim poles slanted upward to a wooden circle at the center of the roof. This skylight, called the *tonoo,* was in turn supported by two sturdy vertical posts in the middle of the *ger*. The entire structure was swathed in several layers of thick wool felt and a final wrapping of canvas to complete a curvaceous balancing act impervious to the great winds that sweep down from Siberia. The top of the metal stove that stood in the center of the *ger* was cut out in a circle so that the *togoo,* the shape and depth of a large wok, fit inside, dipping down into the flames. The stovepipe stretched up and out of the *tonoo,* some 3 meters above the ground. Overlapping carpets covered the floor. Three beds and two chests of orange drawers ringed the circle. A knee-high table stood beside the stove. Low stools were scattered about the *ger*. A mirror on top of one chest was lined with photographs of friends and family stuck into its edges.

There are temporary summer *gers* and long-term winter *gers;* there are *gers* with no floor other than the grass, and *gers* with perfectly fitted wooden plank floors; there are *gers* with a *tonoo* open to the sky, and *gers* with pie-piece glass slipped neatly into each triangle of the wooden circle. But the basic organization of every *ger* in Mongolia is identical.

I leafed through Lkhamsüren's photo album. In picture after picture, straight-faced family members posed in rows in front of Soviet statues or with the ubiquitous inflatable plastic animals of the great communist squares' photographers. Lkhamsüren was tossing handfuls of fresh noodles into the *togoo*. She asked what I ate in Mongolia. I said I had dried soups and things. She asked how I prepared them.

"Just add boiling water."

"When I am done," she said, "you can make your dinner."

"Great, thanks," I nodded, crushed again. Maybe the guidebook was right. Maybe there really was a food shortage. But the *togoo* was full and the kids outside certainly didn't look like they were going hungry. "Smells good," I smiled. Quizzically, doubtfully, she asked if I wanted to try some. "If there's extra," I said tentatively. She ladled a little bit into a small bowl and handed it to me. After she had filled large bowls for the rest of the family, who came in, slurped their dinner quickly, and returned to work, she told me to bring my soup.

"I'm not really that hungry—this was plenty."

"Do you want more?"

It was really good and I was really hungry, and the *togoo* was still half full. "Only if there's enough for everybody."

She laughed, and poured me a steaming bowlful of the mutton-noodle soup called *guriltai shöl*. "The Russians won't touch our food," she said. "They think it's dirty. I didn't think you would eat it either."

The more experience people had with foreigners, the more preconceived assumptions they had about my fears and needs. The fewer images or bits of knowledge people had about life outside Mongolia, the more simply generous they were with their way of life, inviting me into their world rather than trying to adapt it to what they guessed or assumed my expectations and desires to be. Lkhamsüren had not invited me to sleep in the *ger* for the same reason she had not invited me to share dinner: She believed that, as a foreigner, I would not want to lie in a Mongolian bed.

⸺•⸺

We know what we know because of what we have seen, heard, and experienced. In my world, horses are afternoons spent exploring the California foothills or trotting around a ring trying to keep your heels down. Cantering across the prairie because that is how you get from one place to the next is from another century, from the movies, from some imaginary, long-gone world. It is certainly not reality.

The rhythmic pounding of hooves resonated on the dry earth behind me. I giggled, because it *was* reality, because I was in Mongolia and my reality sounded like a John Wayne movie. I stopped. Two men reined in their horses. They didn't ask where I was from. They didn't ask where I was going or how old I was. They just stared at me, and their stares were dull. One of them eyed a truck heading toward us and muttered something to his buddy. I didn't know any of the words, but I knew exactly what he had said. He had said, "Wait until the truck is gone."

I watched him say this. I watched the other one nod. I stood up on the pedals and started riding. People stared and grinned and waved from behind the truck's windows. I thought about stopping them, but what would I say? That I didn't trust the two young men on their horses? That I had seen their eyes and their eyes were wrong? What would I ask for? Protection? A ride? They were going the wrong way. I pretended that nothing was wrong. I told myself that I had imagined it. I told myself that nothing would actually *happen*.

The noise of the truck faded over the hill and the men were back; they were riding in very close, and whatever I saw in their eyes, whatever my gut was screaming at me, I still did not really believe that that border would be crossed, that they would *touch* me, because no one ever had. But they did. One of them reached down and grabbed at my rear panniers, and Greene collapsed to the ground. Feet snatched out of toe clips just in time, I grabbed at one of the horse's reins and managed to keep myself upright as my bicycle fell. The animal was throwing its head into the air. The rider was yelling at me. I let go. The other man was already poking at Greene's panniers with a heavy wooden dowel. He motioned for me to open them. Pretending not to understand what they wanted, I told him cheerfully what was inside, but did not reach for a zipper. I spoke Russian, which was probably a mistake. One of them pointed to my sunglasses, the other to my watch, to my helmet, back to the sunglasses. They wanted these things. They wanted loot. They wanted booty. They wanted ransom. They were robbers, thieves, highwaymen, old-fashioned bandits. They were from the movies, outlaws riding out of the foothills to plunder the stagecoach. But John Wayne was nowhere on the horizon.

I should have been scared, but I was too busy being furious. At them, at their brazenness, at their insolence, at my vulnerability, which I felt like a nakedness. Each of them was stronger than I. Their horses were faster and more agile than Greene. We weren't ten kilometers from Bulgan, but I knew that hours could pass before another truck came down the road. What I did not know was how far they would go. What would they dare? What could I risk? How hungry were they, how angry, how dangerous? I had two pairs of cheap sunglasses in an outside pannier pocket. I didn't even know why I had brought them—in case I lost my good ones, to give away as souvenirs—but I remembered them with relief.

I unzipped the pocket and handed a pair to the leading bully. He laughed. He slipped them on and posed, turning his face to the sun. His partner's demands for my glasses redoubled. Furious, I threw the second pair at him as hard as I could. They landed on the ground and anger washed across his face. For the first time, something sparked in his eyes and it was about me, me specifically, not the generic me—a traveler with a bicycle and panniers full of goodies. Now I was afraid. He was mad at *me*. But then his buddy made a dash for the glasses and if he didn't get there first, his friend would have two pairs and he would have nothing. I was forgotten in the scramble.

Fuming, wishing I hadn't given them anything, relieved at not having had to give them more, retrospectively imagining a calmer, unintimidated me, a me in command of the situation, taking charge rather than reacting, coolly giving up nothing, I practically threw Greene up the rocky slope. At the top of the long hill, I looked back. They were gone, and I knew that I was lucky. I knew that a certain danger had been real. I understood how completely vulnerable I was. What I did not know was that in eight months, this was as close to violence as I would come.

━━•

The bus stop in Bulgan was a dusty, empty space on the edge of town. Quiet brown people sat in the meager shade of a ramshackle shelter waiting for transportation that might or might not arrive. Today, tomorrow, or the next day. They were a tableau of practiced, subdued patience in the heat. I was lucky. I had been there for only a few hours when a short, lopsided yellow bus rumbled in on its way to Mörön. The passengers passed Greene to the back of the bus and laid her on top of the rest of the luggage, then gave me a seat, even though other people were already perched on the bags that filled half the aisle.

There was no suburban sprawl. Bulgan began and ended at the last wooden fence. Past that fence, we were out in the empty prairie. The bus quivered and shimmied and broke down every few hours, but even though the other passengers had been on the move for days, most of them coming all the way from China, everyone was amazingly cheerful. They had become friends on the long ride, sharing the hot days and cold nights, sharing food and drink, sharing, I liked to imagine, the tales of their journeys. From time to time a single voice began to hum, then rose from the hum to form words. Other voices soon followed, mingling, fusing, separating in counterpart, dropping back together, melodies lifting and peaking and longing, ancient and painful and joyful. They sang songs of mothers and horses, songs of loss and birth and searching, harmonies from a deep and simple land where people lived and loved and died within the ancient framework of the nature around them, adapting to it, rather than conquering and dividing from it.

As soon as it had been established that I spoke Russian but no Mongolian, a young woman in jeans and a pink tee shirt had taken me under her wing, making her way forward over the bundles in the aisle to sit beside me. People rearranged themselves to make room for her, as if in collective agreement that she should be responsible for me. Bolormaa had gone to law school in Russia. Slight of build, with glasses beneath her straight black bangs, she had an outgoing confidence that was different from the quiet inner strength of women who had never left Mongolia. She had grown up in a felt tent under a strict Communist regime, yet we had much more in common than one language. It soon felt as if we had known each other for years, as if we had gone to college together, had hung out late into the night over too many cups of coffee, books lying open but mostly ignored on the table.

The only thing about her that I could not imagine for myself was motherhood. Her two-year-old daughter's father was a fellow student back in Russia. Hoping to save enough money to rejoin him, Bolormaa had left her job as a lawyer and taken up the much more lucrative practice of traveling back and forth to China to purchase goods that she then resold for a profit at the market in Mörön. It was a new world. Imported goods and clothing had for decades come almost exclusively from the Soviet Union and its other satellite states. Overnight, Mongolians were having to learn a new set of rules, a whole new game. "We never used to know about buying and selling," Bolormaa said, "we just gave each other whatever we needed." She had invested in children's clothing. Other people imported boom boxes, chewing gum, housewares, televisions. The bus was crammed full of Chinese wares.

At the top of a hill, we passed a large rockpile decorated with empty

⌣· *Ovoo*

vodka bottles, decaying tires, and small *tögrög* notes. (Four years earlier the *tögrög* had been valued at 3 to the dollar. When I had changed money in Darkhan, the official rate had been 350 to the dollar. For $60 I ended up with a few large bills—50s, 100s, one crisp new 500—and enough bundles of ragged 1-, 3-, 10-, and 20-*tögrög* notes to fill a small pannier pocket.) Scraps of rags tied to long wooden poles waved from the middle of the cairn. This, Bolormaa explained as the bus pulled to a stop, was an *ovoo*. Built primarily on passes, *ovoos* are an ancient shamanistic custom. Travelers leave small offerings, or add a symbolic stone to the pile, to thank the gods for keeping them safe in their journeys. Today the specific deities to be thanked may have faded from consciousness, but the custom of demonstrating gratitude continues. Everyone tumbled out of the bus and walked three times clockwise around the spill of rocks, trash, and money, placing a few *tögrögs* in a niche or under a stone. I was to come to love *ovoos*—it was always downhill after that—and to take real comfort in the ritual of leaving a small thankful remembrance that I had reached the top of one more little mountain.

For the rest of the day, the bus bounced through endless, unchanging golden steppe, sometimes following a perceptible road, sometimes bumping through untracked, waving grasses. In the back, Greene lay on her derailleur, her chain flapping loosely. The sun slipped slowly toward the horizon and soon the few short feet of potholed dirt track caught in the bus's bouncing headlights were a narrow tunnel of reality in the mystery of an otherwise ink-black night. Sometime in the darkness, the bus stopped. We would go on in the morning, Bolormaa said, as everyone settled in to sleep, heads leaning on neighbors' shoulders or against cold windows, several of the men rolled up in their *dels* on the grass outside. Shortly after sunrise we rolled off again, but did not go far before veering across the prairie toward two *gers*. Mongolian mail-order: the driver had brought merchandise from China to trade with the family that poured out of the felt homes. They examined the boom box and sorted through the pile of socks, sweaters, and pants, picking, choosing, rejecting, and bargaining. No money changed hands, but when we rattled off again, there was a sheep standing bleating in the aisle.

Late in the afternoon, less than 400 kilometers and more than twenty-four hours after leaving Bulgan, the bus bumped into Mörön. Downtown was a dreary collection of cement buildings—a few stores, the school and the post office, several apartment buildings, the bank and the hotel—but there was a poor former splendor to my spacious accommodations. Faded Oriental carpets and comfortably worn couches decorated the two rooms. The electricity worked sometimes, the water at other times; the radiators, controlled centrally by the city, would not be turned on for at least another month, although the rooms were already deeply cold.

Promptly at seven o'clock that evening, Bolormaa knocked on my door. Within minutes, we had left the cement buildings behind and were walking down a wide dirt street between tall wooden fences. Perpendicular fences cut the dusty land into lots, creating a suburbia of side-by-side homes in rows as succinct as any American tract development. I could not tell one street from the next. Interrupted only by identical green metal gates, the grid of tightly spaced wooden staves felt like a complicated labyrinth. Next to each locked gate was a wooden door. Bolormaa pushed open one of these doors and we entered her family's lot. In one corner stood a wooden shack with two holes cut into the plank floor and old Russian books piled in the corner as toilet paper. Near the opposite fence stood two log cabins. One was where Bolormaa lived with her daughter, her parents, and her two younger brothers; the other belonged to her eldest brother and his family. Two circles in the dirt mapped where both families would build snug *gers* for the cold months. One small *ger* was already standing—Bolormaa's grandparents never collapsed their cozy bubble for the space of a drafty summer house.

As soon as we walked into her house, Bolormaa's mother served tea. Once I had stopped thinking of it as stale bullion, Mongolian tea was delicious, especially when it was brewed with yak milk as rich as fresh butter. Bolormaa's mother had a gentle, accepting face, and the quiet assurance of someone who had learned to make sacrifices without ever relinquishing her dignity. She held the small bowl in her right hand, with the fingertips of her left hand resting lightly beneath her forearm. I touched the fingers of my left hand to my right elbow and reached out to accept the tea, cupping the bottom of the bowl in four fingers, my thumb just below the rim for balance. I had already learned not to hold a tea bowl with my fingers splayed around the sides and an index finger crooked over the rim. I had learned that all food must be served and received with two hands, either literally or symbolically. I had learned that food must be passed into a guest's hands, rather than placed on the table.

In the absence of language, ritual becomes a way of communication, of making yourself a little less foreign. New customs cease to be quaint, primitive, or exotic, and become touchstones, tiny doors into a new culture. I watched people carefully, watched gestures, trying to learn, trying not to offend. Cupping both hands together to indicate particular respect or gratitude when receiving food or a gift would soon become as instinctive as taking off my shoes in a Russian home, not touching the fruit in an Italian shop, or bringing a bottle of wine to a party in America. But even watching carefully, there are things that I will not see. And there are things that I will see, but will misunderstand. One day I will sit on a *ger* floor, studiously copying the posture of the man next to me, right foot planted flat on the floor, knee in the air, left leg curled underneath. I will mimic him exactly, not realizing that this is how men sit, not how women sit.

With the tea, Bolormaa's mother brought the plateful of dairy products—*aaruul, aarts,* and *öröm*—from which every visitor must take at least a nibble. Called *tavgiin idee* ("plate set for guests") in Mongolian, I dubbed it the "welcome plate" in my head. The heap of *aaruul*—curdled milk sundried on *ger* roofs to the hardness of a lollipop, and gnawed or sucked slowly until it softens in the mouth—was supplemented by handfuls of *aarts*— dried curds the size and consistency of Grape-Nuts. Laid artfully on top were slabs of *öröm*—the solid cream that forms on the top of boiled milk as it cools.

Suddenly a small child tumbled through the door. Bolormaa's daughter, Belgüün, had pudgy cheeks and a commanding sparkle in eyes that did not look like everyone else's. Her father was from Cape Verde, Bolormaa explained, and the small girl was a dark-skinned mulatto in a very purely Asian world. "No, people here didn't take it very well at first. But if that's how things work out," she shrugged, "what can you do?" Belgüün was spoiled and demanding and threw flailing temper tantrums, but she reigned un-questioned as the center of the household, doted on and catered to by tot-tering grandparents and eight-year-old cousins alike.

Bolormaa's mother suggested that Bolormaa show me the family photo album, and smiled to herself as we chattered over it in Russian. She boiled meaty mutton bones for our dinner and served us precious Chinese can-dies for dessert. She worried that I would be cold and scared, alone in a hotel room, but trusted her worldly daughter who believed me when I promised that I was used to sleeping alone. "But when you return from Khatgal," she said, "you must come straight here, not to the hotel." Late that night, Bolormaa walked me back through pitch-black streets broken only by the occasional gush of light from *ger*-top *tonoos*. She lit a cigarette and glanced at me. "Mongolian women still don't smoke in public," she said. Then she slipped an arm through mine, grinned, and inhaled deeply. "I only do this when nobody can see."

⁕

Fuzzy baby yaks skittered off the road, then snuck back to lick Greene's panniers and nibble curiously at her tires as I stared from the powerlines to the road to the compass, all telling me to go in different directions. I was on the last leg of the trip back (as it were) to Lake Khövsgöl, and I was going to pedal the whole 100 kilometers. But not more than a dozen kilo-meters out of Mörön, I was already baffled: The powerlines took off over a hill, the most worn of the many sets of tracks turned west, and the com-pass told me to go straight, north. Should I follow the powerlines, because they had to lead somewhere (and the guidebook suggested that they were a reliable method of routefinding)? Should I follow the tracks, on the premise that everybody else who came this way was probably going to Khatgal, too? Or should I ignore both of these tangibles and rely on the theoretical spin of the compass? Khatgal lies almost directly north of Mörön, but the map said to go west for a while before veering north past a small lake. I chose the tracks. Kilometer after kilometer passed slowly beneath Greene's wheels, and eventually I had to recognize the obvious: This road was never going to veer north.

When a vehicle comes down the road in Mongolia and you wave at the driver to stop because you need directions, you are not asking a small favor. If his engine slows to a standstill, it is likely to cough, splutter, and die. "Khatgal," I yelled, as the motorcycle revved in tight circles around me. "No, no, no," the man yelled back over the screaming engine, jerking his head back the way I had come. I glared down the road. Turning around is so infuriating. Undoing what you have done, unraveling the achievement. I heard the man on the motorcycle shout. He took one hand off the handlebars just long enough to point to a vague track leading up the side of a hill. Northeast. *"Bayarlalaa,"* I yelled into the cloud of dust as the engine sputtered and caught and the motorcycle tore away. Silence settled back over the grassland. The compass. Rely on the compass.

Over the crest of the hill, a small lake came into view. A herd of large brown cows grazed on its near shore. As I bounced and skidded several rocky kilometers toward the valley floor, the cows grew larger and odder-looking before finally metamorphosing completely into placid, curious camels. They watched me pitch my tent and walk toward the vivid blue water. Seagulls circled in the sky. An aviary of littler birds called across the water to each other. And floating in the sunset—one perfect white swan. But the squelching, muddy shore was covered in camel dung, and the shallow water was full of shit and algae. I stood scowling at the muck, so picturesque from only a few dozen meters away, then remembered that, like many lakes in landlocked Mongolia, this one was probably saltwater, anyway. So instead of cooking a packet of chili and beans, I ate half a cucumber, sipped frugally at my remaining water, and inhaled the evening glow. The air that filled my lungs was pure and clean. It tasted of earth and grass and infinity. Across the shimmering water, three white puffs sheltered at the base of the hills. When I would pass the lake again five days later, the nomads' homes would be gone. They would have moved on, perhaps following, for part of their journey at least, the road that I could now just barely see, running along the far shore of the lake, heading straight north from Mörön to Khatgal. The compass, the compass, the compass.

I told myself that I had learned my lessons: (1) it is very easy to get lost in Mongolia, and (2) the spin of the compass is not theoretical. I was an inexperienced traveler in a land of no road signs, but I had a tent and a sleeping bag, and being a little lost is part of any good adventure. Today, six years later, as I write this to the sound of helicopters above the New York City skyline and know that the next time I go to Mongolia everyone will tell me to take a personal GPS unit and a cellular telephone, I remember that evening and imagine sitting by the lake checking email, and I know how that connection would have shattered the invigorating, empowering sense of freedom that comes with abandoning yourself to the risks of the unknown.

⸺•⸺

Only ten days earlier, I had envisioned my arrival in Khatgal as a triumphant return to civilization from the wilds of Khövsgöl's lakeshore forest. I had pictured a hot shower and even, in a now absurdly implausible image based on some guidebook comment about increasing tourism, a busload of clean, middle-aged Midwesterners, all incredulous that I had actually bicycled the 100-some kilometers south from the Russian border. Instead, I got one lanky budget-traveler in baggy blue pants.

Daniel was from Switzerland and had been on the road for nineteen months. He appeared on the creaking hotel porch just as I arrived, and helped me lug Greene up the wooden steps and into the dark, capacious building. He laughed when I asked about a restaurant, but said we were welcome to use the hotel's massive iron stove. He chopped firewood and I cooked up the packets of dried soup that Abbas had given me, and over dinner Daniel told travel stories. Or what he had come to think of as travel stories: The tale of a delicious meal in a Laotian village was the tale of how they had tried to charge him two dollars when he knew it should cost only fifty cents, of how had he refused to pay the inflated cost and had argued until he won. The story of a two-day train ride across China was the story of bribing someone to buy him a ticket at the Chinese rather than the foreigner's price, and of how he got away with it for the whole trip. Every story was about *their* cheating and *his* bargaining. The moral was always the value of the penny righteously saved, the pride of pecuniary triumph.

Two of the cheerful young women who ran the hotel joined us in the kitchen, and by the light of a flickering candle (the electricity had not worked in days) we sat up into the night while they taught us to count to ten in Mongolian. Before going to bed I went outside, across the yard, and through a hole in the fence to get to the outhouse. Back in my room, I washed my hands and brushed my teeth using a clever sink contraption made by nailing the side of a large can to a post, then running a screw attached to a wide stopper through a hole in the bottom of the can. After dumping a bucketful of water into the can, you push the screw up and water pours down over your toothbrush into a basin set below the can. It was a long way from a hot shower, but however much I would have loved to turn a faucet and send endless steaming water pouring down over my head, the reality of Khatgal was ultimately much more gratifying than a "return to civilization." I was perfectly happy to trade plumbing for a town still some time away from entertaining busloads of foreigners.

The next morning, wandering through the village, I could hardly imagine ever having expected hot showers or tour buses. Dusty paths ran among log homes. Cows and horses grazed the short downtown grasses. Sheep skulls, goat legs, and random hooves littered the dirt streets like discarded fast-food wrappers. A small boy dipped a pair of metal canisters into the lake and lugged the water home. On a fading, hand-painted billboard, Lenin met with Sükhbaatar, the young revolutionary who in 1921 joined with the Soviet Red Army to drive the White Russians from his country and establish the Mongolian People's Republic. Sitting behind a table draped in red velvet, the Soviet leader made a silent insistent point, one hand raised in emphasis, the other placed in apparent friendship on the Mongolian revolutionary's arm. Stepping over raised doorsills, I followed people into cramped stores. One displayed indifferent piles of tea, matches, butter, cabbage, packets of Chinese noodles, and cigarettes. Another offered soapy Chinese chocolates, potatoes, a lonely pair of shoes, something in squat glass jars labeled "juice" in Russian, and cigarettes. A third sold onions, candles, Chinese gum by the stick, a single sweater, and cigarettes. Farther down the street, people were crowding into a store behind a delivery of bread. Each family in Khatgal was rationed to four loaves per week. *Tögrög* notes clutched in fists over their heads, they pushed forward, trying to get to the bread before there was no bread left to get to.

Daniel had been in Khatgal for a week and had made many friends, including a teacher who had invited him to visit the local school. I tagged along. The whitewashed schoolroom walls were hung with portraits of Descartes, Galileo, Shakespeare, and Genghis Khan. The chalkboard was covered with the vertical curls, dashes, and flourishes of old Mongolian script. Imported from the Middle East via the Chinese Uighurs, the script dates back to the thirteenth century. But in 1941, in conjunction with a massive literacy drive and political expediency, Mongolia adopted a slightly modified version of the Cyrillic alphabet, and the ancient script virtually disappeared. Fifty years later it was making a comeback on chalkboards across the country. Girls in front, boys in back, the fifteen-year-olds sat attentively, two at each wooden desk, while the teacher, a small man in a rumpled suit, asked us questions and translated our answers into Mongolian for the students. Daniel and I told the class how old we were, where we were from, where we had already been in Mongolia, and where we each still planned to go.

All of the students had at least a bit of classroom Russian, so I asked directly whether they had any questions. The response was giggling silence and black eyes skittering away from mine. The teacher asked what our jobs were, how many years we had each gone to school, and what we had studied. Again I turned to the students. I asked how many of them wanted to graduate and go on to university in Ulaanbaatar. This time several of the girls let me catch their eyes, nodding shyly but emphatically, smiling at a crazy dream of a faraway world. I understood that it was expensive to live and study in the capital, but if Ulaanbaatar was far away, I could not imagine what these kids were thinking as they looked at Daniel and me. If Ulaanbaatar was a dream, what were the Alps? What was Times Square? But the ice seemed to have been broken. Hands slipped into the air: Were we married? Did our families own cows and sheep? How many brothers and sisters did we each have?

A girl raised her hand, "What Mongolian food do you like?"

"I was told I would starve," I said, "but people just keep feeding me." We had visited several of Daniel's acquaintances, and every time we walked into a home, we ate. We ate tart new yogurt. We ate *aaruul* and *öröm*. We looked at photo albums—Khatgal in winter, Lake Khövsgöl frozen solid—and drank the freshest, richest milk I had ever tasted. We chewed on the meat of boiled mutton bones while our hosts devoured every bit of meat, gristle, and fat, their strong teeth and sharp knives leaving behind only naked, glistening bone.

A boy raised his hand, "Are there still Indians in America? I heard that they came from Mongolia."

I smiled, "I don't know if they came from *Mongolia,* but, yes, there are still Indians in America."

"What do you think of Mongolian life?" another girl asked. "How does it compare to life in Switzerland and America?"

I answered as I always answered in Russia, that, yes, we had greater material wealth, but that the singing in the kitchen was never as good, by which I meant that the veneer of American life, obsessed with work, money, success, and a permanent happy smile, is rarely stripped down to the essentials of friendship, generosity, and simple pleasure in the same way that it is late at night with a dozen people, a guitar, and a bottle of vodka in a tiny, smoky Russian kitchen, or, I added, over a bowl of *airag* in a Mongolian *ger.* Daniel, his voice and eyes growing intense, spoke of the hospitality he had experienced in Mongolia, of the straightforward, unparalleled generosity of the people he had met. I could not quite reconcile this paean to magnanimity with his proud tales of financial wrangling, but he was fervent and clearly sincere.

I remembered the bus driver trading a boom box for a sheep. I remembered Dölgön asking how much dinosaur eggs sold for in Berlin. I remembered Belgüün's beautiful mixed-race eyes. Then I thought of the singing on the bus to Mörön, and of Belgüün's grandmother, worrying that I would be scared to sleep alone. I thought of a horseman I had seen plodding east from Khatgal, leading a heavily loaded pack camel, and I remembered the silver four-wheel-drive vehicle that had left him in a cloud of dust. And I realized that Daniel and I were both saying a prayer. These children's world was about to be dramatically different from the world of generations of their ancestors, and we were entreating them not to lose touch with the precious ancient values of their culture. It is, of course, one of the great hypocrisies of the western traveler, wanting the people we visit in remote lands to remain charming, simple, exotic, and untouched by the information, possessions, and comforts that we take for granted and are unlikely to relinquish for more than the briefest of forays into more austere lands. But we had found a place that truly touched us and, fairly or not, we wished for it not to change.

Two days later we filled our backpacks with a picnic of cabbage, potatoes, garlic, and onions and set off through *ger*-dappled meadows along the shores of Lake Khövsgöl. The sun was summer-bright, but a sharp breeze already presaged the chill of fall. We built a fire and cooked a feast, then lay on our backs in the fragrant grass. Above us a hawk spiraled silently skyward on motionless wings. At the edge of the meadow, the crystal-clear water of the lake played in colors of the south seas—blues of every perfect hue nature ever made.

I remembered the night I had spent in Mondi, drinking vodka with Sergei and Pasha, still thinking they might wake up in the morning and decide to let me bicycle across the border. That had been two weeks ago, when I had not known a single word of Mongolian, when I had never been inside a *ger,* when Mongolia had been nothing more than a bundle of images in my head. Now I could say "hello" and "thank you" and count to twenty. I knew not to step on the threshold when I walked into a *ger.* I knew not to knock on a *ger* door. I knew that you just walked in. Whether or not you knew the people, whether or not you were expected, you just opened the door and walked in.

I sat up and stared across the lake into the blue horizon. Somewhere just beyond that illusion of sky meeting water lay Mondi. I had been in Khatgal for three days, and I was ready to turn around, pretend I had pedaled in from Russia, and start riding slowly through Mongolia.

CHAPTER 2

A Techno-Dot in the
Eternal Scenery

I stayed on the right road all the way back to Mörön, stayed east of the little lake past the empty space where three *gers* had once stood. I pedaled hard all day and pulled into town with the sunset. Under a drizzling gray sky the next afternoon, I went to the market with Bolormaa. Like many neophyte traders, she did not have a rickety table in the muddy enclosure. She simply stood holding several coats over her arms, asking for twice what they had cost her in China, but willing to bargain. She taught me the prices in Mongolian, and people crowded around to hear me try to pronounce the long, guttural strings of consonants, but no one bought anything. Eventually I wandered off and found bread, cucumbers, cabbage, and little Chinese chocolate cream wafers individually wrapped in red foil. That night before we went to bed, I gave half of everything I had bought to Bolormaa's mother, explaining that it was too much to carry on a bicycle.

Snow fringed the distant mountains and a crisp edge of frost hung on the air when I pedaled out of Mörön the following morning. A small herd of horses sauntered toward the hills, nibbling at the grass as they went, their heavy forelocks flopping over dark eyes. A languorous flock of sheep and goats moved along a distant ridge. Only the Jeep tracks tore the earth apart. As one tracing grew too rutted or muddy, vehicles simply moved over onto virgin land, leaving parallel series of blood-brown scars spreading, veering, cutting deeper and deeper into the pristine expanse.

It's all in who you ask, I told myself, as I rode into the village of Tosontsengel that evening. I passed by a single man, and spied a family of five chatting in front of their yard.

"*Zochid buudal* ("Hotel")?" I asked.

"*Bakhguì* ("No")."

"*Bakhguì?*" I repeated.

"Bakhguì."

"Ah," I nodded, looking off at the hills but making no move to leave.

"Where are you from?" they queried. "Where are you coming from? Where are you going? Alone?!" These were the first phrases I would learn in Mongolian, and again in Chinese, and again in Vietnamese. "You're not scared? How old are you? Are you married?" Seven questions. Seven answers.

When my father heard the Seven Questions, he thought the fifth one justified his fears. But whenever I countered, "Scared of what?" the answers were vague. "Bears?" people shrugged uncertainly. "Wolves? Bandits?" No drive-by shootings, no crack-induced rampages, no automatic weapons, none of the dangers we have come to accept as quotidian when we are safe at home in America.

"No," I shook my head. "I'm not scared."

Then came the words I had been waiting for. *"Tsai uu* ("Tea")*?"* I already knew that once I was inside, I had a place to stay for the night. As I drank the salty, milky tea, the family multiplied. I felt stupefyingly unentertaining with my pathetic vocabulary and blank, apologetic looks to all the questions I didn't understand, but brothers, cousins, grandparents, friends, and neighbors crowded around, watching me as if I were an action-packed movie. They served me a sheep's tail—a delicacy—a hand-sized, bumpy glob of white fat quivering nakedly in a bowl. Pure fat was the one thing I would never learn to stomach. I nervously ignored the opaque blob, and eventually someone removed it and filled the bowl with steaming *guriltai shöl* instead.

I managed to tell them where I was going—south, across the Selenge River toward a village called Arshant. They shook their heads and said there was no bridge. "Bridge." That was not one of the first words I had learned in French, Russian, or German. I had learned "train" and "post office" and "wine." In Mongolian, I learned "river" and "horse" and "bridge." *Güür. "Güür bakhguì* ("There is no bridge").*"* Then came explanations and directions and elaborations, none of which I could begin to decipher. I understood only that there was no bridge.

A child had been sent to fetch the local Russian-language schoolteacher. When she arrived, the young woman explained that the bridge had been wiped out in spring flooding. She said there was a boat in the village of Ikh Uul, fifty kilometers farther east. She said, "The family wants to apologize to you. Their son died one year ago today. He was three years old. Tonight they have gathered to remember him. They apologize if they seem somber. They think you coming on this day is a good omen."

I was still absorbing this disconcerting information when the family matriarch reached out and slipped a silver ring onto my middle finger. Above the gold trim of her dusty *del,* her cheeks were apple-rounded red, and her wise little triangular grin made me want to curl up in her lap like a child. Then her husband presented me with a bulging bag of *aaruul* and a 50-*tögrög* note. To refuse gifts or the small sums of money that often accompanied gifts would be an insult, but small reciprocal presents could always be offered. I gave her a Seattle pen in which a little plastic elevator climbed up and down the Space Needle, explaining that I could see this tower from my home. I gave her daughter a roll of wintergreen Lifesavers, which the girl accepted in cupped palms. She opened the roll and gave one to her little brother, who popped it into his mouth, screamed once, and spit it out into his hand, his shocked eyes darting from me to his big sister and back, the mint too sharp on his tongue in a land of no spices.

To offer payment for food and shelter would be offensive, but money could be given as a gift to young children, who would pass it on to their parents. In the frosty morning, gathered around a crackling stove, I gave each of the two smallest boys a dollar bill. It was a lot of money if you figured it in *tögrögs.* Maybe too much to be appropriate. Maybe worthless if they had no way to exchange it. Regardless, it felt pathetically small and cold compared to the family's generosity. Everyone examined the bills closely, and I understood that one uncle knew what they were worth in Ulaanbaatar. When the notes were eventually tucked into their mother's *del,* she reached out and dumped the rather revolting treat of two forkfuls of rancid butter into my tea.

She said she loved me. She said, "Thank you." Thank me? For drinking three times as much tea as anyone else because you keep refilling my bowl the minute it's empty and I really like it so I don't say no? For turning your son's memorial into the village's evening entertainment? Yet the appreciation was heartfelt and genuine. For sharing a bit of my world? I could show them how many gears my bicycle had and how the brakes worked. I could take pictures and let them look through the zoom lens, but language did not allow me to share much more than technology and smiles. She thanked me simply for being there, a puzzling creature from fantasyland; for wanting to be, as much as a one-night stranger with a thirty-word vocabulary could be, a part of their life and world. And I in turn thanked her, thanked them, for the depth of a hospitality they didn't know was special, for sharing their home with me, for taking me into their world as if I belonged.

The golden-brown prairie turned greener with every rotation of the pedals as the road drew parallel to the river. A thick sweep of deciduous foliage traced the water's route along a sharp spur of hills. I took long breaks, lying in the warm grass just below the breeze, savoring the boundlessness of the resplendent landscape and swatting at the occasional horsefly. A herd of camels tramped languidly through the swaying prairie. Hardy little horses grazed free in desolate stretches of grassland unmarked by the twentieth century. As I rolled downhill into Ikh Uul, a truck pulled up beside me. Two men, a teenage girl, and a shaven-headed boy tumbled out of the cab to ask where I was going.

"Across the river. . . . "

"No bridge," they said. "No boat." They produced a small red plastic bowl and filled it with *arkhi,* homemade alcohol distilled from cow's milk to a clear liquid, affectionately dubbed "Mongolian vodka." As the bowl passed among us, the truck driver increased the volume of each successive question as if at a certain decibel level I would suddenly understand Mongolian. "Follow, we help you," the girl finally managed in Russian. Over tea and fresh yogurt at their friend's house, everyone agreed that there was no bridge. And no boat.

"You must go east to Bulgan, where there is a bridge," came a voice from across the room in precise Russian. I turned to see a young woman standing in the doorway. She leaned into the door frame, her hands clasped together, her long hair pulled back into a low ponytail. Delgermaa had recently finished her studies in Ulaanbaatar and was completing an internship back home at the Ikh Uul school before receiving her degree as a Russian teacher.

"I came that way in the bus," I said, suddenly able to communicate in full sentences. "I don't want to go the same way twice."

Delgermaa glanced back at our host, and translated.

"These people will give you a ride in their truck, then you can go south to Kharkhorin and visit Erdenezuu Monastery," came the response.

"I was told there was a boat here."

"There is no boat."

"Don't people here ever cross the river?"

"Sometimes there is a small plane from Mörön that stops in Arshaant."

"There must be a boat."

"There is a big bridge in Bulgan."

The conversation went round and round like a dog chasing its tail, Delgermaa interpreting timidly but fluently for the room now full of people.

"There must be a boat."

"We can find out when there is a plane."

"There must be a boat."

There was a long pause. Glances that I couldn't interpret flew back and forth across the room. Finally Delgermaa apparently got the go-ahead to admit, "Well, yes, there is a boat, but it's dangerous."

"That's okay."

"No, it's really dangerous."

"Do other people cross the river that way?"

"Yes. But it's too dangerous for a foreigner."

I insisted. I was not going back to Bulgan on a truck. More discussion swirled around the room, and the next thing I knew, I was following Delgermaa across Ikh Uul to the snug log-and-plaster home where she lived with her parents. Although the family still cooked by woodstove and had no bathroom but a squat wooden outhouse across the yard, their house was designed for year-round living, with three separate rooms and bookshelves lining a solid wall. Even in the winter they would not put up a *ger*. Delgermaa's parents were schoolteachers, too. Her father explained that the boat would land well upriver of the road to Arshaant, and that I would need a guide to take me across the hills that stood between the road and the place where the boat would land. He said that in the morning he would find someone to go with me. This time I did not argue. They were going to let me cross the river, but clearly there was no question of letting me go alone.

I rolled out my sleeping bag on the floor next to Delgermaa's bed. After the electricity clicked off at eleven, we lay in the dark and talked. She was twenty-one, married, and pregnant. Her husband had just finished business school and was working for a Chinese imports company. "We did not plan to get pregnant so soon," her soft voice came out of the darkness, "but when it happened, we were happy. Now it is my husband's job to earn money for our own home in Ulaanbaatar, and my job to have the baby. Then my parents will take care of it so I can work."

Like cold pizza on Saturday morning, anything left over from dinner was valid breakfast food. Delgermaa and I were eating *buuz* (mutton and onions steamed in little pouches of dough), dumping them into our tea to reheat them, when her father walked in, followed by a short man with a small army-green rucksack on his back. He would be my Guide across the river, and I instantly had absolute faith in his ability as pathfinder. He wore wire-rimmed glasses and high black boots, and I imagined him as a man who could read the sky, who knew where the animals slept, a man who did not stir the leaves when he walked, a noble Indian scout who would lead me effortlessly through the secret passages of his land.

The Selenge flows north and east some thousand kilometers across Mongolia into southern Russia, where it finally drains into Lake Baikal. At Ikh Uul, it spreads into a web, some strands wide and shallow, others deep and narrow. In the spring and early summer, when snowmelt and thunder-showers swell its banks, the river probably becomes one broad swath of water, but in September it was a tangle of land and liquid, an intricate fili-gree of channels dissecting innumerable patches of solid ground. Guide moved gracefully through the fields toward the river. I dragged my bicycle and its brightly colored bags behind him, leaving a swath of crushed plants and displaced earth in our wake. We came to a wide stream. Guide sat down, pulled off his boots and stuck them into his little rucksack, then rolled his pants into shorts and became my hero as he made three trips through the cold, thigh-deep water, his bare feet balancing smoothly on the rocky bottom. He carried one set of panniers across while I unstrapped, unhooked, and disentangled the rest of Greene's load. Then he returned to lift my bicycle onto his shoulder and repeat the traverse. This time I struggled after him, my feet turning bright red in the biting current. I lurched over the slippery stones, inching forward, tent and sleeping bag tugging at my balance, never more than half an unlucky stumble from a freezing swim.

On the other side, with Greene reloaded and my shoes and socks back on, we trudged through light forest for a short while before coming to a branch of the river too swift and deep to ford on foot. It was a beautiful place   every breeze and rustle and bird call alive in the sweet green air but there was no boat, there were no boat people, and the opposite bank was a steep cliff unconducive to any sort of landing. I looked at Guide. Guide looked away, up and down the empty riverbank, baffled and suddenly un-sure. There was a rustle behind us, and a man appeared through the trees. He and Guide had a brief conversation, then, telling me to wait, they left together. I settled down on the rocky shore with my journal and a bag of crunchy *aarts* from Bolormaa's mother.

Two hours later, Guide returned and announced the obvious: This was the wrong place. We hiked back through the forest to a shallow ford. The day had warmed up considerably, and this time the ice-cold water was al-most refreshing. Sweat dribbled down my back as I pushed Greene through fields of dense, knee-deep weeds. Hordes of tiny insects landed on my salty face, but every time I lifted a hand from the handlebars to swat at them, Greene tipped roughly on the uneven ground, jerking at my arm and crashing into my side. Finally Guide stopped at a narrow stream and pointed across the water into the trees, "See the boat?" I did not see anything, but I dutifully sat down to take off my shoes and socks.

The "boat," when we reached it, was a single hollowed-out tree trunk. It was not dangerous, it was impossible: It would roll 180 degrees the minute it hit the water. Again I looked at Guide. Again he looked away, up and down the bank, as if the situation might suddenly change of its own accord. Then we turned around and retraced our steps. When we arrived back at the last stream we had crossed, two sturdy, barefoot teenage boys were standing on the opposite bank, looking for us. They splashed through the water, picked Greene up fully loaded, and carried her back across in one fell swoop.

I had lost all faith in Guide. It was four hours since we had left Ikh Uul. We had crossed the river four times, only to end up with nothing but dry prairie between us and the village. But the boys knew where we were going. We followed them up the river to the boat: two hollowed-out tree trunks tied together with sticks and wire to form a V. We piled my stuff into the tree trunks and lay Greene across the top. The boys waded the boat farther upstream, then pushed off into the water, one of them crouched at the narrow tip of the V, the other balancing on the back and steering with a long pole. When Delgermaa had told me that the crossing was too dangerous for a foreigner, I had laughed and replied, "That's okay, I can swim." Now, watching Greene cross the thick green water on two tree trunks, those flippant words echoed in my head. I could swim, but my bicycle could not.

Imagining Greene sinking swiftly to the bottom of the murky water, I held my breath until the boys deftly swung their boat along the opposite bank, unloaded Greene and her panniers, and turned the craft around to come back for me and Guide. I was triumphant: nobody could put me back on a truck just because there was no bridge.

On the other side, I strapped Greene's panniers back on. "How much do I owe them?" I asked Guide. "Later," he said, seeming puzzled by the question. The boys were pulling the boat safely up onto the muddy bank. Then we all set off together, and, as we traipsed across sandy islets and waded through channels of cold water, I realized that we had only begun to cross the river. But I had given up putting on my socks or rolling down my pants below my knees, and the two boys could heave Greene high over the water without unpacking her, so each channel-crossing was no longer a thirty-minute event. We passed through a broad clearing where men were mowing hay for the winter, their sickles swinging smoothly through the goldening grasses, and came to a tent where two rugged older men and a third barefoot adolescent seemed to be expecting us.

One of the men was tranquilly distant. Beneath close-shorn gray hair, his deep-set eyes were hooded slits. Only the silent smile in the corners of his mouth took part in the conversation. His companion, however, was energetic and gregarious. He wore an impishly cocked red felt hat and spoke rapid, rusty Russian. The three teenagers worked in manifest respect for him, their strong brown backs moving smoothly to and from the tent as they served bread and *öröm*. Pleasure played in their light grins and their dark eyes were clear and attentive. They built up the fire, filled a *togoo* from the river, and dumped in milk and a handful of tea leaves. I contributed a cucumber, more precious than I had realized, slicing it into the men's cupped, callused hands. The man in the red hat asked the Seven Questions. He asked how I liked his country, "our beautiful nature, our strong people." He expressed the Mongolians' profound pride in their land: "Genghis Khan. Cows, sheep, clean air, pure water—all you need to live." By now I doubted that Guide knew the way across the hills looming ahead of us, but I really didn't care. I had crossed the river and landed, my odd foreignness notwithstanding, in a welcoming circle of rugged men gathered around a fire. "I love your country," I told him, and it sounded so trite and so insufficient, and it was so sincere. And he understood that, and smiled.

However little confidence I had left in Guide's pathfinding abilities, I nevertheless kept an eye on him for the cue that it was time to move on. Eventually he nodded at me and got up. "I need to pay them," I said.

"Later," he shook his head.

"What do you mean, 'later'?" We were saying good-bye to the boys who had ferried us across the river. It was one of those moments, in a land where you don't speak the language, when you are the only one who does not know what is happening.

"The man in the red hat is the boss of the boats. The boys work for him," Guide explained. "He is coming with us. We will pay later."

With the third boy now pushing Greene, the boss of the boats led us on through the fields. We hiked for a quarter of an hour before reaching a robust branch of water. Only then did I understand that we were still in the middle of the Selenge. A boat exactly like the first one lay on the opposite shore. The boy tied his shirt and pants onto his head and plunged in to retrieve it. The sun had been blazing for hours now, and I envied him the swim. But as tempting as it was, I suspected that stripping down to my

〜・ *Greene and Guide are ferried across the Selenge River.*

underwear and saying I would meet them on the other side would not be quite appropriate. After ferrying us all across, the boy asked if he could ride Greene. I knew what would happen, but I couldn't refuse. He would have let me ride his horse. Balance, totter, giggle, balance, crash, his cheeks turning red, the two men laughing at him.

This time we really were across the river. "I need to pay," I said to Guide. "Later," said Boss, "first we must have tea." It had not been an hour since we last had tea, but the three of us set out uphill through dry Grecian landscape toward Boss's *ger*. Goats wandered in and out of the open door, and flies buzzed around the animal parts stored in tubs beneath the beds. As his wife served tea and *airag,* hooves sounded outside and a cheery fellow with a roaring laugh beneath his four-cornered hat ducked through the door and joined us. Then suddenly we were getting up, saying thank-you and goodbye, Guide was outside on a horse with Greene's front panniers slung across the front of his saddle, and the cheery fellow was swinging onto another horse with Greene's rear panniers. While I had been smiling blankly at a roomful of words I didn't know, the conversation swirling around me had somehow resulted in two horses and a second guide joining my trek.

It was the ultimately stupid scene from "Across Mongolia by Bicycle." Two horsemen carried my luggage up a mountain while I struggled behind on a bicycle, like some Victorian lady traveler roughing it alone in Africa with a contingent of natives carrying her steamer trunks. The horses disappeared over a hill while Greene and I fought through a sandy meadow. I was furious. This was stupid. I wanted a horse. Guide was awful. I imagined all sorts of horrible, nasty, mean things to yell at him. He wasn't much of a horseman, either. "Keep the bicycle away from the horse or you'll scare it," he waved at me as I caught up to them. I rolled past him as close as I could get.

Then we were going uphill again. The horses were at the top, with the two men looking down at me scrabbling for a foothold, pushing my bicycle through the rocks. I felt like an idiot. Then the new fellow, his smile stretching ear to ear, swung off his horse, handed his reins to Guide, and slid back down the hill to help me. Grateful, gasping, I reached the top. Then again, straight up an untrailed mountainside. Guide vanished into the forest. Smiley dismounted and, leading his horse with one hand, put the other on Greene's rear rack and began to push. Sweating, panting, I was just steering now, tripping on rocks and branches. I would not even look at Guide when we reached the pass.

Daylight was fading quickly. The Selenge River and Ikh Uul were just visible far below. We picked our way slowly across a cleft in the hills, the slope rising steeply to our right, dropping sharply to our left, a faint trail wending around big boulders. Then on the opposite side of the ravine, we were suddenly standing on a wide dirt road. When he had first crossed the river, I had wanted to pay Guide a handful of dollars, to give him my baseball cap and a pair of socks to replace the rags in which he wrapped his feet. The fourth time he and I had waded pointlessly through the water, and every time Smiley had come running downhill to help me, I had planned to refuse to give Guide a single *tögrög*. But now, through the dusk gathering in the valley below, I could make out the track winding south toward Arshaant. I dug into my pockets and gave each of them a handful of fifty-*tögrög* notes.

When, as we left his *ger,* I had asked Boss for the last time how much I owed him, Daniel's voice had echoed in my head. I had only the vaguest sense of what a reasonable price for the boat rides would be, and I knew that if Boss demanded some ridiculous sum, I would not have the nerve to bargain.

"I don't know," he had shrugged. "It's up to you."

It was the one answer I had not expected. I had looked desperately at Guide, who pulled several bills from his pocket and handed Boss what I guessed to be fifty *tögrögs*. I counted out double that and hoped it was enough to be right.

"No, no, no," Smiley and Guide both said now. "You don't owe us anything."

"Oh, yes, I do."

"No, no."

"Yes, yes."

Guide looked at Smiley, then shrugged and carefully counted out 150 *tögrögs* apiece and handed back the rest. There was a long moment as we all looked at each other. "Will you be all right?" Guide finally asked. "You're not afraid?" I smiled and shook my head. They raised their hands in farewell and turned their horses around. The moon was rising and night falling as Greene and I flew down the hill to the dusky plain below.

In the middle of the night I crawled out of my tent into a silvery vastness truly unchanged since Genghis Khan and his hordes loped east more than half a millennium ago. There was no glow of city lights on the horizon, no ranger station at the edge of the next valley, no quaint general store, no paved road. There was nothing but space, unbounded and untamed. A brilliant moon lit the blackness crystal clear. Moonshadows of every blade of grass danced silently in the wildness. It was the emptiest, quietest place I have ever been. I threw my arms out wide and spun slowly around and around in the dazzling clarity of the night, the stars blurring into ribbons of light above me.

—•—

Mongolia is divided into eighteen *aimags* (provinces or states), and each *aimag* is subdivided into several *sums* (counties). Mörön is the capital of Khövsgöl Aimag, which stretches from Russia in the north to Arshaant in the south. Beyond Arshaant, I would cross into Arkhangai Aimag, one of the most populous regions in Mongolia, where the average population per square kilometer rises to two. Alaska, Greenland, and Western Sahara are less densely populated than Mongolia, as are three Canadian provinces and two Australian states, although of all these, only Greenland and Western Australia cover a greater area than Mongolia. Among sovereign nations, however, Mongolia has the lowest population density on the planet. When my mother heard this, she worried, "How will you find people?" I said not to worry: "They'll find me."

A family stood beside the road, waiting. Long before I saw them, they had spotted me, a techno-dot moving through their eternal scenery.

"Where did you come from?!"

"Ikh Uul."

They stared in disbelief. "How did you get across the river?"

"By boat."

I recount conversations in complete sentences. In reality I understood only tiny fragments of what was said. I knew the word for "river," and guessed at what the question must be. I could not remember how to say "boat," so I used the Russian word and mimed rowing, and watched their faces, looking for recognition. They nodded vigorously.

"Is Arshaant straight ahead?" I asked. ("Arshaant?" I raised my eyebrows and pointed down the road.)

"No, no, no," they shook their heads and pointed across the valley to another track. They had misunderstood me, I thought, or maybe they just didn't know. The Selenge River was at my back, and Arshaant lay south of Ikh Uul. In my mind, the world tends to be a perfect grid. "Arshaant," I repeated. They nodded, and in the dirt they drew a looping diagram of the road climbing a hill, curving around on itself, then turning right and right again. They clearly had no idea what they were talking about. I thanked them politely and rolled off a little way before pulling out my compass. The arrow swung adamantly to the right. I was facing west, not south. Arshaant was exactly where they had said it was. What I had once considered a good sense of direction had disintegrated completely in the vastness of Mongolia.

I turned across the prairie toward the hills. The wind was picking up, and as the road approached the base of the hills it turned to sand. I stood up on the pedals and Greene sank deeper into the soft ground. I got off and walked. Up on a ridge, two horses cantered by, their riders staring down at me as they passed. Whose idea had it been to buy a bicycle instead of a horse?! Then the road turned sharply, straight up a steep, rocky, ungraded hillside. It took me two hours to push Greene to the top of the slope, where an *ovoo's* tattered flags fluttered against the sky. Ominous clouds roiled far away on the horizon. A whirring burst in the air above me. Black wings cleaved the space and echoed through the airy stillness like a clap of distant thunder. The bird rose and dove and disappeared. Sucking slowly on a piece of *aaruul,* I walked three times around the *ovoo* and tucked a few *tögrögs* under a rock. At the bottom of the hill, I filled my water bottles from a narrow stream, then headed out across the gloriously empty golden prairie toward the next hill. Over that hill I turned right again, up another long, sandy valley, pedaling slowly into a growing headwind.

In the gray, windy twilight, I pulled into the quiet residential streets of Arshaant. *"Sain baina uu* ("Hello")," I launched at a teenage girl visible behind a fence. A woman clad in bright blue Gore-Tex riding a twenty-one-gear mountain bike was more than a surprise, more than an oddity. I might as well have been from the moon. I was almost inconceivable. Timidly curious, she approached.

"Zochid buudal?" I inquired.

"Bakhgui," she shook her head, dark eyes shining out of a fairy-tale-heroine beautiful face, black hair drifting to her waist. Her diminutive, bowlegged grandmother appeared on tiptoe beside her, peering over the fence. "Where are you from? Where are you going? Alone? *Tsai uu?"*

There were two houses in the dusty yard. The girl led me past the tiny cabin where she and her grandmother lived, straight into the second, larger home. Up the steps and inside, bicycle and all. Her cousin, a sturdy, big-boned, flat-faced twenty-four-year-old woman named Gerlee (pronounced Gehr-LAY), took one look at me and started cooking. Two ten-year-old girls who had been playing together in a corner went to work mixing flour and water. Delger, the beautiful teenager, chopped mutton and onion. Gerlee directed the girls' dough-making, built up the fire in the stove, and pummeled me with the Seven Questions all at the same time. Delger began sliding great slabs of butter into the *togoo*. The little girls were now dropping spoonfuls of mutton and onion into circles of dough.

I joined them, pinching the edges of the dough shut to make the large dumplings called *khuushuur*. Guests are not supposed to work, but Gerlee was too amused by my awkward, inefficient handling of the half-moons to make me stop. Her thick fingers quickly and fluidly produced consistent designs around *khuushuur* that never fell apart when they were tossed into the bubbling pot of melted butter. Sitting around the woodstove burning our fingers and tongues on the deep-fried *khuushuur,* we ate and mimed and laughed. How old is my father? How old is my mother? Do I have brothers and sisters? How old is my sister? This conversation took half an hour as I slowly learned the words for "father," "mother," "sister," "seventy-three," "sixty-four," and "twenty-four."

The electricity in Gerlee's house was not working, so after dinner we

blew out the candle and went next door. The tiny, elfin shack was lit by a
single bare bulb hanging from the ceiling. It was full of people, but there is
always room for more. We squeezed onto the edge of a bed next to Gerlee's
best friend Altanzuul. By way of introduction, Gerlee recited everything
she had learned about me—where I had bicycled from, that I was not married, how old my parents were. Then she pointed to the tiny, leathery woman
crouched cooking by the stove, a wizened woodcut visage in the dancing
firelight. "That is my grandmother, she is seventy-two." The woman's eyes
sparkled up at me, nodding. There was a well-justified pride in years in the
harshly Darwinian land. As the *arkhi* was passed, Gerlee warned me that by
morning the weather would be very bad. Scattered words of Russian flew
out of the shadows as everyone tried to help her talk to me, to convince
me not to leave in the morning, to spend the day in Arshaant. Shadows
danced on the wooden walls of the tiny home. The guttural rhythms of
Mongolian filled the air. Wordless smiles crossed the room. I said I would
like very much to stay for a day.

•

We woke to weather as gray and unfriendly as Gerlee had predicted. I pulled
on all my layers of polypropylene and fleece. She tossed a light vest over
her short-sleeved cotton shirt, grabbed my arm, and led me outside. There
is a clear division of labor in Mongolia—men's and women's—yet without a concomitant judgment of relative worth, without an apparent sense
of superiority or inferiority. Chopping wood is a man's job, but there was
no man in Gerlee's household, so she had learned to chop firewood as
adeptly as she performed the more traditional woman's job of milking. I
thought I chopped a pretty mean hunk of wood myself, but watching me
swing the ax, Gerlee could barely smother her laughter. I decided not to
try the cow. Altanzuul and Delger arrived, and the three of us set off for
downtown Arshaant. A solid bridge crossed the river that ran through the
middle of the village. On the other side were the usual cement buildings
and dusty streets.

As we passed a dilapidated playground, a young woman approached us
and introduced herself directly to me. Bayarjargal was a Russian-language
teacher at the local school. She had delicate features, wispy bangs, and the
ethereal comportment of a ballet dancer. I had the distinct impression that
she had not run into us by accident. She asked if I would visit the school.
"Sure," I said, not knowing that in that moment I was abandoning my plans
to bicycle from Ulaanbaatar to Beijing. Bayarjargal exchanged a few abrupt

words with Gerlee, and then suddenly she and I were heading across the schoolyard, leaving Gerlee, Altanzuul, and Delger behind.

Children giggled and whispered, looking at me until I looked at them, then ducking their heads away, eyes to their wooden desks. I talked about where I was from and where I was going. I drew the United States on the chalkboard and explained about there being two Washingtons. I spoke Russian; Bayarjargal and a teacher named Enkhtuya translated into Mongolian. Enkhtuya was a starched young woman with an uneasy laugh and a vague wariness, as if she expected to be unpleasantly surprised around every corner. Both she and Bayarjargal wore neat sweaters and long, full skirts, witness to their years as students in Ulaanbaatar and Russia.

When class was over, they led me down the hall to an office where an older man sat behind a desk. He motioned to the chair opposite him. Enkhtuya and Bayarjargal stood against the wall. Tall, thin, dressed in a trim western suit and wearing glasses, the man introduced himself in excellent Russian as Agvantseren. His questions began as everyone's questions began, but quickly veered off in a different direction. Instead of asking whether I was married or had children, he asked why I spoke Russian, how long I had studied it, what kind of work I did in America. Finally, on behalf of the school, he invited me to stay in Arshaant for a few days. "We will provide a place for you to live. Where are you staying now?"

I couldn't remember Gerlee's name. Mongolian names were still a mystery to me, jumbles of meaningless consonants that I had to hear a dozen times before they stuck in my head. Bayarjargal jumped in and told him where I had spent the night.

"We will give you your own room," he said.

"I don't mind living with people, but I'll have to ask if it's all right to stay for a few more days."

"I think you would prefer to stay in an apartment," he said.

The door opened to a graceful, sophisticated woman with high, rounded cheekbones, and laughter etched deeply around her eyes. Baasanjav was the school's biology instructor and vice-director. She had given up a prestigious job as a scientist in Ulaanbaatar to return to Arshaant and take care of her aging parents. Her Russian was impeccable. "What would you like to do while you're here?" she asked. "Would you like to ride a horse?" I said I would love to go riding. "Really riding," I emphasized, preemptively deflecting an assumption that, as a western tourist, I just wanted to have my picture taken sitting on a Mongolian horse. The door opened again and Gerlee stuck her head in. The confident, in-charge young woman with whom I had chopped wood only a few hours earlier was gone. Her cheeks were bright red and she was clearly out of her element. Bayarjargal said something, and Gerlee left with a slam of the door. Baasanjav squinted out the window at the gray sky. "Tomorrow," she smiled, "we will go horseback riding tomorrow."

Followed by a dozen gently swarming, giggling schoolchildren, Enkhtuya, Bayarjargal, and I crossed the schoolyard to a square three-story cement building that functioned as a dormitory for the many children who lived in the *khödöö* (the countryside, the outback)—too far from the village to walk or ride in to school every day. They showed me to a white-walled institutional room lined with four metal cots. They said I could stay there. They said it was hard for me to communicate with Gerlee. They said I had a lot of work to do writing my journal. (I hadn't said a word to them about writing, although I had scribbled a bit in the morning.) They said they had already spoken to Gerlee.

The teachers' contempt was palpable. It seemed absurd in the tiny village, but Gerlee was intimidated by the prim, educated young women, and they were disdainful of her. They wanted to get me away from her. How much as prestige for themselves, how much because they considered her below me, how much because they truly believed that I would be happier alone in the stark, cold room with a dozen kids' faces pressed against the curtainless windowpane staring at me, I couldn't tell. And I didn't put my foot down. I didn't say, "No, I don't want to move in here." I didn't insist on understanding whether they had *asked* Gerlee if I could stay another night at her home, or had simply *told* her that I was moving. I gave in to the confusion of things happening around me in an unfamiliar culture and a language I didn't understand.

They said we should go get my bicycle. We walked up the hill. The air was tense, everyone uncomfortable. Yet even in such awkward circumstances, the rules of hospitality were not broken. Gerlee served tea. I am used to being the interpreter; I am not used to relying on someone else. I was unsure how to take charge of the situation, of the words. Only the night before, Gerlee and I had communicated with mime and forty mutual spoken words. Slowly, convolutedly, simplistically, but directly. Looking into each others' faces. Each others' eyes. Laughing a lot. Now I spoke to her in precise, empty Russian translated by the teachers. "Translated." They did not simply repeat the words we said to each other. They intercepted and rearranged, they added and subtracted meanings, implications, and commentary of their own. This I knew without understanding the words themselves. We all drank quickly, looking at the floor, then we took Greene and left. Back at the dormitory, facing a night alone in the unheated room with children opening the door every few minutes to peek at me, displeasure must have been written all over my face.

"You'd rather be back with those people, wouldn't you?" Enkhtuya asked uncomfortably.

"Yes," I said, finally giving a straight answer. "It was cozy and sociable. I told Agvantseren that I would rather stay at Gerlee's, but then you all announced I was moving here, so I thought Gerlee didn't want me." This wasn't true, of course, or at least it was a distilled version of the truth. At first, when Agvantseren had offered me "an apartment," I had hesitated, wondering whether it would be an imposition to ask Gerlee to stay with her for several days (and, perhaps, somewhere in the back of my mind, actually picturing a private place with plumbing), but by later in the day, I knew perfectly well that she would have welcomed me to stay. What *was* true was that I had been trying to do what the teachers seemed to want, because I assumed that that was the *right* thing to do. Meanwhile they had been trying to give me what they thought *I* would want. They simply could not imagine that I would rather sleep in a Mongolian home than in this room, which, based on what they had seen in Russia, was the kind of room that foreigners liked. In the end, no one was happy.

As tentatively as Lkhamsüren had once offered me a bowl of *guriltai shöl,* Enkhtuya invited me home for the night. She and her tidy house were worlds apart from Gerlee's boisterous, haphazard home around the corner. Enkhtuya had grown up in Mörön and did not know how to milk a cow or ride a horse. At twenty-six she was the youngest of nine children, so when she had left Mörön to come to Arshaant, her parents had moved with her. Her father was not home. Her mother was a tiny woman with sharp, twinkling eyes and a permanent cigarette dangling from the corner of her mouth. Throughout the evening she murmured over and over, "I can't believe it, an American sitting in my kitchen, sleeping in my home. It's like a movie."

Enkhtuya's daughter Oyunga was a bright-eyed six-year-old who Enkhtuya lovingly described as the product of "a mistake of a marriage" in Ulaanbaatar. She was gently urging her to do something, nodding that universal, parental "go ahead" nod. The little girl, her hair topped by energetic pink and red ribbons, her eyes sparkling, squirmed and blushed and pushed into her grandmother's knees for courage, then launched proudly into an English counting rhyme, her eyes darting from the foreign guest to her mother and back.

In the morning I put on a skirt and took my hair out of braids. Enkhtuya wanted me to teach one of her first-year Russian classes. She handed me a textbook and went to sit at the back of the room with Bayarjargal, Baasanjav, and Agvantseren. I didn't know it, but this was a test. The lesson for the day was the difference between "here" and "there." "The chair is here." "The table is there." "Where is the chair?" Several pupils crowded around each book. They whispered answers to each other. I *shooshed* them. They giggled and shrank back into their places. The teachers whispered answers from the back of the room. I *shooshed* Agvantseren—the school's, perhaps the village's, elder statesman—and everyone tittered gleefully to see him treated with such a lack of deference. He grinned and nodded and refrained from prodding the kids for the next minute or two. After class, we returned to the office at the end of the hall, where we were joined by the school principal, a calm, deliberate man for whom Agvantseren acted as interpreter. He explained that Enkhtuya and Bayarjargal had taken a four-month English course in Mörön the previous year, and hoped eventually to teach English instead of Russian. "To help them achieve this goal, the school would like to invite you to stay in Arshaant and teach English for one year."

Completely surprised, I stuttered that I couldn't stay in Mongolia for a year.

"How long can you stay?" Agvantseren countered quickly.

"I have to . . ."—I thought about the blank desert stretching a thousand kilometers south from Ulaanbaatar toward China. I thought about the intimacy and immediacy of daily village life. The point, I reminded myself, was not to pedal every inch of the way—"I have to get to Ulaanbaatar before it snows. But then, maybe I could come back." I had a plan. A goal. A city no more real to me than a name in a nightmare fairy tale, but I was not ready to give up on Saigon. "Not for a year. But maybe for a month?" My brain was scrambling through a new and unexpected set of options, opportunities, and plans, trying to make a decision, to give them an answer, to make a commitment.

"That would be great. Whatever you can do. You don't have to decide now," said Baasanjav, completely unconcerned with planning or commitment. "The sun is out. Shall we go riding?"

I have always loved horses, and always been allergic to them. I went to take an antihistamine. My first-aid kit was gone. I dug through all four panniers; it wasn't there. That made three things gone: my black turtleneck must have slipped down between the bed and the wall as I repacked in the gloomy hotel room in Sükhbaatar; my cable lock had bounced off the top of Greene's panniers somewhere on the rocky road toward Khatgal; and now the first-aid kit. I had other clothes. I had a second bicycle lock. It was as if those things had known they were superfluous before I did. But this was serious. I was in Mongolia without so much as an aspirin or a single bandage. I was heading toward Vietnam without malaria prophylactics. I couldn't remember when I had last seen the bright red kit, but I could not believe that I had just left it somewhere. I was organized. I paid attention. I didn't lose things. At the same time, I refused to believe that it had been stolen. Refused to believe that anyone I had liked and trusted would have taken it. So how? Who? Where? When? I would never know.

Baasanjav and I walked our horses down the road and over a rise into the next valley. She was beautiful in her dark purple *del,* her bearing ancient and regal as she sat her mount with the innate ease of one who has ridden since childhood. She was also intelligent and funny and on a mission to be sure I had fun so I would want to come back. We trotted past a shimmering salt lake and were soon cantering down a long valley. The reins in my hand were unmatched, twisted rawhide strips. The saddle was narrow and stiff, with a straight wooden pommel and cantle. The horses were wild creatures, rudimentarily trained but not tame, not docile. There was not a pampered hair on them. They were ugly, stubby little animals with boxy, oversize heads, but they radiated an ability and a willingness to go forever. Their indomitable spirit and noble energy mirrored the character of the land and people.

When I had said "really riding," I had imagined a scenic hour-long jaunt. Turned out we had a job to do. After two hours in the saddle, we found Baasanjav's cows far down the valley, rounded them up, and turned back toward Arshaant. On the way, we collected other villagers' cows until we were driving fifty head of cattle. Circling back for stragglers, chasing down strays—I was herding cattle. I was herding cattle in Mongolia! And even better—there was not a tickle in my nose, nor a single little red bump on my forearms. Mongolian horses are not like other horses. I am not allergic to Mongolian horses.

In the morning Agvantseren, Baasanjav, Bayarjargal, Enkhtuya, Gerlee, Delger, and Altanzuul walked me out past the end of the village. Greene was loaded with gifts of butter, bread, *tos* (sweet fried flour and butter), cabbage, and literally kilos of *aaruul, öröm,* and *byaslag* (the Mongolian dairy product most similar to western cheese). More than I would ever be able to eat. As little as it had been possible to accept without insult or offense. The dusty road wound clearly down the valley and into the hills. Baasanjav stopped. "Just send a telegram to let us know when you'll be back."

___•___

Hot golden prairie lay silent and pristine beneath an endlessly blue sky. Murky lakes puddled in shallow concavities. I was somewhere south of a village called Tsetserleg, which is somewhere south of Arshaant. The air was still and I could see forever. I had been alone inside the landscape for hours. But now there was a horse rising into the periphery of the vast nothing-ness, and soon it was beside me, the rhythmic thud of its hooves slowing to match the pace of Greene's wheels. I stopped. The teenager reined in and grinned broadly. His body was almost a man's, but his eyes were eager like a child's. He was there yesterday when I arrived in Tsetserleg, when the ugly drunk demanded to see what was in my panniers.

Did I remember him, the youth wanted to know. I understood that this was his question, although we had virtually no words in common. I cer-tainly didn't know the Mongolian for "remember." But I understood, and I nodded. I remembered his horse, a lithe dappled gray. I remembered how easily he sat up there, high on the withers, one stirrup slightly longer than the other, as Mongolians have ridden across the centuries, across half the world once. I remembered how he sat up there, watching, until the ugly drunk finally gave up and a young woman with a baby in her arms invited me home for the night. Now he was pointing into the hills, saying he was on his way home. I nodded and pointed down the road: "That is where I am going." He grinned again, took one last, long look at me, and turned his horse across the prairie.

The hills were not high, but they were muddy and rocky and steep. I was on foot, pushing, when I saw the gray horse stop. The boy was watch-ing me. Then I was rolling down the other side and he was turning away. As I approached the next hill, I saw him stop again. I pedaled hard, shifting down and down, standing, fighting for balance, unwilling to fail with his vibrant young eyes on me. The prairie was flat for a while after that, stretch-ing out under Greene's tires, and the pedaling was easy. Then I heard the galloping hooves, and the dappled gray animal was back at my side. The grinning teenager pointed to the hill ahead of us. I downshifted, hit the rise, pushed harder and harder, but eventually I lost and had to jump off. He was instantly off his horse. With one hand holding his reins and the other on Greene's rear rack, he pushed her up the incline. The hill crested and we were laughing together, breathing hard. He accepted a drink from my water bottle. The only Mongolian I ever saw drink plain water. We needed no words.

After a while we moved on together, out again across the prairie. The glow of late afternoon was settling over the grassland. A herd of horses grazed in the distance. Gentle mountains rimmed the world. He was beautiful, this boy who was almost a man. He rode like a prince. I wanted to take his picture. He circled around me, wheeling his horse in too-tight circles, smiling big at the camera, never as beautiful as he had been unposed, serene and organic in the landscape. *"Tsai uu?"* he asked then, pointing to a lone house just visible at the foot of the hills. I nodded, and we left the road. The grass was lush here. The turf squished soppily beneath Greene's wheels. We negotiated a rickety footbridge over a stream.

His mother and sister had seen us coming and were waiting. The little girl, her cheeks wind-chapped redder than the ribbon in her hair, leaned into her mother's side, torn between uncertainty and curiosity. Inside the wooden home, his father sat on the floor, his left leg curled under him, his back straight along the line of his right leg. His body was powerful. His face had spent decades in the sun, the wind, the snow. He wore a traditional felt hat that rose to a point like a crown above his head. From a tobacco pouch of silvered light-green cloth, he filled a long pipe, and his daughter tonged an ember out of the stove to light it for him. He spoke Russian in a deep, gravelly voice and translated for his family as they asked:

"Do you have cows in America?" Yes, but I live in the city.

"Do you have marmots in America?" Yes, but we don't eat them.

"Do you have spring, summer, fall, and winter in America?" Yes, except in a part of the country called California. Where I grew up.

"Are there still Indians in America?" he asked. "We have heard that they came from Mongolia."

The first time I had heard this question, from the schoolboy in Khatgal, I had unthinkingly brushed it off as the simplistic conceit of a small, isolated nation. Now, looking into his regal, lined face, I thought of the Bering land bridge, and I thought otherwise. "Yes," I said.

He asked if I had cycled from America.

"No," I laughed. "Only from Irkutsk."

He said he would like his son to go to America one day.

"Why not? It's far away and very expensive, but anything is possible."

"Can he ride his horse there?" the strong whisper rasped.

I laughed again. "Quite a ride."

~· *"Can my son ride his horse to America?"*

"What," he insisted, "are the roads like?"

There was a long silent second while my mind scurried through the realization that the Pacific Ocean, which has fringed the geography of my entire life, did not figure in his picture of the Earth. I showed him one of the tiny tin world globes I had brought with me, and explained about the ocean. "This is Mongolia. This is America. This is all water. You need a boat or an airplane to get there." He knew what an airplane was. He had seen them far, far overhead sometimes.

"Ah," he nodded solemnly, and I gave his daughter the globe.

Clouds had been creeping slowly across the horizon, and with sunset the wind suddenly howled in fiercely out of the hills. We huddled around the stove as the storm poured down around us. I pulled a candle out of my panniers and gave it to his wife. She had been tossing dry dung into the fire; now with the same hand she began dumping fresh noodles into the boiling water. The walls were wet where rain blew in around the metal sheets that the father and son had dashed outside to prop over the unpaned windows. After dinner, they showed me where to spread my sleeping bag, on the bearskin that covered the floor between their two beds. Husband and wife crawled into one bed, brother and sister into the other. The candle stump flared and guttered out.

⚓

The prairie buckled slowly into low foothills. Faint tracks occasionally crossed the gentle dips and rises. I had been heading south as best I could within the curves of landscape, but I was lost again. A vague trail led into a narrowing valley. I followed it, ascending slowly along a stream burbling beneath the grasses. The shadows lengthened, bringing the chill of evening on their edges. Then the trail turned sharply and I found myself in light forest, staring up a steep, leafy incline. This definitely was not south anymore, but the only other choice was to turn around. I pushed Greene up the mountain until I came to a clearing where a large *ovoo* afforded some comfort, lending the route at least a past legitimacy. I set up my tent under the trees and boiled dried peas from Seattle and fresh cabbage from Arshaant over a sputtering little fire, then crawled into my sleeping bag.

In the shivering morning light, I walked around the *ovoo*. To my left, the ground rose toward a higher summit. To the right, it sloped downhill. A faint track seemed to wind straight ahead of me, east along the rim to the next saddle. "No," I reminded myself. "Follow the compass. Ignore the road, and follow the compass." South led down across a flowered alpine field. Soon a narrow, sloping ravine appeared. I dragged Greene through the brush and found a meandering footpath. I crossed my fingers and pointed her down the hill. The trail dropped steadily—fainter and stronger, stronger and fainter—and gave out finally into a broad valley. For hours I played hopscotch through the arborescence of streams and tributaries meandering out of the canyons in search of the river. Time and again, I took off my shoes and socks, rolled up my pants, balanced across slippery rocks through freezing water, then pulled shoes and socks back on over glistening red feet.

A round-faced young man in blue jeans and a dark red *del* lay in the grass by a shallow ford. A hand-rolled cigarette hung from the corner of his mouth and a baseball cap tilted backward on his head. A half dozen marmot pelts dangled from his motorcycle. "It's out of gas—do you have any?" he greeted me, nodding at the vehicle. His wooden-stocked rifle was propped on the ground, aimed at a distant marmot hole. He was waiting for the animal to pop its head above ground. He was waiting for someone to come by with gas. He might wait all day, yet it was a waiting that had its own value and no resemblance to impatient western finger drumming, pacing, and watch checking. It had the value of the present—spending, maybe passing, but not killing time.

I didn't have any gas, but I did have a big bag of cheeses, and he had a big bag of *bortsog* (small fried bread twists). So we sat together in the sun and had a little picnic, which is what you do in Mongolia when you come upon someone broken down or out of gas—you share your food and keep him company for a while and help if you can. And if you can't help, you wish him luck, and wade on across the river.

The valley stretched before me, long and flat, but as the afternoon wore on and the headwind picked up, I knew I wouldn't reach Arkhangai (as everyone called the capital of Arkhangai Province, although my map said Tsetserleg) that night. So when a cluster of three *gers* came into view near the river, I turned off the road. It is perfectly acceptable in Mongolia for a traveler to appear at a stranger's home and ask for a night's shelter. I knew this, in theory; in practice, I could not yet imagine asking a question so completely at odds with the conventions of my American upbringing. So I fished for an invitation.

"How far to Arkhangai?" I asked the woman sitting milking a cow.

"Forty kilometers," she estimated.

"Ah." I looked at my watch and squinted at the early evening sky. "No problem. I have a tent."

"*Tsai uu?*"

CHAPTER 3

Twinkle, Twinkle, Little Star

Wandering toward the central square the morning after I arrived in Arkhangai, I instantly spotted the three people in down jackets and hiking boots. The color of our skin was sufficient introduction. Christian was German. Thierry and Claire were from France. They were on their way to Lake Khorgo, 160 kilometers to the west, where they planned to spend several days hiking. A change of pace sounded inviting. So did the ease of French and German. Two hours later, Greene was locked in the hotel and we were all jouncing down the road toward Lake Khorgo in the back of a hired Jeep. Christian wanted to be driven all the way to the western end of the lake, his plan being to hike back slowly along its northern shore, where there was no road. The driver wanted to drop us off as soon as we reached Tariat, the village at the eastern tip of the lake. They compromised and, as dusk turned to dark, the Jeep left us halfway along the southern shore and disappeared back toward Arkhangai.

We built a roaring bonfire and Christian cooked whole wheat pasta and miso soup. Shortly after we had crawled into our tents, my stomach started going funny. Cramps rumbled in the pit of my belly. Waves of chills swept through my body. I crawled back out into the night. The sky was an inky vault ablaze with more stars than a child growing up forty miles from the effulgent glow of Los Angeles could believe existed. Beneath the riot of light, I squatted miserably in the dark. Exhaustion, the first processed food I had eaten in a month, my period, which was two weeks late—I did not let myself consider any more serious explanations for the twisting tightness in my abdomen.

Back in my sleeping bag, trying to ignore my stomach but unable to fall asleep, my thoughts wandered to the question that had been hovering in the back of my mind for a week now: whether or not to return to Arshaant. Returning would mean then taking the train from Ulaanbaatar to Beijing—there would be no cycling across the Gobi Desert in late

November for me—and as much as I wanted to deny it, it still mattered to me to be "the first person to cycle all the way from. . . ." Even if I didn't believe that I *was* the first—the first ever, the first white person, the first westerner, or even the first white westerner since eighteen hundred something—even if I knew that a line on a map did not, could not, define the kind of journey that had drawn me across an ocean, even then I was hesitant to let go of the aesthetically pleasing idea of an unbroken line of ink snaking across a one-dimensional paper representation of the infinitude of people and places I might really get to know if I stayed.

By morning the worst of the cramps had subsided. We took our time drinking tea and packing before eventually setting off west along the lake. A small caravan plodded single-file down the road toward us—a child perched atop mountains of belongings high on a camel's back; a woman on a horse with an infant in her arms; a boy and a girl, six or seven years old, on two heavily loaded horses. Their father's deep-set eyes peered down at us from a pock-marked, bearded face as we showed him our map. I pointed to the end of the lake, where several little squiggles of river drained into the larger body of water. I asked how far it was.

"Far," he said.

"How many kilometers?" I asked, tracing my finger toward the northern shore.

He shook his head. *"Güür bakhgui,"* he said.

"Ys ("Water")*?"* I asked, and held my hand questioningly to my knees, my waist.

He shook his head, leaned forward, and held his hand just above his horse's head. "The water is deep to a horse's ears."

Mongolians' approximations of distances were usually wrong by half. I had learned that if someone said I had 40 kilometers to go, it would probably be 20. Their knowledge of topography, however, was usually infallible. On the other hand, I had been told *"güür bakhgui"* before, and the rivers didn't look like much on the map. Christian was also inclined to disregard the warning and assume that we could get ourselves across. We thanked the man and kept going. The hills were trimmed in trees turning autumn yellow. The water was a deep, pristine blue. We ate a leisurely picnic lunch on a perfect sandy beach, then late in the afternoon we reached the western end of the lake. Several strands of river spread into marsh. Christian and I took off our shoes and tried, the mud sucking at our feet, but again and again we were stopped by channels of water too wide and deep to wade across, and by the sight of increasingly dubious-looking mud beyond them.

There was no bridge. And this time there was also no boat. No rickety pier. No old fisherman willing to give us a ride, as I would have looked for anywhere else in the world. But Mongolians do not traditionally eat fish, so they don't fish, which means that they don't have picturesque little rowboats just waiting to ferry hiking tourists across the water.

Eventually we admitted defeat and continued west down the road until we came to a small *ger* encampment. Being part of a group was very different from being a solo traveler. Christian did things differently than I. He passed right by the women milking cows and approached the men chopping wood.

"Sain baina uu?"

"Sain. Ta Sain baina uu ("Fine, and you")*?"*

Christian swung his backpack to the ground and took out a pack of cigarettes. A culture of its own, smoking, to which I was not an initiate. He shared the cigarettes around. The men smoked, their inhalations interspersed with long, satisfied silences and incidental questions about where we were from and where we were going.

"Tent?" Christian eventually queried, miming, "Can we put up our tents and sleep here?"

"Of course," the men nodded. *"Tsai uu?"*

We followed them inside. Christian passed out more cigarettes, and candy to the children, but it felt more like an invasion than a joining, our backpacks massive in the modest home. We spread a map out on the low table. A half dozen adults pointed eagerly to familiar place names and read them out loud. They were fascinated by the paper depictions, but did not relate them to the geography they knew. Our host took my pen and drew his own map. Fifteen kilometers to the bridge, he said, drawing a straight line. Above the line he drew a circle. *"Jijig nuur* ("Little lake")." From the bridge, he drew a line to this little lake. "Ten kilometers," he said. Only then, he made clear, could we turn back along the northern shore of Lake Khorgo.

In retrospect, an extra day or two does not sound particularly daunting. At the time, given the continued grumblings in my stomach, it seemed overwhelming. It turned out to be more than the others wanted to take on either. So the next day we headed slowly back the way we had come. After only a few hours, we heard the rumble of a truck. I asked the statuesque woman behind the wheel how far they were going. To Ulaanbaatar, she said. Christian, Thierry, and Claire wanted to be dropped off in Tariat. They were still determined to spend some time on the northern shore. But when the truck stopped to let them out, I asked the driver to take me all the way back to Arkhangai.

And so began one of the most wonderfully Mongolian evenings of my trip. I was riding in the open back of the truck with twenty men and a goat. A young veterinarian warned me that we were in for a long, hard night. "I know, I know, no problem," I dismissed his protective cautions with false bravado. The rattling, bumping ride had already sent my stomach into convulsions. Every jounce of the truck shot pain through my belly, and with sunset the temperature had begun to drop quickly. I pulled my legs up tight to my chest and shivered, trying desperately to keep smiling. I was sitting on a bag of something, between the goat and an older, bespectacled gentleman. He reached over and wrapped his sheepskin-lined *del* around me.

As the stars slowly multiplied, the men's voices rose into the evening sky. The veterinarian began translating the songs for me. Enveloped in the woolly *del,* I was warm now, but it still felt like somebody was walking through a minefield in my abdomen, and getting blown up at every step. It was a struggle to look interested in his sweet explanations. I closed my eyes. When I woke up, the truck was stopped in the middle of starlit blackness, an open *ger* door spilling yellow light onto the prairie. It was the driver's brother's home. "We will sleep here," the veterinarian said.

I tried to take just a nibble of *öröm* from the *tavgiin idee,* but someone handed me a large piece of *aaruul.* I had developed quite a liking for *aaruul's* odd—chalky, smoky, sour—flavor. But now suddenly the smell turned my stomach and my throat clenched at the taste. I slipped it into my pocket. *Arkhi* was being poured, the small bowl passed to the man sitting to the right of the host. Holding the bowl, the man began to sing. After a few notes, voices from around the *ger* joined in until everyone was singing. At the end of the song the singer downed the alcohol, then the bowl was refilled and passed to the next man to initiate the next song. By the light of two candles and the heat of the fire they sang graceful, painful, hopeful songs; and as the cramps subsided, I giggled with the pleasure of being there instead of in a tent somewhere speaking French.

The man to my left emptied the bowl of *arkhi.* Our host refilled it and raised a toast to me, the alien, the guest, then passed it to me together with a 500-*tögrög* bill. *Arkhi* was often accompanied by a monetary token. All other milk products are white, the color of good; *arkhi* is "black" (clear) and, to apologize for serving something of a bad color, the drink is offered with a small bill—usually 20, 50, or at most 100 *tögrögs.* I swore to myself that I would not leave in the morning without making a generous gift to our host's youngest child. But first—it was my turn to sing. I had been dreading this. I can't sing. My inability to approximate, let alone carry, a tune, is a source of endless amusement to my friends, who just shake their heads and wince when I blithely chime in with the car radio. People who cannot sing tend to know fewer songs than those who can, so ever since I had realized what was coming, I had been frantically searching my pathetic little repertoire. "Amazing Grace"—can't come close. "America the Beautiful"—"spacious skies and amber waves of grain" and then I'm lost. Anything from *My Fair Lady* or *The Sound of Music* or *Evita*—only if I'm singing along with the record. And worst of all, whatever I started, I was going to have to finish on my own. No one else was going to know the words.

The veterinarian translated as I spoke: "I have come to this country where the hospitality is so inconceivable that it is hard for me to believe that we all live in the same world. But I look at the stars here, so many, so beautiful, so close, and they are the same stars as in my sky, and I know that it *is* all one world. I would like to sing a children's song about these stars. . . ."

"Twinkle, twinkle, little star. . . ."

In a land lived by the rising and setting sun, it was long past midnight when a strapping woman with a vigorous laugh and thick, powerful fingers reached into the pot bubbling on the stove, grabbed at a sheep's head, pulled at it, cut at it, handed me a large chunk. Everyone watched expectantly. My stomach had settled. The hot, salty meat tasted wonderful. *"Amttai* ("Delicious")," I grinned as I chewed. One of the men grabbed his tongue and pointed to the meat in my hand. I took another big bite and repeated, *"Amttai."* Fat I couldn't handle; tongue was no problem.

There is a reason for everything, and that night of Mongolian faces in firelight shadows, of song in the dark, was the reason behind the disjointed European camping trip. Those hours in the *ger* were worth every moment of the cold, jarring truck ride. The *arkhi* and *airag* continued to make the rounds. *Airag* is twice sipped lightly from its large bowl and passed to the next person; then, on the third round, each person drinks a full bowl. *Arkhi,* on the other hand, is drunk to the bottom three times, although "to the bottom" in Mongolia means leaving a sip in the small bowl. I was worried about what the drinks might do to my stomach, but the circle of expectant, appreciative eyes made it impossible to refuse. Eventually everyone squeezed two and three to a bed or spread mats in concentric circles on the floor. I slept squished between the veterinarian and a wooden chest, and woke to a stomach of knots. I stumbled through the morning rituals of pulling on clothes, rolling up sleeping mats, peeing in the prairie, wanting nothing but to curl up in bed for the rest of my life. From a large bowl of leftover mutton parts, the men were cutting bite-size chunks and dumping them into their bowls of tea to heat. I wanted to be laughing along with them, but I could barely, grimly, manage a few polite sips of tea. I wanted to be the kind of person who can ignore discomfort and pain. These people deserved so much more from me. But I was a pathetic, crumpled thing.

Back in the truck I curled instantly into the bespectacled gentleman's shoulder, closed my eyes, and willed myself not to throw up. It was a beautiful day, a beautiful way to see Mongolia, and I was missing it all. In the early afternoon, we reached Arkhangai and pulled up in front of someone's home. I wanted to be reveling in the company, but I was just appalled by the prospect of food. I said I had to go straight to the hotel. "I'm sorry. I'm really, really sorry. I'm not usually like this. Really. Thank you. I'm sorry. Thank you very much." They wished me well, but I knew my abrupt departure was a bad, ungrateful act. Back at the hotel I collapsed into bed and fell immediately asleep. I had not given our host's child a generous gift. Or anything at all.

___•___

I spent the next two days sleeping a lot and eating very little. Alone in the cold cement hotel room, I huddled in my sleeping bag and drank most of my precious supply of powdered hot chocolate. It was not quite my fantasy of lolling naked in a plush, well-heated room after a long hot shower, with a spoon and a pint of Ben & Jerry's New York Super Fudge Chunk, but satisfaction and comfort are relative things. I sat on the floor and cleaned Greene. I disassembled parts I didn't know existed, then got out the repair book to find out how to put them back together. With a toothbrush and a pile of cotton swabs, I cleaned clogs of dirt from every nook and dip of her chain, chainwheels, and freewheel, then flipped her over and spun clean oil into her gears. I adjusted wearing brake pads, pumped up her tires, and duct-taped a broken brace on her rear rack. I wiped her down and reorganized her panniers until she looked almost as good as new, all ready to go.

Nestled in the top of a valley ringed on two sides by jagged rock peaks, Arkhangai had about it a hint of alpine village charm rather than the Wild West air of other towns I had seen. I roamed the downtown streets, slowly collecting every vegetable I could find—cabbage, turnips, garlic, onions, and carrots. I also found, tucked into niches and corners behind unmarked doors, a barber shop, a watch repair, and a bookstore. Among the old, party-line texts I found a Russian-Mongolian phrasebook and a set of postcards. Next door, however, the post office had only domestic stamps. The clerk showed me how many of them it would take to send a postcard to America. She couldn't fit them all onto an envelope. Besides, she said, if she sold me that many stamps, she would be out for the rest of the month.

Back at the hotel, standing by the stove stirring my vegetable soup, I met Bat, a forty-year-old geologist from Ulaanbaatar. He peered into my pot.

"You put carrots in it?" he wrinkled his nose. "Carrots are for horses. Did you not know where to buy meat?"

"I wanted it without meat. In America I only eat meat a few times a month."

"In Mongolia," he said, shaking his head, "if it doesn't have meat, it's not food."

I asked him if there were public baths in Arkhangai. He didn't know but said he would find out. The next day he announced that he had found a shower. He would take me there at noon. I packed up soap, shampoo, a towel, clean socks and clean underwear. I had not been near hot water in four weeks of almost daily cycling. At noon Bat made a call from the hotel phone. They said to call back at two. Phones were fairly rare, and I was a little surprised that municipal baths would have one, but it certainly was convenient. At two o'clock the answer was the same—try back in an hour, the water isn't hot. The delay, I realized, was not about getting an appointment; there was a problem with the plumbing. At three o'clock they said to come at four, the water was sure to be hot by then. At four o'clock we set off across town, eventually turning into the courtyard of a white, three-story, L-shaped institutional building.

"What is all this?" I asked Bat, as we headed for a door off to one side of the courtyard.

"Wait here," he said, and went inside.

A minute later he reappeared and beckoned to me. A smiling woman in a white smock and cap sat in a small, neat room behind a little metal desk. This was not at all what I had imagined Mongolian public baths would look like. I handed her the 100 *tögrögs* Bat had said it would cost. She hopped up and led me to a little white-tiled room. She pointed to the hot water faucet and said there was enough for about five minutes. Then she smiled again, and shut the door. Bat had made a deal with the psychiatric ward of the Arkhangai hospital to fill their water heater for me.

Afterward he invited me back to his room. I curled up on the couch and he tucked a thick, scratchy blanket around me. I had not been so warm or clean or comfortable in what felt like a very long time. He made me hot, sweet Russian tea. He offered to give me a massage. I drowsily knew that I should say no, that I was pushing the boundaries of propriety just by being there, but a massage sounded better than anything in the world. Better even than chocolate ice cream. I lay down. His hands moved expertly over my back and legs, fingers digging into pressure points of exhausted muscles. He took his time, kneading wonderfully deep and slow. "Roll over," he said after a while, and I knew it was the beginning of the end, but I rolled. Bat was intelligent and handsome, and as his fingers moved down my face and shoulders, I vaguely considered staying. But when they reached my breasts, I opened my eyes and shook my head. It wasn't what I wanted that night. He began working on my feet, then my calves, then slowly over my knees, and I didn't get up and leave until his hands wandered between my thighs.

Like a premonition, the thought crossed my mind the morning I left Arkhangai that somewhere in this vastly hospitable nation there had to be such a thing as a bad *ger*. A teenager on a horse whistled at me. He called out winningly, "Sleep at my *ail* ("a group of gers, family, household"), go on tomorrow." It was seven o'clock, the headwind was getting stronger by the minute, and Khotont, the next village, was at least an hour away. Driving a single sheep ahead of his horse, he led me to two *gers* not far off the road. His mother and teenage sister silently served us *airag* and *öröm* and left to milk the cows. His sullen, wiry grandfather talked sharply at me, repeating the same question several times, disapproving that I did not understand. None of them seemed pleased or curious. The boy asked if I had *valuta,* the Russian word for hard currency. I had never heard this word, this question, in Mongolia. The warning flags flew up. "No," I lied, trusting that whatever experience had taught them their interest in foreign currency was still insufficient for them to realize that I had to have dollars with me— more than $1,000 in cash strapped to various parts of my body, several thousand more in travelers checks in Greene's panniers.

Next thing I knew, I was alone in the *ger* with the dour old man. He snapped something about "Khotont today." At this point, my mind should have been scrambling for exit lines as I dashed for the door. Instead, even as I was telling myself that I would have to sleep lightly and keep a watchful eye on Greene, I sat there, trying to persuade an overtly unfriendly man to let me spend the night in his home. "Sleep—here—Khotont—tomorrow," I said. Just as with the bandits on the road to Bulgan, my reflexive reaction to the intuition of danger was not to heed my apprehension, but to drop my head and forge stubbornly ahead as if nothing were wrong.

The old man snorted irritably, handed me two pieces of *aaruul,* and motioned me out the door. Then he tied the door shut, got on a horse, and rode off. The boy was kneeling on the ground nearby, his arm plunged inside a still-living sheep's belly, pinching the aorta closed in an age-old method of slaughter that wasted none of the animal's nutrient-rich blood. He barely even glanced up. I wandered toward the cattle pen. The women were no more interested in me than the men, but eventually the girl motioned me into the second *ger.* Never saying a word, she handed me a bowl of dirty *airag.* Then she reached for the ring on my middle finger, the gift from Tosontsengel. She tried to pull it off, demanding the silver band be transferred to her finger.

It was after eight, darkening and blustery, when I sped away, fleeing into the dusk, throwing the old man's *aaruul* to the wind, wanting no part of his poison near me. Ruts and bumps were no longer discernible, only the color of the road lighter than the grassland. I was moving fast, my legs pumping a visceral desire for as much space as possible between myself and their dark, warped emptiness, not worrying about sand or rock or hole, just pedaling headlong into the blackness, witches flying in the night sky behind me, on and on, exhausted legs tireless now. Eventually the few electric lights of Khotont appeared out of the night. But this was not France, where a bartender or a couple out for an evening stroll would point the way to a charming *pension.* There would be only dark rows of wooden fence lining empty streets. The hills around me were a fragrant bed of grasses. My little blue tent was sure and cozy.

I was drifting off to sleep when my body suddenly threw itself into convulsions trying to out-twist the cramps. Nightmares of *airag.* Fantasies of Ulaanbaatar doctors. I writhed and whimpered and jammed my knuckles into back muscles, which seemed to relieve the pain a little. I begged the night for the oblivion of sleep and woke in chilly predawn light to find the agony had ebbed away.

⸺•

When Genghis Khan ruled what would become the largest empire the world has ever seen, stretching from Korea across the Middle East as far west as Hungary, his capital was a sprawling *ger* encampment in the steppes of the

Mongolian heartland. His son and successor, Ögödei, who wanted a home more grandiose than his father's *ger,* had his architects turn Karakorum into a city of buildings and solid walls. Even so, when Genghis's grandson, Kublai, became Great Khan, he did not stay in Karakorum, choosing instead to rule from the cities of Dadu, which would later become Beijing, and Shangdu, also known as Xanadu. Following Kublai's death in 1294, the vast Mongol empire began to disintegrate. Borders quickly shrank inward from all sides. But the site of Genghis Khan's original capital—some 300 kilometers south-west of Ulaanbaatar, almost precisely in the center of the country, and known today as Kharkhorin—ultimately remained under Mongolian control.

It was here, in the late sixteenth century, that Altan Khan, intent on spreading Buddhism across his country, ordered the construction of a great monastery called Erdenezuu Khiid. Once full of *gers* and numerous temples, once teeming with monks and their apprentices, once the heart of a deeply religious land, the monastery enclosure was now a largely empty expanse of weeds. Two dogs chased each other around the yard. A cow nosed at a locked door. But smoke curled from a chimney, and inside, worshipers were once again tracing the circumference of a small temple. Three sides of the hall were covered in a melange of dried leaves, golden figurines, hand-stitched clothwork, candles, and offerings of food and *tögrög* notes. The reds and blues and glowing coppers shown like long-unexplored treasure clutter in an old aunt's dusty attic. Incense wafted up through multicolored cloth streamers. Monks murmured and chanted, their red garb an undulating background to the burnished gong in the center of the room. From the ashes of Soviet domination, their world was slowly reviving in the ancient air of the steppes.

I pedaled into Kharkhorin on September 25. That night the first blizzard of winter swept down across the prairie. I was sharing a hotel room with two Japanese backpackers. We all fell asleep with our fingers crossed that the bad weather would pass quickly, but in the morning the storm was still raging. Yumiko, who had spent a year in Kansas and spoke colloquial, collegiate English, and Satomi and I spent the day huddled under our covers, talking or playing cards or writing in our journals. Every once in a while, one of us dashed across the freezing floor to peer out the window. Snow blew sideways through the bare tree branches that scraped against the foggy glass, and beyond that was nothing but an impenetrable wall of white. We fell asleep early, but after a few hours I woke in the dark to the now-familiar cramps clawing their way up my body, and spent the rest of the night tossing and turning, eventually throwing up in the bathroom down the hall, where a small snowdrift had piled up inside the window. Sometime after dawn, I finally slipped into a profound, exhausted sleep.

When I woke up again, beaten and drained but in no pain, sun was pouring through the window. The branches outside were motionless beneath a brilliant azure sky. It was a perfect riding day. Except that I had never ridden a bicycle in snow. I had become reasonably adept at rocks and mud, but snow was a new mystery. Nevertheless, in one of the stupidest travel decisions of my life, I compulsively opted to leave Kharkhorin.

It was early afternoon by the time I set out, slipping and sliding and falling. Snow and dirt and ice gathered squeaking and scraping on Greene. It took me two hours to struggle eleven kilometers to a fork in the road. Powerlines led uphill above a vague trail. A slightly wider road dropped down to the left. I looked at my compass. The road headed southeast. Ulaanbaatar lies *north*east of Kharkhorin. I tapped the compass. I shook it. I pointed it in various directions. I spun the dial. It would not change its mind. It was four o'clock now and well below freezing. I was eleven kilometers from a hotel in one direction and had no idea how far from anything in the other direction. I rolled onto the left fork. Rocks lay in ambush beneath the snow and ice. I had one foot on the ground and my eyes glued to Greene's front tire. I almost rode right into the river. Daylight was turning to evening. I was clearly not on the main road out of Kharkhorin. I still was not more than fifteen kilometers from the hotel. And I just stood there, glaring at the chunks of ice twisting down the swift, dark current.

The crashing rumble of a truck turned me around. Brakes squealed, and a jovial leather-jacketed man landed in the snow beside me. In an inebriated slur of German and Russian, he offered me a ride to the paved road. "No, thank you, just across the river." His teenage sister reached down from the back of the truck to hand us a plastic bowl of *airag*. Another man, two women, and two small children were crowded in the cab with the driver. We drank the *airag* and Jovial offered me a ride to his home in Arvaikheer, 150 kilometers southeast of Kharkhorin. "No, thank you, just across the river." Jovial and Greene and I clambered up into the truck bed with fifteen-year-old Gerelmaa, and the vehicle plunged through the freezing river, its spinning wheels digging deeper into the ever-widening muddy scars along the banks.

"No, thank you, just across the river," I had said. But as we bounced down an indecipherable road across kilometer after kilometer of frosty, glittery, empty steppe, I didn't seem to be telling them to stop the truck and let me off. I was shivering in my layers of fleece and polypro. Bare-handed, her feet in light socks and short, thin boots, Gerelmaa seemed impervious to the cold. She babbled at me nonstop, always somehow expecting me to understand, surprised at the end of every long explanation or question that I had absolutely no idea what she was talking about. Jovial, meanwhile, as boring as any drunk in any dive bar in any city in the world, asked me over and over what my name was, why I didn't stay in Mongolia, why I didn't marry a Mongolian. Then he asked if I had heard what was happening in Russia.

"No, what?"

"There are two presidents."

"What do you mean, 'two presidents'?"

"I don't know."

"Who? How can there be two presidents? What happened?"

"I don't know, but there are two presidents in Russia now. Why don't you marry a Mongolian man and stay here?"

Bang-zzzzrrrhhh! The truck dipped sharply and we were stuck, the right rear wheel spinning deep in snow and mud, going nowhere. For a while, everyone just looked at it in that patient, waiting Mongolian way that I had found so charming—until I was cold, tired, and afraid that I could literally freeze to death overnight. Why wasn't anybody *doing* anything!? Three *gers* huddled not a kilometer away in the twilight. Why wasn't anyone going for help, or at least for hot tea? Eventually they started gathering stones to pile in front of the tire. Longing for the *gers,* feeling guilty for being such a wimp, I reluctantly clambered down from the truck to help. But no little stones were going to get us out of this. As darkness descended, it was finally decided that the women and children should head for the *gers.* I had never thought I would accept being "women and children." I'd be tough. I'd hang with the guys. I was off like a shot, trudging through the moonlight. Gerelmaa carried one child piggyback while the other little boy skipped through the snow and I just wished we could get there faster.

The small family in the nearest *ger* quickly made room for us when we walked in, a group of strangers appearing out of the night. I sat selfishly close to the stove, took off my shoes, and held my feet to the metal until it scorched my socks. After a while, we heard the crunch of heavy tires on snow. They had succeeded in extricating the wheel. Gerelmaa had to nudge me to give my snug stoveside seat to the men just in from the cold. Jovial had sobered up and turned into a pleasantly charming fellow, still encouraging me to go on to Arvaikheer with them. But I was not getting back on that truck. I was in Mongolia and I had learned. I did not need to look at the sky, look at my watch, sigh, say, "That's okay, I have a tent," and wait for an invitation. I turned to our hosts and asked, "May I sleep here?" and the truck roared into the night without me.

_____•_____

It was warm, almost hot in the sun reflecting off the snow when I left the huddle of three *gers,* following a vague road and my compass, straight east now. A hunter growled past on a motorcycle. Then, as he lay prone in the prairie, his rifle trained on a distant marmot hole, Greene and I passed him. We played leapfrog for several hours, bumping over rocks, crunching through ice and snow, wading through freezing streams, until in the early afternoon a black snake of pavement welled up on the horizon. Like a deep gulp of oxygen after staying too long beneath the waves. Like a western plane from a Soviet airport. Like a language I know after one that I don't. Fantasies of Snickers danced through my head.

I had indeed missed the main road out of Kharhorin, and was farther south than I had hoped to be, but there was no snow on the pavement, no sand, no rocks. The sun shone over the rolling plains. Horses grazed beyond clustered *gers.* Feather-legged falcons drifted effortlessly across the sky. I slowed as I approached a congregation of short, black-robed men gathered in a meadow, then almost fell off Greene as the monks suddenly became vultures, flapping their massive bodies awkwardly into the air. I rode all day, pedaling down the kilometers. Coasting downhill at dusk, I almost missed the turnoff to Erdenesant. A half dozen industrial buildings loomed over the small, wooden-fenced village. The hotel was three rooms in an unmarked apartment building. Two policemen from Ulaanbaatar were also spending the night. I asked if they knew what was happening in Russia.

"Tanks in the streets of Moscow."

"Whose tanks?"

"I don't know, but there may be war."

In Lün the next night, a faded wooden *"Zochid Buudal"* sign listed askew above the hotel entrance. The manager cooked mutton and potato stew on a hot plate on the floor while his children romped around the room and didn't need Nintendo to keep themselves amused. I slept fully clothed in my sleeping bag in a drafty, unheated room, and was on the road again by 7:30 A.M., the sun not yet above the horizon. Ulaanbaatar was 130 kilometers away. At noon I saw a *ger* suspiciously close to the road. A hand-lettered sign read *"guanz"*—a Mongolian diner. I stopped for a quick plateful of *buuz.* I was not yet halfway to the capital. The next *guanz* was one of a

⌣· *The pavement again!*

cluster of three on a road beginning to feel like a highway. Fifty kilometers to go. At 7:15 P.M. I came around a corner to the city glittering in the valley below. The full moon was rising. My odometer, set at zero when I wobbled off from Irkutsk, now read 1,675 kilometers.

The next morning I stretched clean and naked and warm under a single sheet. Radiators pumped heat into the fifth-floor room, and hot water poured from the taps in the bathroom. On the streets below, there were sirens and traffic lights and almost as many Mercedes as cows. Over the bridge at the Bayangol Hotel, there was round-the-clock direct-dial international telephone service and satellite television. The major news from the world was that Michael Jordan had quit basketball, Michael Jackson had been accused of child abuse, oh, and there had been an attempted coup in Russia. Calls to the United States cost eight dollars per minute, but the connections were good. While vapid Southern California sitcoms and pictures of Moscow's burning Parliament flickered across the television screen, I reassured my father that I was alive and well (a little white lie), and asked my mother to send a new first-aid kit care of poste restante in Beijing.

In the high-ceilinged dining room of the Ulaanbaatar Hotel, I ate omelets and instant coffee served on a white tablecloth. The desolate backwater capital of characterless parallelogram Communist buildings felt like a booming metropolis. The empty department-store shelves seemed to overflow with goods. There were Snickers and apples in every kiosk, and Coca-Cola that tasted like the nectar of the gods. I ate dinner in the hotel's dollar restaurant with a German couple who were working to reintroduce the wild horse to the Gobi Desert, and barely made it back to my room before suddenly, violently, losing everything I had eaten all day. After five peaceful nights, the cramps had returned with a vengeance. Shivering in spite of all the radiators, jamming knuckles into back muscles, I tossed and twisted through the night.

When I am in Russia, I swear I will fly out of the country rather than let a Soviet doctor touch me. In Ulaanbaatar I was ecstatic to be able to go to a Russian hospital. The soldiers and advisors whom the doctors were there to serve had left Mongolia; the cavernous hospital echoed eerily and the physicians were bored silly. Two of them settled into chairs in the exam room to chat while a third examined me. I told her that I had skipped a period, but knew I was not pregnant. She nodded, and quickly located a line of pain from my sternum down along my right ribs. "You have to be very careful what you eat and drink in this country," she said, shaking her head and handing me two foil packages of little pale green and big dull red pills. As I took the medicine, I thought of Lkhamsüren. This doctor, I knew, would never have eaten her *guriltai shöl*. To this day I do not know what was wrong with me. I also do not know whether it was the pills, the massive purge of the night before, or just coincidence, but the cramps never came back.

The circus was closed. The movies were all Chinese or American. The opera was not performing that week. But the post office was open and well stocked with beautiful stamps. I wrote a long letter, found a photocopy machine, and mailed twenty copies home. I found the U.S. embassy and inquired if they had received any letters for me. The pinched vice-consul informed me coldly that the embassy did not appreciate being used as a mail stop, but she would check—what was my name? she asked.

"Erika Warmbrunn."

She whirled around, eyebrows raised, "Warm . . . ?"

"Yes," I giggled, "I'm sorry."

"Do you know you're on the State Department Watch List?"

"My father panicked, but it's all right, I've spoken with him."

She didn't seem to see the humor of it. "I have to officially cable the State Department and report that you have been found."

"Yes," I sighed, "I have been found."

I ran into Christian and we went to dinner at the Bayangol. The Coca-

Cola still tasted good, but already less ambrosial than it had the first day in the city. Almost every foreigner I knew in Mongolia was there: the wild-horse couple at one table, Thierry and Claire at another, Yumiko and Satomi at a third. Yumiko said that an hour after I left Kharkhorin, another foreigner arrived on a bus, a tall bearded man from Switzerland. According to her, Daniel would be arriving in Ulaanbaatar in the next few days, but I never saw him again. Then, on the way out of the restaurant, I saw one more fa-miliar face. Zölöö, one of the first Mongolians I had ever met, light-years earlier in Sükhbaatar, was celebrating her birthday with two friends. The food in that cold sea of red plastic chairs and orange tablecloths was not half as good as the meals I had eaten in the simplest Mongolian homes, but the girls saved up, and three times a year—on each one's birthday—they treated themselves to the prestigious plastic surroundings.

The next day I bought a plane ticket back to Mörön. When I had left Irkutsk two months earlier, I had really wanted to arrive one day in Saigon able to say, "I cycled every inch of the way." Mondi had ruined that plan, had edited the trip down to "every inch of the way from Khatgal to Saigon." (Later there would also be the truck ride out of Kharkhorin—did twenty kilometers count?) And then, in a small village in the middle of Mongolia, they had invited me to stay, to live with them and teach them English. And the great spontaneity battle was engaged: Let things happen, learn to let things happen. Understand that it does not all have to fit the plan, the idea, or any other neat little package. Understand that being a part of daily vil-lage life is a much richer experience than any unbroken line on a map. It is about here and now, not about the story you will tell at home. And, ulti-mately, it will make a better story than any line on a map.

My twenty-eighth birthday was only a few days away, but instead of bicycling across the border into China as I had once planned, I was making arrangements to leave Greene in Ulaanbaatar and sending Baasanjav a tele-gram saying that I would be in Arshaant by the weekend. I knew that, once there, I would fantasize about Snickers and apples and hot showers, but af-ter a week of cement apartment buildings and plastic restaurants, I was ready to go back to the scruffy horses and eager children, all of us tiny in the vast landscape.

~· *Buyanjargal and Myagmarsüren in class*

Part II

TEACHING IN ARSHAANT

A Small World in a Vast Landscape

CHAPTER 4

A Fair Trade

In the middle of Arshaant's dusty schoolyard, children ran in and out of a *ger* carrying firewood and rugs. I had missed the actual building of the *ger,* an amazingly quick production that had been repeated in yards all across the village in the month since I had left: A few neighbors gather to help, and in a matter of hours a cozy felt tent has sprung up and the family is ready to move from their drafty summer home into the *ger* where they will spend the winter. Inside the *ger* in the middle of the schoolyard, a single metal-framed cot snuggled against one wall, an assortment of chairs and stools ringed half the perimeter, and a low dresser sat in the far curve. Carpets lay in a horseshoe around the stove, and two tumbling piles of chopped wood framed the doorway. This was my home. They had built me a *ger.* They had built me my very own *ger.*

I had been worried that Baasanjav had not received my telegram. I had been worried that the teachers' impulsive September eagerness would have faded. I had been worried that they would think me irresponsible and unreliable, because my telegram had said I would arrive on Saturday and it was now Thursday. I should have known. "Late" in Mongolia is measured not in minutes but in days or weeks, or not at all. In a land without telephones, where every traveler is at the mercy of the elements, "I'll be there Saturday" means probably within a week and if you don't appear at all, everyone understands that there was no gas, or the river flooded, or unexpected guests kept you at home. Patience runs deep in lands where time is still the passing of the seasons rather than the tick of the minute hand. It did not matter whether I arrived Saturday, Sunday, Thursday, or next month. It did not matter if I arrived almost a week later than my telegram had said. It didn't really matter that I had sent a telegram. I was here, now, and that was all that mattered.

When I had gotten off the plane in Mörön, with no idea how I would continue on to Arshaant, the only person I knew in town was standing at the gate. Spread out over its 1.5 million square kilometers, Mongolia is a very small world, where around any corner you might run into someone you know. Bolormaa was waiting for a friend who was supposed to bring Belgüün a pair of shoes from the capital. Instead of shoes for her daughter she got me, insisting that I stay with her rather than at the hotel even before asking why I was there. When I told her where I was going, she laughed, "That's easy. I just came back from China again. I have to spend a few days at the market here, then I'm going to Arshaant to sell whatever is left. I have relatives there. We'll go together."

A few days stretched into almost a week while Bolormaa worked the market in Mörön and her brother Batgal repaired his Jeep and searched for gas, but one afternoon we were finally under way. For every half hour of driving, twenty minutes were spent repairing flat tires and tinkering under the hood, and by the time we arrived at the banks of the Selenge, the sky was already pink with the setting sun. Batgal hollered across the river. Two men on the other side waved back, then stepped out onto a creaking contraption of metal boat hulls covered with rough wooden planking and pulled it toward us along a cable stretched above the water. As I once again ferried across the Selenge River, I wondered vaguely if this was what everyone had meant in September when they said "bridge." The final nighttime dash through hills and shallow crystal streams was miraculously accomplished without a single flat tire, and we reached Arshaant before Bolormaa's relatives had gone to bed.

Her cousin was a vivacious woman in her mid-forties whose husband was a gentle, pigeon-toed man who seemed to take up no space in the energetic rumpus of their home. Their two little boys were cheerful, rambunctious imps. Their daughters were teenagers with ready smiles. Fifteen-year-old Buyanjargal co-opted my attentions from the moment we arrived. Emotions lit and shadowed the broad planes of her face with the vivid changeability of high weather on a bright summer day. Frustration brought her arching eyebrows glowering down over dark almond eyes; easy pleasure dimpled her cheeks with a wide grin. Excitement coursed through her long child's limbs that would soon be those of a young woman. Her relatives had not been expecting Bolormaa, but they knew I was coming. They knew that an American was coming to teach English. "They knew," Bolormaa translated over bowls of *buuz* the next morning, "because the school has been building you a *ger*." She had to say it several times before I began to believe her.

Then Agvantseren and Baasanjav ducked through the door. As far as I could tell, no one had left the yard that morning; no child had been sent running across town to deliver the news that I had arrived. But the teachers knew, and they had come to take me to my *ger*. My *ger*! Turning around and around in the center of the small home, elatedly taking in every little detail, I was clearly in the way as the finishing touches were still being arranged, so I went shopping. One store had potatoes and onions. Another had flour, for sale by ration card only—three kilos per person per month. And that was the extent of the food available in Arshaant's stores that day. I found a pen, and several flimsy copybooks for my lesson plans; only later when I sat down to write did I realize that the pen was not a ballpoint. I walked back to main street, but none of the stores had ink.

That afternoon we gathered in the principal's office. He asked if my *ger* was all right.

"It's perfect," I said, still hopelessly charmed by the cozy home.

"The school handyman will come build your fire in the morning," he said.

There was a neat pile of kindling next to my stove, and an old Russian paperback to use as tinder. I told them that I was perfectly capable of building a fire. They nodded, unconvinced.

"He will come do it for you," Agvantseren repeated. "And there will be a television."

"That doesn't matter," I laughed. "It's great the way it is."

"The television will be here soon."

"I don't need a television, but I should probably have a lock on the door."

"Yes, of course we will get a lock—you should use it when you're asleep, or not at home—and the television will be here by the time the electricity comes on tonight."

"It's all in Mongolian, I won't understand anything. But I could use something to keep water in."

"We'll find a pail. And the television will be here soon. Is there anything else you need?"

I sheepishly showed them my new pen and asked if they had ink. The principal passed me a small glass jar. From the land of ATMs and email, I glanced helplessly from the pen to the ink and back. I had no idea what to do. Baasanjav quietly reached over, opened the pen, and deftly drew ink into the chamber. No wonder they didn't believe I could build a fire.

I was up early the next morning, and had a fire crackling happily by the time Handyman walked in. He surveyed the *ger* carefully, found nothing amiss, and shoved an additional log into the stove. A gangly, dark-skinned man of few words, he had been told to take care of me, and was taking his responsibility seriously.

Almost as soon as the first wisp of smoke had drifted up out of my stove-pipe, the visits had begun. I would hear pounding footsteps, a second of dead silence, a giggle or a whisper, and then the door would be flung open. Standing outside, their figures perfectly framed in the low doorway, a gaggle of children would peer in and dare each other to enter. Some groups were braver than others. They would swarm inside and then press immediately back against the door, the kids in front trying to hide behind their friends, the kids in back pushing forward until they suddenly found themselves in front and started trying to duck to the back again. In this constantly re-volving pattern, they would watch me eat, watch me write, watch me rinse dishes. Then suddenly, as if responding to some call I could not hear, they would turn and dash out across the yard, the door slamming gently behind the receding footsteps.

A group of sixth-grade girls braved the doorsill en masse. They tumbled in, giggled, whispered, blushed, looked at the floor, the *tonoo,* each other, anywhere but at me, the object they had come to see. "Hello," I said, and black eyes and giggles caromed off every curve of the *ger.* Only one of the girls held her head high and looked straight at me. Until I was able to re-member her name, I dubbed Bat-Ölzii "Indian" in my mind. Even more than the weathered faces of grandparents, the silky-skinned thirteen-year-old's ancient eyes and solemn face mirrored Native American visages and echoed long-ago eastward migrations. I looked at her and pointed to the bed. "Bed," I said in English. *"Krovat,"* I said in Russian. *"Or!"* she said in Mongolian. *"Or,"* I repeated, and again giggles bounced around the *ger,* but now most of the girls were looking at me.

I asked them to tell me the words for "stove" and "wood." They taught me "sleep" and "ax" and "school." In Mongolian I asked the girls how old they were. In Russian I asked what they wanted to do when they grew up. Russian was compulsory for all students, but most of them were too shy to try out their classroom language. Only Bat-Ölzii never giggled, squirmed, or slipped into whispered conference with the others. She was brave. When she didn't understand something I said or could not find the word she wanted in Russian, she glanced down in concentration, the curve of her cheekbones flushing with a hint of red, then brought her clear, steady eyes back up and asked me to say it again. Slowly, carefully, she translated for her friends as they explained that they hoped to become teachers and doctors and journalists.

That afternoon I set out up the hill toward Gerlee's. She would already know that I had arrived, and I was determined not to let the teachers co-opt me completely. The sun was out. The air was warm and motionless and the skies were flawlessly blue, but the river was edged with ice. Gerlee's mother and grandmother were sitting by the stove drinking tea when I walked in. They welcomed me like a long-lost daughter, with a warm cheek-pressed-to-cheek greeting. Her grandmother immediately chose a thick bit of intestine out of the pot on the stove and handed it to me. As I searched for scraps of meat and tried to make good slurping and licking sounds, Gerlee's mother explained that Altanzuul had moved to Erdenet and that Gerlee and Delger were in the *khödöö*. But they would be home the next afternoon and I had to come back to see them then. She said this in complete, full-speed sentences. I was lucky to pick out the key words.

"Gerlee today *khödöö*," I repeated. "Gerlee tomorrow here. Me tomorrow here???" She responded with a stream of affirmative-sounding Mongolian accompanied by enough nodding that I knew I had understood. I gave each of them an apple. The fruit was accepted in cupped hands. Gerlee's mother cut herself a small bite and put the rest carefully in a drawer, "for Gerlee and Delger." I used up the rest of my Mongolian explaining how I got back to Arshaant and how long I would be there and where Greene was. "My bicycle is in Ulaanbaatar" is one of the few Mongolian sentences I remember to this day.

Minutes after I arrived back home, Pippi Longstocking popped through the door. The little girl wore a dirty green *del* and horizontally striped woolen stockings. Half her hair had escaped from skinny, unruly braids. She made it clear that I was to come with her. I had no idea who she was or where she was leading me, but I followed her back across the bridge. She chattered earnestly as we climbed the dusty hill into the labyrinth of wooden fences, staring hard to see if I had understood what I supposed to be an explanation of where we were going. But I could only shrug apologetically and wait to see where we ended up. We ended up at Gerlee's. Pippi's name was Tüvshinjargal. She was Gerlee's littlest sister and had proudly taken it upon herself to bring me home after school. Her grandmother did not know why I had returned any more than I had known where I was going, but when I walked in she immediately and unquestioningly set to cooking, as if it were perfectly logical for me to be back again, as if she had not just finished feeding me.

⚓

English classes were an extracurricular activity. When the students had been asked if they wanted to stay after school four days a week to study English, almost every one had raised a hand. The teachers had selected those they thought would profit most, those most motivated and able to learn quickly, those most likely to continue their education beyond Arshaant. Buyanjargal once showed me a picture of herself and her fifth-grade classmates. Of the dozen children in the photo, three were now in the ninth grade. The rest had left school. Most were in the *khödöö,* working. Tenth grade was the final year of schooling available in Arshaant. The few students who would continue beyond the tenth grade would go to Mörön for two years and then perhaps on to Ulaanbaatar. The list for English classes was whittled down to forty-five, divided by age into three groups. Baasanjav showed me to my classroom. Afternoon light streamed through dusty windows into the bare but spotless room. The dull pink walls were undecorated, and the students sat on hard stools behind flat wooden desks. She handed me a list of the kids in each group. Then she left. And never came back. They had decided that they trusted me, and no one ever came to observe one of my classes.

It was perfect. The kids knew that I spoke no Mongolian. Speaking to them in English was not an act, not a classroom exercise. Especially in Group One, the twelve- and thirteen-year-olds, most of whom did not yet know more than a few tentative phrases of Russian, they knew they could not ask for translations. They had no recourse but to listen and try to make sense of the odd new sounds.

"My name is Erika." I flapped my arms, encouraging them to repeat after me.

Nothing.

"My," I waved my hands like a sideshow conductor.

"My," Bat-Ölzii whispered bravely.

"My."

"My," several voices repeated together.

"Name."

"Name." They all chimed in.

"Is."

"Is!"

"My name is Erika."

∽· *Enkhjargal and my Seattle Mariners baseball cap*

"My name is Erika," they chorused unevenly.

I laughed and pointed at Bat-Ölzii and said, "My name is Bat-Ölzii." I pointed at Buyanjargal's little brother, "My name is Battur." I pointed to a little girl in a ragged plaid coat, "What is your name?"

"My name is Enkhjargal," she stated precisely. Enkhjargal was eleven years old. She had chipmunk-rounded cheeks and short, scraggly braids. Her fingers were invariably stained with the ink of a leaky pen; papers stuck out of every corner of her notebook; and her eyes captured every thought in the room.

The Group Two students were a little older, with more experience in Russian. "My name is Tsengüünjargal," said a girl with a narrow face and long fingers, sitting up straight to answer, then slouching back against the wall.

"My name is Chuluunbaatar," muttered the only boy in the class.

"My name is Otgontuya."

"My name is Enkhtsetseg."

I had my work cut out for me just remembering their names. Narantsetseg means "Sunflower," while Sarantsetseg is "Moonflower." Sarantuya is "Moonbeam," Enkhtuya "Peacebeam," Enkhjargal "Peace-Joy," and Bayarjargal "Happiness-Joy." Mongolians have no inherited family name, only a given name, and a patronymic that is generally reduced to an initial or entirely disused. The girls were suns and moons and flowers; the boys were heroes—Enkhbaatar was "Peace-Hero," Batbaatar "Strong-Hero," and Sükhbaatar "Ax-Hero." My attempts to wrap my tongue around the seemingly endless strings of syllables and to attach the right *-jargal, -tsetseg,* and *-baatar* to the right face were a continuous source of glee to the youngsters.

Buyanjargal was in Group Three, together with her best friend, Delgersüren. A full head shorter than Buyanjargal, Delgersüren had the bouncy energy of a gymnast and delicate features that promised to mature into striking beauty. The girls (there were no boys in Group Three) were like fifteen-year-olds anywhere—the leaders and the followers, the confident and the insecure, the popular and the striving emulators. But unlike their media-barraged western counterparts, they still moved with the natural ease of children, rather than the self-consciousness of adolescents trying too hard, too soon, to mimic the adult images of the world around them. Without the daily bombardments of impossibly perfect characters selling them perfume, success, and unattainable physical ideals, they were at home in their bodies.

Only sixteen-year-old Sarantuya seemed uncomfortable in her frame. She had a dark mole high on the bridge of her nose, and features that seemed lost in her heavy face. Her smile was less forthcoming than most of the girls', and she wore the expression of a woman caught in the inescapable drudgery of hardworking days. Myagmarsüren, also sixteen, was more comfortably outgoing. Already less of a girl than the others, her laugh had matured beyond a giggle into a resonant expression of pleasure. Without in any way excluding herself from her schoolmates' society, she conveyed a poised air of independence they did not yet have. Then there was Khongorzul. She was oddly fair-skinned, her hair tinted a surprising red in the sea of pure ebony heads. Whenever I asked her a question, her eyes widened in terror, her fingers fluttered and clenched in her lap, and she scrunched deeper into her seat, twisting her dropped head sideways to ask for help. And her friends helped her, murmuring answers that she then whispered unsurely back to me.

If the girls were particularly quick to help Khongorzul, they did not sit silently even when the best of them were on the spot. Answers were whispered across the room at every question. And it was not just the kids. Enkhtuya and Bayarjargal did it too. At first, I could only interpret the immediate looks to each other as a negation of independent thought, and did not understand why it was accepted. Yet it was open and shameless and somehow not cheating. Slowly I would come to realize that in a society where every creature had to be individually survival-tough, there was a compensatory sense of community and mutual aid. In a land where people lived among the other creatures as if in an ancient agreement that every creature was part of the whole and had the right to do what it must to survive, there was little sympathy for pain or weakness, but there was also little sense of competition.

After classes I crossed the schoolyard back to my *ger* and barely had my coat off before the door opened and dinner arrived in the arms of the school's rotund, splay-toothed cook. I had said that I would be happy to cook for myself if the school provided the food, but they had insisted that she would prepare my meals. Some days she would trundle across the yard herself with a dish of mutton and turnip and a big smile. Some days she would send a pair of schoolgirls to deliver a pot of mutton and potato. Every few days she would send over a loaf of freshly baked bread, and once she left a bowl of sugar, which I knew was not available in any store in the village. Another time she concocted a miraculous salad of shredded cabbage and carrots that most Mongolians would have considered horse food. I told her that the raw vegetables were delicious, and within minutes a little girl arrived with two more platefuls.

Just as Cook left, Bolormaa and Buyanjargal arrived. Bolormaa was impressed. No one lives alone in Mongolia. "If I had a *ger* all to myself, I wouldn't even prefer to live in an apartment," she said, looking around and shaking her head. I served them tea from the thermos Cook had brought, and then dished out the mutton and potatoes, refusing to let them help. I gave her and Buyanjargal my two forks, and ate my share with a knife. Finally I could return a hint of the immeasurable hospitality Bolormaa had showered on me. As Buyanjargal ate, she asked over and over whether the television worked.

"Sure, it works," I shrugged.

She checked the plug anyway, and pointed to the on-off switch: "This is how you turn it on."

"Yes," I grinned, "I know that."

Eventually Bolormaa stated the obvious, which had completely escaped me—Buyanjargal wanted to watch television. "Oh, of course," I nodded at the teenager, who immediately switched it on and dropped to the floor with her arms curled around her knees. Television was still a relative novelty in Arshaant. Everyone who visited after the electricity came on in the evening asked why the set wasn't on. Was it not working? Did I not know how to turn it on? While Bolormaa and I laughed about my luxurious queen's life, all alone in my very own *ger,* Buyanjargal stared at the little black-and-white screen, even more interesting than a real, live American.

⸎

Tüvshinjargal found me again the next afternoon, bouncing with eagerness to guide me home to her big sister. I promised to visit after classes. "Now—work—five o'clock—home," I said, stringing together words without any of the prepositions, conjugations, or auxiliaries that would turn them into sentences. But she seemed to understand, and at five o'clock she was back, bouncing impatiently in front of my door. I crossed the yard to the kitchen and told Cook not to make me dinner, I would be eating at a friend's ("To-night—food—no—friend—home—eat"), then followed Tüvshinjargal across the bridge and up the hill.

By nature Gerlee and I would not seek each other out and become friends, but I felt badly about the way she had been treated, about the way I had allowed her to be treated, in September. She was pushy and posses-sive, but she meant well and she was why I was there. If she had not invited me to stay for a day in September, I would not have been living in my own schoolyard *ger* in October.

Her home was alive with the chatter of three or four little girls busily mixing and rolling and cutting dough. Gerlee was patient and helpful with them, and they were all clearly having fun. They happily looked to her for guidance, and were proud to show her their work. Watching her with the kids, I saw a Gerlee who was in charge without being bossy, instructive without being aggressive, a Gerlee I really liked and, trusting the little girls' instincts, really respected.

After dinner a friend of Gerlee's accompanied me down the hill, speak-ing incomprehensibly slurred Russian the whole way. Drunk and chival-rous, he was seeing me home. Gerlee had probably given him very specific instructions. But I was not going home. I was going to say good-bye to Bolormaa before she left in the morning. The dark mazes of wooden fences were still a mystery to me, however, and if I didn't follow the precise route that I knew, from my *ger* to Buyanjargal's, I was unlikely to find the right gate in the right fence. We entered the schoolyard. His job was almost done. He asked for the key to my *ger*.

"I'm not going home," I said. We were standing right in front of my home.

"Key."

"No. I'm going to a friend's."

"I live over there," he tippled, complementing the non sequitur with a vague wave into the night.

"That's nice. Goodnight."

"Key?"

"No."

"I'll come with you." It was a cavalier offer of protection against the dark night. It was a drunken gentleman's offer to guide me wherever I was going, even though he had no idea where that was.

"No, thank you, I know the way."

"I live over there," he repeated. There was a muddled pause as he peered into the darkness, then swung his head back to me. "Goodnight."

"Goodnight." I turned around and bumped into the principal, his little son in tow, on their way back from the outhouse.

"Where are you going?" he asked. Everyone always asked where I was going. Anyone who saw me leaving the schoolyard called out, "Where to?" Crossing the bridge: "Where to?" Climbing a hill toward someone's home: "Where to?"

"For a walk," I would call back, or "Over there." If I said, "To the store," it set off a storm of concern about what it was I needed. If I said, "To Gerlee's," I immediately had a guide. But no matter how vaguely I answered, everybody always knew where I had been. "So, you had dinner with Gerlee last night?" "So, you went to the store this morning? What did you need? Did you find what you needed? Is everything okay?"

"I am going to a friend's," I answered the principal.

Drunk said something to him in Mongolian.

"You left your key there?" the principal looked back at me.

"No!" It was like the party game Telephone, except that the message got all fuddled and convoluted without any whispering. "I have my key, I'm just not going home."

"Do you need help?"

"No, I know the way."

"You're not scared?"

"No."

"I will come with you."

"No, really, it's okay. Really."

They let me go, shaking their heads, watching me the whole way.

Buyanjargal's home reminded me of a living room from someone's sitcom-perfect suburban childhood. She and her little brothers were sprawled on the floor playing jacks—but without metallic stars, without a rubber ball. They played with animal bones and a piece of chain. Their mother was simultaneously minding the tea on the stove and sewing patches onto a worn-out pair of pants. Their father sat nearby, dreamily smoking his pipe. The television was on, the volume turned up high, nothing but gray static on the screen of a set that looked like the Soviets had rejected it in the 1950s. Bolormaa was working on her accounts in the neat notebook she kept of all her transactions.

As ten-year-old Battur abandoned the game of jacks and asked if I wanted to play chess, his mother dropped her work and began cooking me a meal that I knew there was no point in trying to refuse, no matter how full I already was. I had not played chess in years, and had never been particularly good. Checkmate loomed almost immediately, but then suddenly I made a few swift captures of my own, Battur made some inattentive mistakes, and I cornered his king. In spite of the loss, he wanted to play again. He was quickly down to his queen and a few pawns while I still had my queen, a rook, and a bishop, and was wondering at the ten-year-old's nonchalance in the face of inevitable defeat when he checkmated me. Without a hint of triumph in his eyes, his irrepressible sparkle burst at me across the board. Only then did I think to wonder whether he had been told to let the guest win the first game. I never beat him again.

The kids' classes were easy. Teaching the teachers—Agvantseren, his daughter Bayarjargal, and Enkhtuya—was more complicated. It seemed to me that the most significant thing I had to offer them was the opportunity to hear American English and to practice their oral skills, so I hoped to simply lead them in discussions. I should have remembered all those "Conversational French" classes. "Just Talking" was always easier said than done. When I spoke English to Enkhtuya, she either answered in Russian or, if she didn't understand, she winced and looked to Agvantseren for a translation. Bayarjargal shrank quietly into her seat, caught between a bashful reserve in the presence of her loquacious father and a desire to please him. The women were learning English because it was practical, what I might call a career move. Agvantseren was doing it out of intellectual thirst. His English was purely self-taught. He learned because it was fun. And he was good at it. "I just want to be able to read a newspaper and understand the radio, but the girls will become English teachers, so you should concentrate on what they need," he said, and proceeded to commandeer the conversation with the enthusiasm of the eager student he had no doubt always been.

"What are you doing last night?" he asked me, knowing better than I did how to start a class.

"What *did* you do last night?" I corrected him.

"What *did* you do last night?"

"Last night I ate dinner and had many visitors. What did *you* do last night?"

"Last night I—eat?"

"*Ate*. Today I eat. Yesterday I ate."

"*Ate*. Last night I ate dinner and watch television."

"*Watched* television."

"*Watched* television, yes. Watched."

"Enkhtuya, what did you do last night?" I asked.

"Last night I . . . ate dinner and watched television," she parroted Agvantseren although she did not own a television.

"Who cooked dinner?" I asked her. She blinked and turned to Agvantseren.

"To cook," I said quickly, before she could get a translation. I mimed cutting and stirring.

"I," she whispered tentatively.

"You cooked dinner?"

She nodded.

"Who cooked dinner?"

"I?"

"I cooked dinner."

"Yes."

"I cooked dinner. Say the whole sentence."

"Oh. Yes. I cooked dinner."

"Bayarjargal, what will you do tonight?"

"Tonight I . . . will? . . . cook dinner and watch television."

⁓•⁓

It was Sunday morning, the only day of the week when there were no classes. With the door flung open to the springlike sunshine, I set about cleaning my bubble-home. Daily *ger* routines were very organized, and I tried to imitate the sense of order that allowed life in such a small space to remain uncluttered. Outside of the three cities, there were no trash cans—because there was no trash, because there was no packaging. Only the imported Chinese and Russian candies came in wrappers, which the Mongolians tossed thoughtlessly into the pristine prairie even as they exalted the purity of their land. They could not yet conceive of how a few bits of waxy paper could multiply into the moldering trash heaps of a packaged-products environment. Tea stems were spit out and cigarette ends flicked at the floor around the stove in the evening, but in the morning everything was swept up and tossed into the fire. Dishes were washed, beds quickly reconverted into sitting space.

I was sweeping when Handyman appeared, as he did several times a day, to protectively check on me. My usual thermos of tea had not been delivered that morning, so I served him chamomile-mint tea made with tea bags from Seattle. "American tea," I laughed as he sipped politely. It tasted as little like tea to him as the salty Mongolian brew had first tasted like tea to me. A few hours later, he came back to say that lunch was ready. Across the yard in the school cafeteria, the fuzzy black legs of the animal that was now lunch were jumbled in a corner of the kitchen entryway. Inside, a huge iron stove devoured hefty logs while the students' meal bubbled in meter-wide *togoos*. We sat at a little table behind the stove. A small bowl of tea was put in my hands. It had been made without salt.

He and Cook stared at me expectantly.

"No salt?" I asked.

"No salt," they nodded proudly. "Like your American tea. Is it good?"

Mongolian tea without salt is bitter, colored water. They were sipping at their own bowls and it obviously tasted as bad to them as it did to me. If I said politely that it was good, I would be stuck with a month of flavorless brown liquid. "American tea with salt is bad," I said. "Mongolian tea with salt is good. I like Mongolian tea. I like Mongolian tea with salt. Mongolian tea without salt is bad," I said, actually managing the explanation in almost grammatically correct Mongolian. Everybody looked at everybody else. Cook reached into a bag and grabbed a fistful of salt. With a grin and a flourish she tossed it into the steaming vat of tea and we all burst out laughing. Then we dumped out our bowls and refilled them with the flavorful, salted brew.

After lunch I went for a walk. I followed the river out of the village and found a path that led along the crest of the fading green hills. A handful of *gers* dotted the riverbank below. A child and a bent old woman crossed from one felt home to another. Yaks foraged along the slopes. Somewhere a dog barked. I climbed up to a small rock outcropping and looked back over Arshaant. Agvantseren claimed that the village's population was 3,000. I counted maybe 200 homes; even multiplying by five or six people per household, I couldn't raise the local population much above 1,000.

Suddenly cries of "Erika!" echoed up from the valley. Four small, running figures pulled up at the river, waving their arms high and calling my name. One figure waved her red jacket like a flag. I waved back and sat down to wait for them. The girls splashed through the river and dashed straight up the hill. Buyanjargal, Tüvshinjargal, and two of her friends collapsed panting and laughing around me. They pulled off their soaking shoes and wrung out their socks, then we continued down the trail together, the eleven-year-olds vying to hold my hands on the narrow path. We crossed a stream on two saplings laid side by side, the children far more surefooted than I. The path grew wider, but Buyanjargal walked so close to me that our shoulders brushed against each other.

Americans stand a yard apart and talk loudly. They hug hello and good-bye but do their best never to bump up against a stranger in a ticket line. In Mongolia, incidental physical contact is constant—people push and crowd and stand pressing against each other—but explicit demonstrations of affection are rare. Only once or twice was a warm cheek pressed to mine in greeting or farewell. American kids have their own bedrooms with their own televisions, computers, and phone lines. Mongolian families live in one room and share beds. Privacy, by western standards, is nonexistent. Whenever I opened my journal, someone pulled it out from under my pen to leaf through it. One evening Bolormaa had shown me notes from her lover in Russia. I had smiled at the pictures on the cards and handed the private missives back to her. She shook her head and told me to read them. Now, as Buyanjargal chattered in a garble of Mongolian and Russian, her face so close to mine that I could feel her breath in my ear, I tried to overcome my American need for individual space, but found myself claustrophobic in the airy valley. Eagerness to taste the world danced in her eyes. She was bright and hungry to learn. She was also a demanding, possessive show-off who wanted things her way. She reminded me of myself.

We drank from a clear, cold spring and tumbled in idyllic meadow grass beneath a sky that had never known smog. When daylight began to fade, we turned back toward the village. As we walked, the children began to sing. Buyanjargal stopped to recite a poem. Then they all wanted to show me a Mongolian dance. In their wet shoes and socks, in the sunset light of a valley unchanged in centuries, the children danced and sang in the rocky, dusty road. Their clothes were worn and patched, but their parents were not wondering, terrified, where their daughters were. It was a world where little girls were free to wander off impromptu for a Sunday afternoon without warnings about the myriad dangers of the streets. Maybe living without plumbing was a fair trade for living without fear.

CHAPTER 5

"Thirteen!"

I very quickly developed a new respect for the energy that teaching takes. Two classes in a row left me exhausted. "One." I held up one finger. "Two." I held up two fingers.

"One," they repeated in ragged unison. "Two. Three. Four. . . . "

I held up eight fingers and pointed to Baasanjav's son.

"Eight," came a squeak from the other side of the room.

"Eight," the little boy parroted, grinning at me. Baasanjav's son Batbar and Buyanjargal's brother Battur were winsome ten-year-old boys with explosive twinkles in their eyes. "They don't really know how to study yet," Baasanjav had admitted, "but the exposure will be good for them." So they sat in on classes, and I tried to include them in the lessons. I looked over at Enkhjargal and held my finger to my lips, then held up four fingers to Nomonjargal, a bright twelve-year-old with a slender face and mischievous smile. Budding rebelliousness expressed itself in feigned laziness and too-loud laughter when he answered correctly. "Four," he barked.

"2 + 3 = " I wrote on the chalkboard and pointed to Bat-Ölzii.

"Five."

"Very good."

"8 − 2 = "

"Six!" The squeak burst from the corner. Her eagerness was almost uncontrollable, and only when she tried especially hard could Enkhjargal muster the restraint to keep the answers to herself.

Groups Two and Three, those few crucial years older, were already moving more quickly than Group One. They sped through one to ten and kept going right on up to twenty. I had taken hundreds of hours of first-year language classes, but had never taught one. I was making it up as I went along. I left the plus and minus and equals signs on the chalkboard and pointed to them as I spoke, but I stopped writing the digits. I wanted them to have to *hear* me. I wanted the sounds to come to life inside their heads.

"Twelve plus one is. . . ."

Tsengüünjargal raised her hand, then snatched it back down when she realized what she had done. Until we reached thirty-three, thirteen was the most difficult word they would encounter. I grabbed my tongue between my fingers: "th-th-th." Fifteen kids burst out laughing. They didn't know where to look. Their teacher was holding her tongue and blowing through her teeth. Teachers didn't do that. But these were the brightest, quickest students in the village. They squirmed and blushed and dove in. They grabbed their tongues: "Th-th-th. Th-th-th."

"Thteen."

"Thriteen."

"Thirteen!"

Had I left Ulaanbaatar heading south on my bicycle, instead of west on an airplane, I would, about now, be arriving in China, but as the kids' gleeful shouts brought a rush of tears to my eyes, I knew absolutely that no line on a map could ever rival the innocent vivacity of the young faces victoriously trumpeting "thirteen!" The trust and excitement in their black eyes were like the heartbeat of a bird in the palms of my hands, a healthy baby bird that believed I could teach it to fly. Surrounded by the uneven timbre of their fervent voices now counting to twenty, I could not fathom how I had landed in such a magical place.

⟋•

The morning light was a brittle, translucent coral as I crossed the schoolyard. Nestled self-sufficient in its valley, the village might still have been asleep but for the curls of smoke climbing from the stovepipes. If I lit a fire before trudging to the outhouse, the sharp edge of frost would already have melted from the air inside my *ger* by the time I returned. I tossed a slice of bread on the stove to toast, then on top of the toast a bit of *öröm,* which melted deep into the bread like a big slab of butter. I had come to love my mornings. The brief sunrise hour was the only time I could rely on solitude. I would pour a cup of salty tea and write, or prepare lessons, until the first inevitable visit officially began the day.

The door cracked open. "Hello," I said. "Hello. *Sain baina uu?* Hello."

"Khello," one dared to try. The rest of the group collapsed into hysterical laughter.

"*Sain, sain,*" I nodded emphatically. "Good, good. Hello."

"Gello!" another one burst out. "Gello!"

A group of eight- to ten-year-old boys had discovered me and taken to thundering in on their way to class in the morning. There was Frog, a short boy in dark blue corduroy with bulging eyes who made himself right at home, proudly throwing out his little chest and sitting on the bed or at the table while his friends watched in awe. "Hello," he said. "Hello. Hello. Hello. Hello." There was Bully, a big, solid boy who stood in front of the group and barked loudly in his own made-up guttural language. He knew that I did not speak his language and that he could not make sense of my sounds, so he invented a new middle ground.

And then there was Erdenedalai—a wise nine-year-old dressed in purple. He came at first with the group, then later on his own. He stood at the door, not shy or nervous, just polite, until I pointed to a chair at the table. Then he sat across from me, still, his eyes bright and clear, and pointed to various things around the *ger*. A sharp nod acknowledged every item as I named it in English. He never attempted to repeat the English, but carefully told me the object's name in Mongolian and then patiently corrected my pronunciation. Unlike Bully, Erdenedalai had immediately grasped that our two languages were interchangeable, that if we gave each other the keys, we could unlock the meanings in each other's sounds. He spoke slowly and clearly, watching me closely, and repeating or drawing or carefully miming any words that brought a puzzled squint to my forehead.

One day he came to tell me that there was a truck in town selling apples for fifty *tögrögs* apiece. The intense little boy walked in, sat down at the table, and with our very, very few common words explained all the details. What was being sold, where, for how much. By the time I got there, the apples were gone, but as long as I was out on main street, I decided to go shopping. As a rule I hate shopping. Afternoons at the mall are not my idea of a good time. But in Arshaant exploring stores had quickly become both habit and pastime. In lands where supplies are irregular at best, shopping is dictated by availability rather than need; because stores are few and stock is haphazard, any open door merits a visit. Browsing store shelves was also one of the few forms of diversion in the sleepy village. My supply of candles and matches was running low. As the days grew shorter, the hours between sunset and seven o'clock, when the electricity usually clicked on, grew longer. In the first store, which carried mostly flimsy math textbooks and cabbage, I spied a large burlap bag of powdery white things the size and gnarled shape of gingerroot.

"What are those?" I asked.

The clerk explained. Her words were a stream of meaningless sounds.

"To eat?" I asked.

She laughed and handed me one. It tasted something like a dried fig rolled in powdered sugar. It was fruit. I bought half a kilo. But she did not have candles or matches. In the next store, on a shelf below a half dozen bolts of colorful *del* material was a large carton of white candles. I knew the word for candle. I even knew the word for match, but there were no matches. The only other store open that day was tucked into the corner of an abandoned factory yard. Its dark shelves displayed three or four metal pots and pans, a kettle, a dozen bottles of imported whisky, a sack of potatoes, and a small heap of box matches.

On the way home from this stunningly successful shopping trip, I stuck my head in my neighbors' door to ask if I could borrow their ax. My pile of kindling was also almost gone. Their little boy was home alone, but I knew the word for "ax." He showed me where it leaned against the wall. Then he showed me his new puppy, which promptly followed me home. I had scarcely made my first chop when the boy's father appeared. I don't know which sight upset him more—the ax in my hands, or the little animal inside my *ger*. He kicked the dog out, took the ax, and swiftly shredded a log. It would be weeks before he trusted me to chop my own kindling. Less than an hour later, Agvantseren walked in. News traveled quickly. He had come to tell me that he understood that Europeans liked dogs, but the puppy might be dirty or sick, and he strongly advised against allowing it inside. She was a healthy, energetic, roly-poly thing and I continued to let her visit, slipping her the mutton fat that I otherwise tossed guiltily into the stove, knowing that every other person in town would gladly eat it.

On a blustery day of scudding gray clouds, the wind blew walls of dust through the village, which was deserted as if everyone were hiding from a coming gunfight. Three horsemen trotted side by side down an empty street, shadowy figures in the brown cloud. Only the tumbleweeds were missing. Gerlee came by that evening with a couple of friends in tow. "There is a dance at the Club," she said. "Will you come with us?" No street lamps lit the way. The moon was hidden in the cloudy sky, and we made our way by memory and the echo of other voices in the darkness. Wrapped in coats and scarves, everyone stood leaning against the walls of a narrow wooden hall. Two stoves barely took the edge off the frozen air. Boys approached girls, not really looking at them, and held out a hand. Not really looking at each other, they danced until the song ended, then dashed separately back to the walls.

After a while the man in charge of the few scratchy cassettes put on a tape of imitation electronic Madonna. A clutch of young men in their twenties, including two with the unmistakable fake leather jackets and swagger of time spent in The City, responded to the music with hard-hitting, floor-pounding stomps. Dancing they had seen on television, I suspected, but had rarely practiced. I joined their circle in the center of the hall. Gerlee, who couldn't believe that I did not know the waltzing Mongolian dances, watched wide-eyed. I couldn't chop wood. I couldn't milk a cow. But, as far as she was concerned, I sure could dance. Looking at me afterward with a newfound respect, she shook her head: "I can't do *that*."

⚓

Some days there was a visceral thrill to teaching. One afternoon I decided it was time for a field trip. Group Two followed me outside. "This is a tree," I said, running my hand up a thin, struggling trunk at the edge of the schoolyard. "What is this?"

"This is a tree," came a voice from the back of the group.

I walked over to where Otgontuya was standing and pointed back at the bare branches. *"That* is a tree. What is that?"

"That is a tree," she grinned triumphantly.

I pulled her the two paces to the tree, put her hand on the trunk and walked away. "What is that?"

She squinted in concentration. *"This* is a tree."

"Yes, very good!"

White flakes had begun floating out of the sky. "What is this?" Enkhtsetseg held out a hand, a drop of white turning to water in her palm.

"That is snow."

"What is this?" someone else pointed to a horse across the yard.

"What is . . . ?"

"What is . . . *that?*"

"That is a horse. What is that?"

"That is a horse."

Suddenly a dozen teenagers were grabbing and pointing at everything in sight: "What is this? What is that?" Cow, school, rock, fence, sheep. In the long run, a few of them would at best remember a few of the new words, and much of the energy coursing through them came from the sheer novelty of a teacher taking the classroom outside. But I also felt the connections being made in their brains, like Helen Keller suddenly grasping that the symbols in the palm of her hand *meant* something, that they named the objects and sensations in the world around her. It was that crucial moment in language-learning when the new word suddenly connects to the *object,* rather than being just a funny way of saying the old word. Suddenly English was not an arbitrary classroom exercise or a translation of Mongolian, but its own way of interpreting the universe.

It was snowing harder and we headed for my *ger.* Chuluunbaatar—a lanky fifteen-year-old with the body of a young cowboy, who was still as embarrassed when he got the answer right as when he didn't have a clue—swiftly built up a fire while we learned "bed, table, match, stove, candle. . . ." Otgontuya grabbed the sleeve of her *del:* "What is this?" *"Del,"* I answered, laughing; "there are no *dels* in America." The wood crackled in the stove, their eyes shone in the dim light, and laughter filled the felt bubble. I mimed horses. I mimed cows and sheep. Laughing, bouncing, and learning, the children stayed longer than the hour scheduled for their lesson. I was late getting to the teachers' class.

"Have you ever been to Ulaanbaatar?"

"Yes, I have been to Ulaanbaatar."

"Have you ever been to Moscow?"

"No, I have never been to Moscow."

"Have you ever eaten a hamburger?"

Enkhtuya stared blankly at me for a second, then dashed her eyes to Agvantseren.

"Do you know what a hamburger is?" I queried quickly.

"No?" She shook her head nervously, as if that might be the wrong answer. There are plenty of people in the world who have never heard of a hamburger, but I had not met many of them. "The whole sentence," I said. And it made me unreasonably happy to hear her enunciate, "I do not know what a hamburger is."

By the time class was over, the snow was piling up on the ground. The teachers fretted among themselves about how cold I would be, then Enkhtuya invited me home for the night. Her mother was in Mörön. Her father sat on a low stool cleaning his rifle while Enkhtuya prepared *buuz,* refusing to let me help. His back was bent and his wrinkled fingers trembled slightly as he worked, but he was still a tall and powerful man. He was going boar hunting in the morning. His limpid eyes smiled at my mangled attempts to speak Mongolian. They glowed when I forced his daughter to brave a sentence of English in response.

Probably in an attempt to flatten the rolling Mongolian "r," Enkhtuya had a habit of throwing her chin and lower jaw off to the side when she spoke English, muffling and torquing her pronunciation. After dinner I sat her in front of a mirror and showed her what she was doing. I showed her my flat American "r." I showed her how my lower jaw stayed aligned with my upper jaw. "Are." She tried to copy it. "Car." She tried again. "Parade." Her chin dove off to the left. "Flower." We started to giggle. "Horse." More giggles. "Married." She collapsed laughing on the floor, her restrained demeanor finally dissolving with the involuntary slide of her jaw. We sat laughing and working in front of the mirror until finally, with her chin held between her hands, she was producing one clear, flat "r" after another. "The car and the horse are in the parade. . . . "

We were still giggling when some friends dropped by to play dominoes. I had had a set of dominoes as a child, but all I had ever done was line them up and knock them over. I had never actually played the game. Everyone was ready to tell me which piece to move or not to move, but nobody explained the rules, and there was little patience while I thought or played hesitantly. It was a seeming contradiction that I had also experienced with Greene: while everyone had always been very protective of her, often bringing her right inside their homes for the night, no one had ever treated her gently; people pushed and poked at any part that moved or looked like it might. It did not make sense to me that in a country where material goods were so expensive and hard to come by, they were not treated with great care. But Mongolia cannot afford things that need to be coddled. Everything, and everyone, is expected to stand up to whatever life doles out. Like their animals and possessions, people are expected to be hardy. Until I learned to play, I would lose.

Enkhtuya's father got up long before dawn. I watched his leathery face drinking tea by candlelight and was back asleep before I heard him go. I never saw a sickly or bedridden old person in Mongolia. Did they all go directly from bent and wrinkled but strong and lucid to dead? Remembering my own grandmother, frail in her nursing-home bed for years, I asked if that happened to elderly people in Mongolia. "Oh yes," Enkhtuya said, "often before an old person dies, they won't get out of bed for days."

⸙

Tüvshinjargal touched her forehead to the stone of the small white temple. Like Katya across the border to the north, the little Mongolian girl with the wind-chapped cheeks and skinny braids had been born just in time to grow up without the fears and interdictions of a totalitarian state. I had been on my way to Agvantseren's, hoping to borrow something to read. But the sky was bright blue, much of the snow had melted, and it was a perfect day for a hike, so I had taken a circuitous route. There was a white spot in the hills behind Gerlee's, and I didn't know what it was. That was all the direction I needed. As I passed near their yard, Tüvshinjargal had come running out to join me. We had hiked up the hill together, and I had given her a *tögrög* note to tuck under a stone as she circled the structure three times in a ritual that her generation had never known as a crime.

Then she had wanted me to come home with her. Now, having finished the inevitable bowl of quickly prepared *guriltai shöl,* I got up to leave and Gerlee got up to come with me. Much as in America we walk dinner guests down the driveway to their car, she always walked me a little way down the road. "Where are you going?" she asked, confused, as I started into the hills. I was still on my way to Agvantseren's, but even more than a book, I wanted to climb the rocky ridge above us, to work up a sweat and stretch stagnating muscles. Eating mutton twice a day and rarely walking farther than across the schoolyard or up to Gerlee's or Enkhtuya's (to eat more mutton) was almost as much of a shock to a body grown accustomed to daily cycling as daily cycling had once been to a body accustomed to little more regular exercise than walking to the car to drive to the bookstore. It felt as if every muscle in my body were turning to mush. This was impossible to explain. I could tell Gerlee *where* I wanted to go. I could point. But I could not explain *why.*

"I don't know," I said, because I didn't know how to say "to hike, to look around, to get some exercise." I didn't even know the words for "It doesn't matter, I just want to walk."

"Where?" she repeated loudly, taking "I don't know" to mean "I don't understand."

I could tell her I was going to Agvantseren's, but then she would try to lead me down the shortest route across the village, and I would still be standing there, shaking my head and not following her, trying to walk into the hills, unable to explain.

"I go there." I pointed. "I can go alone."

She followed my finger. There was nothing there. Rocks and grass. A few patches of snow. She looked back at me, frustrated. She wanted to help. I had to be going somewhere. I had to be looking for something. But she couldn't figure out where, or what, or how to help. Walking for the pleasure of walking or wanting to be outside because the sky is blue and the air feels good in your lungs does not necessarily make a lot of sense to someone who spends days at a time, regardless of the weather, herding sheep and cattle. Gerlee's mystified eyes followed me as I set out toward the ridge. She knew that she would never understand me.

At the top of the spur, breathing hard and covered in a light, satisfying sweat, I perched on a rock. Behind me, the next valley stretched toward the horizon like an undiscovered country reaching for the sea. In front of me was "my" village. The valley that had still been a golden green only a few weeks earlier was now a collage of brown and white, earth and snow. Dropping down the opposite side of the ridge, I followed a vague path into the maze of fences and pushed through a wooden gate into Agvantseren's yard. Bayarjargal was nursing her daughter (there had been a husband, briefly, somewhere). A thick woolen sweater she had just finished knitting lay on the stool beside her. Several younger siblings were studying or reading. Agvantseren was not home. He had gone to the *khödöö* to visit his wife. I had known that he had ten children. I had known that Bayarjargal was somewhere in the middle. I had not realized that Tsengüünjargal and Nomonjargal were also part of the family. No wonder they were among my brightest students. The minute I opened the door and stepped inside, Bayarjargal stopped nursing, and the kids abandoned their homework to serve tea and fresh *öröm*. I told her not to cook for me.

She looked uncomfortable. "Why not?"

"I've already eaten."

"Let us cook you *buuz*."

"No, I'm really not hungry."

"At least *buuz* with tea." *Buuz* cooked in tea were smaller, but no less work to prepare. I didn't want them to go to all that effort. I wasn't hungry. But Bayarjargal was upset. Confusion showed in her eyes. Genuine distress. She was at a loss. This was wrong. It was wrong not to feed me. She looked at her younger siblings. They glanced at each other, at me, and back at her. Tsengüünjargal's hand had stopped halfway to the flour. They, too, knew how things were supposed to be done.

"Okay," I relented, "*buuz* with tea."

She relaxed. The children went to work, chopping, rolling, and crimping. Bayarjargal pulled out her photo album and I settled down to look through pages of straight-faced studio shots, Pioneer Camp pictures, and holiday photos from Red Square until the *buuz* were ready. I was, slowly, learning how things were supposed to be done. And learning to do them that way.

CHAPTER 6

So Kiss Me and Smile for Me

The school building was filled with that dead cold that gets into your bones and makes you think you will never be warm again. It was milder outside, where the sun danced on the snow and the cold was alive under a cloudless sapphire sky. Agvantseren said the radiators would be turned on eventually, but it wasn't really winter yet, and heat was very expensive. In the freezing classroom, I began teaching the kids the Latin alphabet. I wrote the twenty-six letters on the chalkboard and taught them "The Alphabet Song." I wrote all the words they knew on the board, letter by letter, spelling out loud as we went.

Group One had become exceedingly rambunctious. The class was moving too quickly for Batbar and Battur to keep up, and I was no longer new and fascinating enough to keep them wide-eyed and quiet. They bounced all over the place, laughing and whispering, looking to Nomonjargal for approval and finding it. The lessons that were over their heads were moving too slowly to challenge the older boy, so he amused himself by egging on their antics, and I was not sufficiently experienced to either juggle three separate levels of learning in one classroom or to be a firm disciplinarian without just sounding mean. So the three of them joked and horsed around, distracting the whole class, except for Enkhjargal, whose big, wise eyes just watched quietly as I got more and more frustrated.

Enkhjargal was the best student in the village. She deserved anything and everything I possibly had to give her, and with my attention constantly diverted by the boys, I knew she was not getting the encouragement or the challenge that she deserved. "She could keep up with Group Three," I thought, and finally saw the obvious solution. After class, I told her and Nomonjargal to start coming with Group Two. With a little effort, Nomonjargal would also be perfectly capable of keeping up, and the challenge would do him good. Indeed, the next day his swaggering leadership disappeared when he suddenly found himself the little boy in a group of older girls. And without their leader, the boys in Group One calmed right down.

Group Three had also grown boisterous as the teenagers' awe of the American Teacher faded into the nonchalance of daily habit. Their rambunctiousness was good-natured, and I reminded myself that none of them had to be coming to English classes—they were all there to have fun. But after a particularly unruly hour, during which I found myself responding to the energetic chatter with snappish discipline, I wondered if I would end up making them hate me. Then, the next day, they focused and paid attention, absorbing new information like desert plants drinking in a summer rainstorm.

"I am from America. Where are you from?"

"I am from Mongolia."

"Is she from China?"

"No, she is from Mongolia."

"Is he from Russia?"

"No, he is from Mongolia."

"Where am I from?"

"You is—are—from America!"

"Yes, I am from America." I laughed, and drew a stick-figure family on the chalkboard. "This is me. This is my father. This is my mother. Father, mother, sister, brother. This is my family. I have one sister and no brothers. How many brothers and sisters do you have?" I drew a menagerie on the board. "This is a cow. This is a horse. My family has no cows, no horses, and no yaks. How many yaks does your family have?"

It was snowing again, sifting steadily down. The flakes that fell through the *tonoo* tinkled and sizzled as they landed on the stove. I slipped several large logs into the fire before going to bed, arranging them to smolder slowly through the night. In the morning the valley was quilted in perfect, powdery white. In front of my door, the snow reached halfway to my knees. Inside the outhouses, the drifts buried my ankles. This time the snow was here to stay. Sarantsetseg, the school's twenty-three-year-old accountant, had invited me home for dinner. She had a bold, ringing laugh and eyes that flashed with quick, ironic humor. Her jauntily pursed lips were painted a brighter red than Enkhtuya's or Bayarjargal's would ever be. She seemed too large a personality to stay long in the quiet village. That evening she came by to find out if I still wanted to hike up the hill, in spite of the snow.

"You can spend the night," she offered.

"Should I bring my sleeping bag?"

"Of course you can bring your sleeping bag."

I had learned how different our assumptions could be. I had learned that when I was asking one question, it could come out sounding like another one altogether. I had learned to be explicit. "I only want to bring it if there are not enough blankets for everybody."

Sarantsetseg laughed at me. "We have plenty of covers for lots of guests. You don't need to bring your sleeping bag." I grabbed my toothbrush and we set off up the hill. "My father," she giggled, "asked if you would sleep in a Mongolian bed, or if you would think it was dirty. He asked what you would eat for dinner. He asked if you would not be scared by such a big family."

Sarantsetseg was the oldest of five children—two girls, three boys, the youngest twelve or thirteen. By any standard I had grown up with, seven people living in one circular room would define the depths of poverty, but as I bicycled across Mongolia, I had begun to question what defined poverty. Her family's cozy *ger* was lined with beautiful carpets and finely painted chests, the children were plump and energetic, the familial love and respect were palpable. It was not an easy life, but it was not a poor life.

Only once, in a lone roadside *ger* south of Arshaant where I had stopped to ask directions, had I had seen real poverty, the poverty that is about the struggle to survive. Four barefoot children ranged in a clump watching their mother talk to me, then invite me inside. There were no smiles on their faces. There was no curiosity in their blank, staring eyes. Their mother's eyes, too, were the dead eyes of a beaten animal whose existence has become merely the habit of putting the next foot forward in the meaningless, endless, lifeless routine of the hours and days. My attempts at conversation, at smiles, were lost in the dusky, dirty *ger*. There was no fear, just the apathy born of hardship and futility—uncomprehending, listless acceptance, even the energy to question burnt out. They were the first and only downtrodden Mongolians I encountered. Yet however poor, however much they didn't understand or care who I was or why I was there, they were still prepared to share what they had. As I left, the woman handed me five long sticks of dry, flavorless *aaruul* already spotted with mold. I gave her a cabbage. I gave the children large handfuls of candies. They nodded soberly, but even candy could not elicit grins from the worn young faces.

Sarantsetseg gave me a high, western-style chair. My knees were on an even plane with the traditional low table. I switched to a low stool and caught the subtle smiles of approval on her parents' faces. Sarantsetseg told me I could take off my shoes. I started unlacing them, assuming she was telling me nicely that they were dirty. "You probably think it's very odd of us to keep our shoes on inside," she apologized. "It's just that in Mongolia we spend so much time outside, it's not worth always taking off our shoes just to put them on again." I thought I had learned. The only foreign country Sarantsetseg had ever been to was Russia, where everyone leaves their shoes at the door. I laughed. And laced my shoes back up. "In America we don't always take off our shoes when we go inside, either. It's perfectly normal to me to leave them on."

Every time I visited a home, the world of the village got smaller: Sarantsetseg's sister turned out to be Sarantuya, from Group Three. And the cousin helping her knead the dough for *khuushuur* was Orgoltsetseg, a bright tomboy from Group One. Sarantsetseg's father, a robust man with a body like the trunk of a squat oak tree and a twinkle in his eyes, asked if I played chess. We settled on the floor with the board between us. He warned me whenever I was about to make a bad move, pointed out a better one, and effortlessly beat me twice in quick succession. When the *khuushuur* were ready, Orgoltsetseg handed us a bowlful, and he and I ate over the chessboard as we continued playing.

For all the ritual surrounding food—the tea and the *tavgiin idee,* the sharing of *airag* and *arkhi,* the feeding of the guest in vast quantities—the actual eating was devoid of ritual. There was no gathering together, no waiting until everyone was served. Food was utilitarian. It was not to be savored. It was to be eaten before it got cold. I knew that the evening was an occasion, having the foreign guest come to dinner, so it was odd to me to eat while we played, instead of in a circle including the rest of the family. But there was no dining room table to gather around, no upstairs bedroom for the kids to be called away from. A half dozen people living together in one room hardly lack for quality time together. We ate, we played, I lost. And the gathering together came later, around the television, to watch the wildly popular Mexican soap opera "Simply Maria." Broadcast from Moscow, the serial was dubbed into Russian, the Spanish still audible behind the translation. As the wealthy Mexicans moved elegantly through the melodramas of their splendid mansions, Sarantsetseg looked at me and shook her head.

"You are a very simple woman, aren't you?"

I wasn't sure what she meant.

"To live in a *ger* and travel by bicycle."

I caught the swivel of her gaze between the television and my lumpy clothes and daily braids. "You mean compared to Maria?"

"When you are used to that, you must be a very simple nature to be able to live in a *ger*."

"I don't live like that. I have one room, no servants, I never dress as well as she does. . . . " It is always a difficult differentiation. Just as I cannot understand the difference between having $2 billion and $3 billion, Sarantsetseg could not really see the difference between my Toyota hatchback and Maria's Mercedes. And, all things being relative, the trappings of my simple Seattle apartment *were* probably closer to Maria's mansion than to Sarantsetseg's *ger*.

"And you are short for an American."

"I am? No, not really." I looked at the screen. None of them seemed particularly tall. "I'm not tall, but I'm pretty average."

"No, you're not," Sarantsetseg shook her head confidently. "You are short for an American. I watched basketball on television. It is a fun game. I like Charles Barkley very much."

⚈

Fall break had started. Most of the kids whose families lived in the *khödöö* were already gone. I asked Agvantseren how I was going to eat during the vacation.

"Cook will come in to fix your meals," he stated.

"No, she won't," I said. "It's her vacation. I just need some food and some utensils, and I can cook for myself."

"But you don't know how to cook," said Enkhtuya.

"I'm not a great chef, but I cook for myself at home."

"Not over a fire," Bayarjargal pointed out.

"No, but I cook over a fire when I go camping." Three blank faces looked back at me. And then I tried to explain camping to people who lived in tents and cooked over a fire every day. "For fun we walk into the wilderness and sleep in a tent and cook over a fire." It didn't make much sense to me either just then. "I live alone," I tried again, "and I don't eat in restaurants all the time. I cook my own meals."

"But in America all your food is prepared, you just unfreeze it or something."

I had to admit that it was possible to live on frozen food that came in colorful cardboard packages on its own plate, but explained that it was also possible to buy fresh vegetables and meat (albeit dead, hairless, and neatly trimmed), which I then cooked myself. Eventually I seemed to have con-vinced them that I was not completely incompetent. Enkhtuya took me to the kitchen to collect a cleaver, a cutting board, a big pot, salt, tea, pota-toes, turnips, cabbage, and a chunk of mutton. We dumped the lump of meat in a small pot and took it to my neighbors' unheated shanty, which also served as their refrigerator. She pushed aside a goat leg to make room for the pot on top of a rusty metal barrel next to various other woolly ani-mal parts. Then Agvantseren invited me home for dinner. They still didn't really believe I could cook.

Agvantseren's *ger* had a refrigerator. In it were stored dishes, silverware, and flour. I had seen similar refrigerators cum cabinets in many homes, and could not understand them. Who had managed to sell all those refrigera-tors to people who had little or no electricity? Did they not know what a refrigerator was supposed to do? In a half dozen trips to Russia over the previous decade, I had witnessed the years' dramatic changes, but in Mongolia I tended to assume that things had always been the way they were now. "No," Agvantseren explained. "Just two years ago, everything was dif-ferent." The hotel had functioned. The public baths had been open regu-larly. There had been sugar in the stores and flour for sale without ration coupons. Arshaant had had electricity twenty-four hours a day, and the re-frigerators had functioned as refrigerators.

"Maybe things will get better again soon," he concluded, glancing over at Bayarjargal, who was busy cooking. She never got a word in edgewise when her father was around. She scarcely said three sentences the whole evening, just cooked while he and I talked. Agvantseren was a gently domi-neering man who had educated himself well in a time and place where this was not easy to do, and he wanted the best for his children. "Maybe," he grinned, "they will even get to see America one day." He said it in the way I would say, "Maybe one day I'll have a picnic on the moon."

"Maybe things will get better," he had said, with a shrug that was not particularly hopeful, but was also without any bitterness. Russians in the 1990s carry inside themselves the profound pain and shame of seventy years of having been so lied to by their own. The Mongolians were already much more free of recent history. They had shed the previous seven decades like a skin. It was a foreign skin, not their own; they had left it behind and bore little residue of pain. The history they carried within themselves was an ancient history of pride.

Nonetheless, Mongolia still lived in the overwhelming shadow of the monolith to the north, and the events in Russia were making people nervous.

Rumors of revolution and pictures of tanks in the streets of Moscow were disquieting in the southern steppes. Although Mongolia had recently been able to broaden its horizons by turning to China for trade in certain goods, its economy remained inextricably linked to Russia. We discussed the need for Mongolia to become truly independent of its two huge neighbors. I mentioned the sweater I had seen Bayarjargal knit, and went on at some length about how she should start a business. I assured her how well such sweaters, and similar socks and gloves, would sell to tourists in Ulaanbaatar. The idea made her smile, and I wished she would really do it. If the country were going to continue its move away from traditional self-sufficient nomadism toward the perceived improvements of televisions, motorized vehicles, and Chicago Bulls tee shirts, it would have to find a way to support the import economy without bleeding itself dry.

⸱⸱⸱

In the early twentieth century, Mongolia supported a vast network of more than 700 monasteries. As many as one-third of the country's males were monks or monastic students. While these monasteries were hardly bastions of chaste holiness—drunkenness, promiscuity, and abuse of power ran rampant—the populace remained steadfast in its devotion to the system—a system that was not to survive the Communists. Religious persecution intensified throughout the 1930s, culminating in two years of bloody purges during which tens of thousands of monks were dispersed back into the countryside, or simply disappeared. The vast archipelago of monasteries was reduced to four poor buildings, and of these, only Gandan Khiid in Ulaanbaatar was allowed to continue functioning, even nominally, as a place of worship.

The monks, however, had not gone quietly. C. R. Bawden writes in *The Modern History of Mongolia* that in 1932, at a monastery called Bandid Gegeen, "lamas by the hundred [were] forcibly secularized, 400 of them being expelled from the lamasery in a single day. . . . The local authorities . . . affronted the common people as well as the lamas by their desecration of sacred objects, tearing off the wrappers of volumes of the scriptures and burning the books themselves, digging out holy relics embedded in stupas, stripping the oracle lama of his special vestments and helmet in full view of the people, and so on."

These acts sparked a great uprising against the Party, led to the establishment of a rebel government at Bandid Gegeen, and contributed to the outbreak of civil war across western Mongolia. In the long run, however, the monks were no match for the Soviet-supported Communists. By 1938 the struggle was over and for the next fifty years the Communists could claim to have won. Yet when religion was again legalized in 1990, there was an immediate resurgence of belief and practice. The few standing monasteries blossomed again into houses of worship, and new monasteries began springing up all across the country, quickly attracting a new generation of adherents.

At the edge of Arshaant, just beyond the last home, one small *ger* sat behind a carved fence. A prayer wheel stood in the yard. A circle had been worn into the dirt around the base of a tree adorned with colorful ribbons and small *tögrög* notes. Inside, incense wafted through the *ger*. More ribbons waved down beneath the circle of sky. Buddhas and candles clustered under a poster of the Dalai Lama. Two monks sat along one curve of the *ger,* muttering their chants. A teenage apprentice stoked the stove. An American visitor slipped onto a low bench and held out her hands to the warmth. The eldest monk smiled at her and clanged his cymbal. Outside, hidden beneath long prairie grass, lay the gray stone foundations of Bandid Gegeen.

⁓•

The days were flying by. I woke up punctually at eight. I made a fire. I boiled salty tea with fresh yak milk. For the vacation week, English classes had been moved to the morning, and each group met every day. They started at ten, three in a row until one o'clock, then back for the teachers' class from two to three-thirty. The afternoons then disappeared into the little necessities of daily routine: fetching water from the river (an increasingly difficult project as the ice grew out from the banks), making tea, doing dishes, preparing the next day's lessons, cooking dinner, chopping kindling. My neighbor now trusted me to use his ax. Or at least allowed me to do it.

One morning I walked into my classroom and it was warm. The radiators had been turned on. Our breath was no longer visible on the air. The kids and I no longer spent the hour with our hands scrunched up into our sleeves, stamping our feet to keep warm. In Group Two I wrote a paragraph about myself on the chalkboard: "My name is Erika. I am twenty-eight years old. I am from America. I have one sister and no brothers. My family has no cows and no sheep." As I wrote, the students copied the sentences into their notebooks. We read the paragraph together, then I told them to rewrite it about themselves. What these kids had learned in a few weeks was amazing. When I thought about the time I had spent in my first-year college Russian course memorizing a new alphabet, when I thought about the sheer quantity of information I was throwing at them, it was simply astonishing to see how much they had absorbed. Tsengüünjargal and Enkhjargal finished first. Tsengüünjargal sat in her corner sighing and whistling under her breath to let everybody know that she was done. Enkhjargal kept writing, making up additional sentences on her own.

In Group Three, while everyone else was still copying my paragraph, I discovered that Buyanjargal and Delgersüren were already writing their own. Someone in Group Two had told them what the exercise would be. Copying my paragraph was practice they needed: practice writing the new letters, practice seeing each new word as its own entity. Just as all those teachers in Southern California had once had to tell me, there was a purpose to the preliminary part of the exercise.

Then I realized that they had not just skipped half of the assignment. Buyanjargal had Otgontuya's notebook on her lap. They were copying her essay instead of composing their own. Buyanjargal was a great kid. I loved her energy and eagerness, and cherished her family like adopted kin. But I knew her games too well, and this time I wasn't playing. I reached down, took Otgontuya's notebook, and walked away. When everyone had finished, I asked each student in turn to read her paragraph out loud. I peered over the girls' shoulders as they read, checking spelling and correcting pronunciation. I didn't ask Buyanjargal or Delgersüren to read. Buyanjargal held out her notebook. I shrugged and shook my head. I told her I wasn't interested. I told her it was not her own work. I knew that what they had done was not about cheating per se (it couldn't be, in an extracurricular class with no grades). It was about thinking she didn't need the steps if she had the final product. It was about wanting to be ahead and show off. I knew. I had been there.

The next day, I began class by writing short dialogues on the chalkboard.

"What is that?"

"This is a pen."

"How many pens do you have?"

"I have three pens. What is that?"

"This is a book."

"How many books do you have?"

"I have one book."

The principal had requested that before leaving, I run a public exam to demonstrate what the students had learned. I had proposed that instead of an exam we would stage a little performance.

"Is he from Russia?"

"No, he is from Mongolia. Is she from America?"

"No, she is from Russia."

"What is her name?"

"Her name is Masha."

"Are they hungry?"

"No, they are thirsty."

I called Buyanjargal and Myagmarsüren to the front of the classroom and handed Buyanjargal my gloves, the woolen balaklava I slept in every night, and a Seattle Mariners baseball cap. After the incident with Otgontuya's notebook the day before, Buyanjargal had followed me home. It had taken me a second to recognize the look on her face when she stepped into my *ger:* she was fifteen years old, had gotten in trouble at school, and, I had suddenly realized, *I* was the authority figure. Unsure of how bad the situation might be, scared of how angry I might be, wishing she could just make it all go away, Buyanjargal had nevertheless held on to her natural pride and defiance as she asked for Otgontuya's notebook back. I was not interested in punishing the girls; I knew that their own chagrin would be more than "punishment" enough. Still, I did not want to make it too easy. I refused to give her the notebook, saying that I would give it back to Otgontuya myself. I said it with a smile, with no hint of the cold shoulder I had allowed myself in class, and she had seemed to understand my point: that I was disappointed in her behavior, but that the incident would have no further repercussions.

Now, called up to perform in front of the class, she and Myagmarsüren blushed and giggled. Field trips and props and skits, all things I had taken for granted in grade school in Southern California, were new to them. This was not how they were used to learning, but their eyes sparkled and grins burst across their bright red cheeks. Buyanjargal especially was clearly loving every minute of it.

"Hello. How are you?"

"I am fine, thanks. And you?"

"I am cold. How many hats and gloves do you have?"

"I have two hats and four gloves." *(Give other student a hat and two gloves.)*

"Thank you."

"You're welcome."

Afterward I said in English, "Please memorize these dialogues at home for our final performance on Thursday the eleventh." In Mongolian I pointed to the dialogue on the board, said "at home," covered my eyes, recited a few lines, and said "Thursday." Chatter exploded around the room when they realized what I was saying—they were going to perform in English in front of the whole school!

I had decided that a song would add to the spirit of the event, but had of course been stymied by my lack of repertoire before finally realizing that one of the few verses I knew (and whose tune I could roughly reproduce) was sentimentally perfect. I began teaching Groups Two and Three the refrain to John Denver's "Leaving on a Jet Plane."

> So kiss me and smile for me
> Tell me that you'll wait for me
> Hold me like you'll never let me go
> Because I'm leaving on a jet plane
> Don't know when I'll be back again
> Oh, babe, I hate to go.

It wouldn't be a jet, but I would be leaving, and I had no idea when I would be back again. The children would not be children the next time I saw them. Many would be parents. Many would have scattered away from the village. I would come back. But most of them I would never see again. Over the final short week of classes, we began and ended every hour slowly learning the song. Leaning against my desk watching their guileless, unspoiled faces—"Don't know when I'll be back again"—part of me wanted to stay in Arshaant for a long, long time—"Oh, babe, I hate to go."

⁘

Buyanjargal looked at my vegetables and shook her head. She reached for the knife: "Smaller, you have to cut them smaller." Turnip, potato, and cabbage weren't exactly broccoli, shiitake mushrooms, and red bell peppers, but I was about to attempt a vegetarian stir-fry. "No," I told her, holding on to the knife, "you don't have to cut them smaller." In Buyanjargal's world, of course, vegetables weren't really food. At best they were garnish, and all across her vast country they were chopped into the same diminutive sizes. "I know this is bigger than you have ever seen them chopped," I added, "but I promise they can be cooked like this."

She had dropped by when I was making my lunch the day before, too, and witnessed something even more upsetting than the oversize vegetables: a packet of freeze-dried chili and beans dumped into a small pot of boiling water. I had been avidly looking forward to the insta-food—carried across an ocean because I had been told there was no food in Mongolia—because while there was plenty of food, there was little variety and absolutely no spice. I warned Buyanjargal that she probably wouldn't like the chili. I looked up the word "spicy." I told her she didn't have to finish it. Then I gave her a small bowlful, just as Lkhamsüren had once given me, sure I wouldn't like *guriltai shöl*. Buyanjargal sniffed at it and glanced up at me, a little concerned. Then she slipped a spoonful into her mouth. Her eyes went wide and she reached for the bread I was holding ready. With her mouth full of bread, she looked at me again, her eyebrows high on her forehead. Was it really supposed to taste like this? She had braved her way through half the bowl before giving up. Now she threw her hands up in despair and left, shaking her head at me and my incomprehensible food.

That evening, just as I settled in to prepare the next day's classes, Buyanjargal's little brothers burst through the door. She had told her mother about my inedibly hot, strange food out of a packet. She had told her about my huge vegetables. And her mother, sure I was starving, had sent the boys to save me. "Come to our house!" they chirped. I was annoyed. I was touched. I put away my notebooks and went with them. Their father was playing cards with a few friends when we walked in, and their mother was scrubbing clothes on a rough washboard. She had clearly not been expecting me. It turned out that Battur just wanted to play chess, and Buyanjargal wanted to know if I would take a picture of her family.

As word had spread through the village that I had a camera, kids had begun crowding into my *ger* to ask for photographs of themselves and their friends. People I didn't know approached me: "Hello, will you take my picture?" Families wanted to pose in many different combinations. I had learned to say, "I don't have enough film. I can take one picture of everybody together." I had learned to say, "There's not enough light now." While Battur cornered my king, Buyanjargal and I discussed the fact that they were in school in the morning, I taught in the afternoon, and by evening the light was gone. Finally we decided that I would come back early the next morning—after sunrise but before they left for school. My shreds of Mongolian were improving: it was an entire conversation that didn't involve any of the Seven Questions. That settled and the chess game duly lost, I said goodnight and headed home. The sky was pure black crystal, and I walked slowly, basking in the moonlight that reflected off the snow as if there were no night. When I had said I wasn't hungry, Buyanjargal's mother had not insisted on feeding me. And now, for the first time, she had let me walk the three minutes home alone. Just when people in Arshaant were beginning to treat me a little less like the Foreign Guest, I was about to leave.

Becky grinned and spread her cards on the table. Ace-high flush. Beat my three kings. Through the picture window, sunrise was glowing over the Seattle skyline. Time to make omelets for breakfast and go home to bed. As she scooped the pile of change across the table, the sounds of children running and yelling outside my *ger* woke me up. Vacation was over. A circle of pale morning sky hung above the *tonoo*. A thick slab of ice covered my water bucket. I pulled on the brown corduroy *del* Enkhtuya had lent me and slipped a couple of logs into the stove.

There were times when I considered taking up the school on their original invitation to stay for a year, but when my subconscious turned to home, to all-night poker games and sunrises over Puget Sound, I knew it was time to move on. Saigon was still out there, and I needed to finish what I had begun. I needed to do what I had said I would do. I had been in Arshaant for a month. I had, for however brief a moment, lived in Mongolia, waking up every day in the same bed, interacting every day with the same people, developing relationships rather than snapshot images. A month is not a very long time, but it is much longer than a day. Chopping my own kindling and walking home alone meant that, if only in some tiny way, I belonged. And that tiny bit of belonging was infinitely more comforting, if less glamorous, than all of the attention and care lavished on me when I arrived in the evening and left again the next morning. The month in Arshaant had been about having a life, rather than escaping from one. But even the profound satisfactions of that life were, I knew, dependent on moving on before it all faded into the truly quotidian. Somewhere in the back of my mind, wanderlust was nibbling again.

Moving on, however, was more easily said than done. Few vehicles ever passed through Arshaant, and if it snowed again, none might come or go until spring. A small plane made a semiregular Mörön-Arshaant-Erdenet run, and from Erdenet there was a nightly train to Ulaanbaatar. The flight schedule was always subject to the weather, the vagaries of fuel availability, and the airplane's state of repair, but it was due through on Friday, November 12. Agvantseren had put me on the passenger list at the post office, but as of Tuesday, mine had been the only name, and if there were not enough passengers, the flight would be canceled. Agvantseren told me this, and then he asked the inevitable question, "What happens if you leave later?" My visa would expire on November 20, the train to China ran only twice a week, and I had no idea how problematic it would be to get caught in Ulaanbaatar with an expired visa. But this was Mongolia. I laughed and shrugged my shoulders—I would leave when I left.

Our performance was scheduled for three o'clock on November 11. At one o'clock we gathered to rehearse. I was disappointed to find that several of the kids had not learned their assigned dialogues. I was even more disappointed when I peeked out into the hall shortly before three o'clock and there were only a dozen students hanging around. Some of the girls changed into their official dull brown school uniforms with white frilly aprons, and we kept rehearsing. Around three-thirty people started showing up, and by the time Agvantseren came to tell us that it was time to start, it was four o'clock, the blue and green hall was packed, and the dialogues were all memorized. Group One opened the show, singing the Alphabet Song, then stepping out in pairs to recite their dialogues.

"Hello, what is your name?"

"My name is Battur."

"How are you?"

"I am fine. How old are you?"

"I am ten."

Virtually no one in the audience understood a word of English, but each pair of students, mistakes and all, was greeted with energetic applause. Groups Two and Three then performed their dialogues, and for our finale they sang "Leaving on a Jet Plane." The goodwill in their efforts was painfully gratifying and, miraculously, the tune seemed to approximate the real thing. Afterward, the principal presented me with a notice of appreciation hand-printed in the beautiful swirls of old Mongolian. Agvantseren came next, handing me several homemade envelopes full of *tögrög* notes collected by the students and teachers. Finally, Enkhjargal came forward to present a small bird that her father had carved out of horn. Then someone put on the tape of pop music that had been played at the Club. "We heard you dance very well," said Agvantseren. "Will you dance for us now?" So I danced. To the two tunes on the tape, played over and over. A few of the braver students joined me, while the rest of the school stood watching and applauding.

That night I made my way up the hill to Enkhjargal's home. Her mother, whom I had never met before, quickly made *tos* and concocted Russian-style tea with milk and sugar. I had never seen Enkhjargal as quiet as she was that night, sitting behind me in the shadows. The Mariners baseball cap we had used as a prop in class was an odd gift to give a girl, but Enkhjargal's eyes widened like saucers when I held it out to her. She took it in two cupped hands and held it in her lap like a priceless treasure. Walking back to my *ger,* the infinitude of stars above the village seemed almost within reach, the Milky Way a blaze of twinkles splashed across the sky like a pebbled path in a stream. Then the wind began to blow.

By morning the skies were heavy gray. I built a fire and the snow started drifting down. At ten o'clock the post office said that there were enough passengers to merit a flight, but now the weather might be a problem; come back at noon to find out if the plane can fly. I went to Buyanjargal's to say good-bye. At noon the post office said they would know at two. There were several inches of snow on the ground and it was still falling. My door opened and Enkhjargal's parents ducked in. As I served tea, I realized that the Mongolian ritual had become habit—the tea was as automatic as "Hi, how are you?" So was the absence of any need to know why someone had dropped by ("Hi, what's up?"). It was a life lived in the moment. They are here, greet them and serve them tea. If they have a reason for being here, they will get around to it.

I had given their daughter a supermarket giveaway-night baseball cap— a tiny token of appreciation and encouragement for my brightest and most eager pupil. Now they had come to give me a metalwork heirloom passed down for generations from father to son. I could not refuse, could not protest that it was too much, when they presented the small *ochir*. A traditional prayer tool of Tibetan Buddhist lamas, the *ochir* is a brass casting of palindromic arches symbolizing the power to realize active compassion. I could only accept it in two cupped hands, my eyes even wider than their daughter's had been the night before when I gave her the silly cap.

At two o'clock the snow was still swirling down and the post office said to check back in the morning. Farewells were reprised—at Gerlee's, at Sarantsetseg's, at Agvantseren's. *Guriltai shöl* was slurped, presents were spontaneously pulled out of drawers and pockets. They promised to write and I promised to return. Outside, a few stars peeked through the unraveling cloud cover. The wind was still blowing.

At seven o'clock on the morning of November 13, I peered out at a still and starry sky. At eight-thirty I walked to the post office in sunny, nose-hair-freezing air. They said to check back at ten o'clock. Shortly after ten, Agvantseren came by in a bright blue *del* with an orange sash. It was the first time I had seen him wear anything but a suit. He had just been to the post office. They had said to come back at one. At one o'clock the post office was closed. At one forty-five they said the plane would leave Mörön at two-fifteen. At two-fifteen we walked to a snowy field at the edge of the village, where a wind sock had been hung on a fence post. Shortly after three o'clock a little plane roared out of a dip in the hills and landed in a cloud of snow. A cluster of kids broke and ran after the twelve-seater, swarming under its wings as it turned and taxied back. Baasanjav slipped two little chocolates into my pocket and Arshaant shrank away to a dot, then a memory.

⌣· Bicyclists south of Pingyao

Part III

BICYCLING IN CHINA

*Chasing a Man Across the
Middle Kingdom*

CHAPTER 7

Pedaling into a Rice-paper Painting

I dreaded the Beijing train station. Even at 5:00 A.M. it would be engulfed in the impenetrable, thronging masses of the planet's most populous nation. There would be hordes and crowds and curious swarming mobs, and there was no way for me to get off the train in one fell swoop. With her panniers on, Greene wouldn't fit down the narrow corridor. I was going to have to get her out onto the platform, leave her there at the mercy of innumerable curious, probing fingers, and fight my way back onto the train through the other disembarking passengers to get her panniers. Then, surrounded by poking, prodding, questioning people, not knowing a single word of Chinese, I was going to have to load her and make my way out into a completely unknown city, somehow managing to look like I knew what I was doing.

After three months in Mongolia, I had come to feel at home there. I knew how things worked, knew what to expect. Now, as the train drew close to Beijing at the end of the forty-hour journey from Ulaanbaatar, I was once again facing the challenge of the unknown. After a month of slow, settled village life, it felt like beginning the journey anew. The familiar trepidation and excitement were knocking around inside of me as I made a neat pile—two front panniers, two rear panniers attached to each other like a saddlebag, a tightly tied bundle of sleeping bag, mat, and tent—and tried to work out the quickest way to pick it all up. I rehearsed. I rearranged the pile. I practiced again. The train grumbled toward the station. I rolled Greene into the corridor. Soon the platform stretched alongside, cold, dim, and almost empty. Only a handful of scattered figures waited sleepily to greet arriving passengers. I carried Greene down the steps onto the platform, turned around to dash back onto the train, and heard the Vietnamese students with whom I had shared a compartment yelling my name. They were leaning out the window right behind me, holding out all my stuff. No one even looked at me as I loaded Greene and headed for the exit.

The broad boulevards were almost empty in the pale dawn. A lone street sweeper's straw broom rasped down the sidewalk. A single figure moved through slow-motion tai-chi exercises. One yellow taxicab buzzed down the avenue. The pavement was patched with ice. I pedaled tentatively, balancing carefully across the white slicks. And then it opened before me— the plaza that had first entered my consciousness as a killing field, and would remain ever after inextricably linked with the image of one skinny man facing down a tank. I turned south, away from Mao Tse-tung's huge face staring out over Tiananmen Square's 100 acres of flagstone. The scattered individuals were multiplying quickly. Shop owners were opening their stores, setting out displays of bright clothes and fresh vegetables. Steam rose from sidewalk noodle stands where people slurped their breakfast out of huge bowls held close to their mouths. And all around me were men, women, and children on bicycles.

I found the sprawling budget-travelers' hotel and settled into a room with two other backpacking tourists. Our window looked out on a freeway embankment that bore five intertwined circular scars where carefully planted flowers had been uprooted: The 2000 Olympic Games had just been awarded to Sydney, Australia. The freeway, the dense urban skyline—to eyes grown accustomed to felt tents and log cabins and endless rolling hills, it felt like midtown Manhattan.

It was already a week since I had flown out of Arshaant, landing in Erdenet only to find that there was no transportation from the airport into the city. A small group of us had set off straight across the snowy hills, but by the time we had reached the station, the train was long gone. We had spent that night at someone's friend's apartment, and the following evening caught the overnight train to Ulaanbaatar. Four days in the city and two more nights on a train had then brought me to Beijing, 1,500 kilometers as the crow flies from my schoolyard *ger*.

In my hotel room, I flipped Greene over and spun her back wheel; its orbit was as wobbly as a badly thrown Frisbee. Fearing a bent rim that could never be replaced in China, I opened my trusty repair book and discovered that one of the tools in my bag was called a "spoke adjuster" and that what you did with it was called "truing the wheel"—loosening tight spokes and tightening loose ones until evenly balanced tension brought the wheel back into a perfect circular spin.

Several hours later, with Greene trued and cleaned and ready to go again whenever I wanted, I locked her in the room and set out to explore Beijing on foot. Five months later I would fly back into the Chinese capital on my way north. In contrast to the kaleidoscopic heat and noise of Saigon and Hong Kong, Beijing would seem drab and deserted, but arriving from Ulaanbaatar, Beijing was a vivid, bustling metropolis, its streets and sidewalks overwhelmingly colorful rivers of bicycles, buses, and pedestrians.

Knowing that the reality of a crumbling string of bricks could never live up to the spectacular photographs and the legends of being the only man-made structure visible from space, I nevertheless joined a vanload of tourists traveling out to the Great Wall. Construction of a tamped-earth barrier had begun more than 2,000 years ago. Over the following centuries and at the cost of many lives, the wall had grown and served very efficiently as a military highway, but failed completely to stop the armies of Kublai Khan. We followed a path from the parking lot past vendors' stalls, only a handful of which were open in the chilly off-season, then climbed up a forested hillside to the top of the wall. Snow lay in shadowy niches. Uneven staircases led up to turrets and back down, then up again to the next one, and on, as far as the eye could see, across the dips and ridges of the brown winter hills, as if to infinity. And each of us at some point found ourselves glancing away from the brick, up into the pale sky, searching for

the moon, trying to imagine the unimaginable. The storied serpent of ancient brick felt alive, immutable, and more impressive than anything I had
ever imagined it to be.

Over the next week, struggling to learn the numbers from one to ten
as I bargained for and savored Beijing's abundant street food—hot yams,
steaming bowls of noodles, crunchy crêpelike concoctions—I discovered
the fabulously helpful convention of finger-counting. Even with local
customers, vendors regularly supplemented spoken prices with finger
symbols similar to American sign language. I learned to watch fingers as
automatically as I listened to words. I learned to bargain with my fingers,
too, which would always be more fluent than my tongue's mangled attempts
at Mandarin.

I met a British poet from the Isle of Guernsey, and together we went
to the movies—technicolor, warp-speed kung fu battles in which the
women were just as tough as the men—and braved our first monolingual
Mandarin restaurant, pointing cluelessly to the squiggles and squares on the
menu, not knowing until the dishes arrived what we had ordered.

I learned my way around China's two currencies—the RMB and the
FEC. The RMB (which I learned to call *kuai* instead of *yuan,* like "buck" instead of "dollar") was the true national currency; the FEC was what the bank
gave to foreigners. Because it could be exchanged for dollars, the FEC, although theoretically identical in value to the RMB, supported a healthy black
market and traded on the street for RMB at a very advantageous rate.

I learned the most ubiquitous and dreaded of Chinese phrases, the two
words of legendary status among travelers: *mei you.* Literally "not-have," it
is the negative answer to the question *"You mei you . . . ?"* ("Do you have . . . ?"
or "Is there . . . ?").

"Do you have hot water?" *"Mei you!"*

"Is there a hotel?" *"Mei you!"*

"Is there a paved road?" *"Mei you!"*

In the affirmative, the answer was a simple *"You!"* But the answer I
learned to expect was *"Mei you."*

I collected my new first-aid kit at poste restante and a pile of precious
letters at American Express. Instead of making me homesick, missives from
afar had the odd effect of making me feel welcome in new, unfamiliar cities. They made me feel somehow real. In one of the countless cheap restaurants lining the streets around the hotel, over a plate of dumplings that
I wanted to call *buuz* but here were called *jiaozi,* I sat for hours and wrote
Volume II of the letter home. Twenty- and thirty-year-old Americans,

Europeans, and Australians filled the restaurant with loud laughter and travel tales.

One of them was a bearded man from Chicago named Kirk. We ate noodles, drank beer, wandered the streets together, and one night I gave him a massage until my roommates returned. When I loaded Greene and rolled her out of the hotel on the morning of November 30, Kirk came to see us off. He and a friend were heading first north, then south via Xian toward Yangshuo. He joked that if I rode fast enough, I could catch up to them. "We can visit the terra-cotta warriors in Xian together," he laughed. It was a laugh that would resonate across the next seven weeks and 2,700 kilometers.

⋅

It is one thing not to know the language around you: background chatter is noise rather than snatches of conversation; shopping is slow, complicated, and imprecise; menus are confusing jumbles of letters. It is altogether another to be truly illiterate. I stopped at an intersection and stared helplessly at the road sign. They were pretty, all those dots and sweeps and angles, all those precise, flowing lines and elegant dashes. They were also profoundly meaningless. I looked at them and did not see language.

I had tried to maintain a southwestern course, but in the confusion of Beijing's sprawling suburbs, my maps seemed unable to agree on where anything was located. I had a map of China in Pinyin—the standard transliteration of Chinese characters into the Roman alphabet—and a province-by-province atlas in Chinese characters. The atlas quickly proved more useful than the map. Less than an hour's ride from the capital, Pinyin had disappeared from the road signs and my atonal attempts to pronounce the transliterations on the map met only with blank, uncomprehending stares. In the atlas, even though I could not read a single squiggle or dash, I could determine a route by working backward from the next big city—the next place in larger-type squiggles and dashes (in this case Taiyuan, 600 kilometers southwest of Beijing).

I usually had no idea what the name of the next town or village was. When I stopped to ask directions, I would just point to a set of characters I had circled on the page, and follow the nod, or the shake of the head and the pointing finger. Of course, sometimes there was no one to ask. Then I would stand at an intersection looking up at a sign, down at the atlas, up at the sign, down at the atlas, searching for a matching series: "Three characters, the second character is a bottomless triangle on top of three parallel dashes. . . . " It was slow (it was all slow), but it worked, and over the next two months I would become quite proficient at it, although the only two characters I would ever actually learn to recognize had nothing to do with road signs.

After hours of dusty, gritty, trafficky pedaling, I came to a fork in the road. It was three-thirty, the next town on the map was thirty kilometers away, and this was northern China in late November; it would be dark by five o'clock. I was a fool to head up the twisting, icy mountain road. But I was a fool in what was suddenly no longer greater Beijing. The traffic, the noise, the grime gave way abruptly to mountain stillness. An endless horizon of jagged papercut mountains receded into silent, pink haze. I remembered lying in the hay beneath an infinite farmland sky in France, or pressing my face to a train window as it sped through liquid green-golden sunlight along the Rhine, and seeing suddenly that Monet and the German Romantics hadn't made up what they put on their canvasses. Now I saw that the Chinese artists hadn't made it up either. I was pedaling into a rice-paper painting. My trip into China had begun.

Thirty kilometers to the next town *on the map.* I had not ridden thirty kilometers when a cluster of low stone houses appeared along the road. A young man with the resigned air of an eternal graduate student found me a few minutes later, standing uncertainly in front of a two-story barracks-style building wondering if this were the local *lüguan.* My phrasebook listed three different words for hotel—*lüshè, lüguan,* and *binguan*—in ascending order of comfort. *Binguans* were expensive, carpet-and-hot-running-water establishments that charged FEC. They existed only in the larger cities. *Lüguan* covered a fair amount of middle ground, while *lüshè* seemed to indicate clearly that I was just looking for a place—any place, no particular standards required—to stay for the night. *Lüshè,* therefore, was the most appropriate word to use in small villages.

Unfortunately, I would never manage a consistently comprehensible pronunciation of *lüshè,* and usually had to fall back on *lüguan,* as I did now. The young man nodded and led me inside to the hotel manager. She handed me a form. Name, address, passport number, where I had come from, where I was going. The usual information, I assumed. I didn't know. I couldn't read anything on the piece of paper. I didn't know where to write my name. She tapped a space on the form with her index finger and handed me a pen. I printed carefully. She stared, crinkling her forehead. As far as she was concerned, I didn't know *how* to write my name. I pulled out my phrasebook and found the word "address." She nodded and pointed to a blank space. I found the word "American." She almost smiled, took the form, and wrote that in herself. I pointed to my passport number. She nodded, copied it onto the form, and decided that that was enough information. She slipped the paperwork into a drawer and got up to lead the way down the hall to a cement-box room with a drafty window, a thermos of hot water on the table, and a pair of rubber thongs, and a plastic basin tucked under the bed.

"Chi fan ma?" she asked. I shook my head helplessly and handed her the phrasebook. She found "dining hall," then "dinner," and raised her eyebrows in a question mark. I nodded vigorously. Chi fan was a phrase I would come to know well. Meaning literally "to eat rice," the addition of ma turned it into a question that seemed to function broadly as both "Are you hungry?" and "Can I get something to eat?"

Each language one learns makes the next one easier, due not only to an expanded etymological base, but to a broader linguistic frame of reference. In Mongolia, it had taken me weeks to grasp the concept that questions were formed not by word order or intonation, but by the addition of a single word—either uu or ve—to the end of a sentence. When I had arrived in China, however, and read that to form a question, the word ma is added to the end of a sentence, the once-puzzling structure made immediate sense.

On the whole, I would be amazed to discover the simplicity of basic Chinese grammar—no verb conjugations, no tenses, no declension of nouns—and the short Chinese vowel-consonant syllables would prove much easier to learn than the endless consonant clusters of Mongolian. The problem, for my amusical ear, was that Chinese is a tonal language. I simply could not hear, let alone re-create, the four different tones that can turn the word chi from "to eat" into "pond," "a unit of length equal to one-third of a meter," or "the color red," and fan from "cooked rice" into "sail," "commonplace," or "to turn over." Every time I walked into a restaurant and asked to eat, I knew that I might actually be asking for a "red sail" or a "commonplace pond," or, quite possibly, saying, "Hello—the unit of length equal to one-third of a meter turns over."

The young man had been waiting discreetly in the hall. Now the hotel manager told me to follow him. We crossed the street and he pushed aside a heavy quilt covering a doorway. There was one small wooden table in the room, two chairs, a bed. Restaurants, I would learn, were often no more than a home with a table and a willingness to cook for others. A young woman jumped up when we walked in and waved us to the table. She served us leaking glasses of tepid, bitter tea, then disappeared into the kitchen. After a while she returned with a huge ceramic bowl of steaming stew. Rabbit meat swam around rabbit bones, and one rabbit eye stared up at me out of a rabbit skull. They watched me eat. They smiled at me. They laughed at the chili tears in my eyes as the delicious stew burned down my throat.

I handed them my atlas. They pored over the book, as fascinated by the maps as most Mongolians had been, and equally unable to tell me where we were on the page. Adjusting Greene's handlebars before leaving Beijing, I had tugged too hard, snapping the odometer wires, and my attempt to repair them hadn't held. Now not only did I not know where I was, I didn't even know how far I had gone.

Being lost in China was more intimidating than being lost in Mongolia. Compared to the sunlit northern plains, where "lost" could always be corrected with a turn across the prairie (and knowing exactly where you were was somehow spiritually irrelevant), the Middle Kingdom felt like a profound mystery whose secret depths could swallow a person whole. Voluminous baskets of corn spilled over on tile rooftops, and piles of cornstalks lined the rock walls of misty mountain villages. The world was a palette of yellow and gray. Stone and corn and winter-dead brown trees. Men gathered around outdoor pool tables, the green felt rectangle a shock of color in the pale landscape. Children played tag, squealing and laughing, peeling around stone walls, skidding to a stop at the pool table to see who was winning, then tearing off again.

My odometer was clicking away (thanks to the help of the young man at the hotel the night before), the plastic burned off, wire ends twisted and duct-taped back together. I knew that I had gone twenty kilometers, thirty, forty, but I still didn't know where I was. A sign indicated Beijing to the left when I thought it should be to the right. I was heading south according to the map, west according to the compass, winding inexorably up into the mountains. The road crossed high above train tracks. I stopped to stare down at the determined black lines barreling into a tunnel in their undeterrably linear quest. A guidebook I had seen in Beijing said it was a twenty-two-hour journey to Xian. Twenty-two hours *by train*. How many would it be by twisting, turning mountain road? How many weeks would it take me to pedal what the book called an overnight trip? I took a long drink of water and continued up the hill.

On the other side of the pass, rounding a downhill curve at thirty

⌣· *Men gathered around outdoor pool tables, the green felt rectangle a shock of color in the pale landscape.*

kilometers an hour, I rolled onto a long, narrow patch of ice. I held Greene steady. Continuing in a straight line I would be safe, but a straight line led straight off the edge of the mountain. I had to try to follow the curve of the road. Greene's tires disappeared silently from beneath me. Cartoonlike, my bicycle and I hung in the air, parallel to the pavement. Then we dropped. Greene's panniers hit first. Then my left knee, left hip, left elbow. My neck snapped hard across my shoulder. The crack of helmet hitting pavement exploded inside my head.

A nasty concussion might not have killed me, but it probably would have kept me from leaping up and dragging Greene to the side of the road before a small white car came careening around the corner. Stunned, my chest heaving, my heart thumping wildly, my head pounding, I reached up and touched my helmet gratefully. To this day, I believe that it saved my life. I looked out across the valley. The various browns swam briefly before coalescing into winter-frozen fields. I looked down at my odometer. The digits lay there, clear and imperturbable. I moved my head, stretched my arms and legs, examined Greene and straightened her handlebars. We were fine.

We were both fine. It was all okay. I could keep going as if it had never happened. I swung out onto the road, and slithered straight across it into the stone mountainside. I stumbled back across the pavement and sat down. I sat there for a long time before I tried again.

As it dropped into a valley, the road broadened and curled into a busy traffic circle. A stone marker was carved in Pinyin as well as Chinese characters: Yixian. Yixian was on my maps! I showed the atlas to the crowd of men who gathered the minute I stopped. I pointed at the next village.

"Xiling," they read. "Twenty-two kilometers," said their fingers.

"Lüguan you mei you ("Is there a hotel")*?"*

"You, you," several of them nodded.

There was certainly also a hotel in Yixian, but in the early days of the trip I was intimidated by the complexities and options of larger towns. Later I would find myself eschewing the adventure of the villages in favor of the relative anonymity of the savvier cities.

The hotel manager in Xiling was a handsome man in a leather jacket, named Ting. Or something that sounded like Ting to me. It had taken the better part of three months in Mongolia, but by the time I had left Arshaant, I was able to hear Mongolian names. Now I was back at square one. Ting sent the receptionist to lead me through an empty, cavernous restaurant to a cozy back room. She sat down across from me, and soon the plates began arriving: white, starchy mushrooms; leafy green vegetables; pork and carrots. Rice and tea. We grabbed chopsticks from the jar on the table and dove in. At a second table, a half dozen men sat over their meal, watching us. One of them, a young soldier, picked up a bottle of green bamboo liquor, crossed the room, and poured us each a shot. And then another and another. He knew a few words of English, but would not attempt to speak them. Instead, he wrote his question on a napkin and passed it to me. When I answered out loud, he just shook his head and handed me the pen.

For me, the thrill of language is the moment of looking a stranger in the eye and communicating. The fun of language is learning to turn a new and unfamiliar set of sounds, a new logic, often, into direct human communication. Grammar is a useful tool, but I have never been much good at sitting in a classroom memorizing declensions. Language is profoundly alive, and for me a new language lives on the tongue and in the eyes, not on the page. In China, the opposite was true: more often than not, English was a paperbound exercise, learned from a book, rarely heard, even more rarely spoken.

I neatly printed the words—"I am from America"—and passed the napkin back across the table. The young soldier read it, grinned and nod-ded, and took the pen to compose his next question. This dichotomy between written and spoken language would continue to fascinate me all across the country. Often, faced with my incomprehension, people would reach for a pen and then hand me a scrap of paper covered with characters. I would stare helplessly at the paper, amazed that anyone could imagine that I would be able to understand written Chinese when I couldn't understand the spoken language. "I can't read," I learned to say, a sentence I had never imagined having to learn in any language. I was more than halfway across the country before fully understanding that while dialects in China vary to the point of mutual incomprehensibility, the written language remains universal. Thus movies made in Beijing are subtitled for audiences in Hong Kong, and vice versa. Based on this experience, I would finally understand, it was perfectly logical for people to assume that I could read what I could not hear.

In Xiling, I slept with my woolen balaklava on my head and my sleep-ing bag tucked under two heavy quilts, my breath visible on the air. In the morning, the right side of my neck was so stiff from my fall the day before that I could not sit up or lift my head to look out the window. I had to roll over onto my stomach and pull myself backward up onto my knees, letting my head follow my spine. I could feel the deep bruises all along my left side, but did not bother digging down through layers of clothes to look at them. The previous day's haze had disappeared to reveal a beautiful cypress valley surrounded by jagged peaks. Silhouetted against the bright blue sky were tiled roofs and swooping imperial eaves. I had spent the night a stone's throw from the Western Qing tombs, where the Yongzheng Emperor (who ruled 1723–1736) and several of his successors were interred together with an entourage of their consorts, wives, and concubines. The square behind the hotel was lined with knickknack shops and kiosks, mostly closed for the winter.

"They always cheat you. They see a white person, and all they want is your money. They always charge you ten times the real price. You have to bargain for everything. It's always a fight." These were the stories I had heard in Beijing travelers' cafés. And they were true, except for the "always" part. For every time someone charged me five times the local price for a bed or a meal, someone else refused to let me pay at all. I had rolled Greene into the cement-box room in Xiling without asking how much it cost. I had not asked how much dinner cost. I had not asked the price of the hot rice por-ridge, cold tofu, and pickled vegetables that Ting and I shared for breakfast.

▲ *At the turn-off to* **Erdenet.** *Five boys dashed their horses up the prairie for a closer look at Greene and me.*

▶ **Two members of Lkhamsüren's family**

▲ *Basaanjavd (second from right in back row) and her extended family*

◀ *Learning the ancient script*

▶ *A young boy and a foal*
at Lkhamsüren's

▼ *Inside a well-to-do ger*
in Arkhangai Province

▲ *In front of one of Arshaant's three or four shops*

▶ *With Sarantseteg in front of my ger*

◀ A motorcycle marmot hunter

◀ The insta-crowd, in China

▼ Somewhere north of Lenshuijiang

▲ **The Great Wall.** *The storied serpent of ancient brick felt alive, immutable, and more impressive than anything I had ever imagined it to be.*

◀ *Beijing*

▼ *A village street near Yangshuo*

▼ *At work in the rice paddies along Highway 1 south of Hanoi*

▲ **Lunch in a Cat Ba home.** *As our mutual anonymity evolved into a connection between individuals, I wished I had more time to explore Vietnam.*

◀ *Hanoi prepares for Tet.*

▶ **1545 kilometers to go.** *The only road sign I saw that hadn't been changed to Ho Chi Minh City.*

▲ **Bich Dong.** *A realm of dark waters so thick they are the liquid cousins of the earth.*

▲ **Life on the water north of Hué**

The money itself didn't matter much. The bitter taste of being taken advantage of did. I knew that I was not a cool, savvy traveler. I was not like Daniel. I would give in to the exorbitant price and pedal on, frustrated, mad, and hurt. Fear of this hovered in the back of my mind as Ting, the receptionist, and I wandered through the halls and ramparts, then down a long spirit way under the watchful stone eyes of carved animal figures.

When I was ready to leave, Ting handed me a bill for dinner. Eight *kuai* (about one dollar). I asked about the room and breakfast. He shook his head and reached for the phrasebook. He found the words "foreign" and "friend." Then he found the word "lunch" and looked at me.

I shook my head.

He found the word "late," and mimed a mountainous road. "Laiyuan— 110 kilometers," he said.

"Go tomorrow," said the receptionist.

"Yes," a little voice inside my head concurred, "stick around, explore the village beyond the main street; you are not in a hurry, the journey is not in the kilometers ticked off the map. You will never catch Kirk in Xian."

"No," I said, "I go today."

Memories of northern China are memories of cement and cold, of the bone-deep chill that spread through me as soon as I stopped pedaling, of cement floors and walls that sucked away any hope of warmth, of coal stoves and feeble radiators fighting losing battles. The road had perfectly duplicated Ting's mime, switchbacking sharply up into the raw winter mountains. In the middle of one switchback, a big blue truck lay on its back just below the edge of the road, its thick black tires reaching helplessly toward the sky. It was the only spot of color on the frigid brown slopes. Standing on the pedals, my shoulders and arms working as hard as my legs, sweating in the crisp, icy air, I climbed slowly toward the village at the pass, where I fell asleep in the early winter darkness to the howling of a bitter wind and imaginings of sleet and rain and snow.

But daybreak revealed only freezing air beneath an azure sky. A river wound across high plateau ringed by distant papercut mountains. All day long I had to stop every few kilometers and jump up and down to send blood back into my aching toes. The sunlight was devoid of any warmth. I reached for a drink, but there was only ice in my frozen-solid water bottles.

In Laiyuan late that afternoon, the hotel receptionist handed me a registration form. "Name?" I said, having looked up the word. "Name," she said.

"Where?" I said. "Name," she said, pointing, and I wrote my name. She looked at the slip of paper I handed her, and shook her head. She wanted something she could read. I held out my passport. "Name," I pointed, but the simplistic designs meant no more to her than the more intricate ones on the registration form meant to me.

The half dozen men who had gathered around us began launching suggestions. At one point the chatter seemed to resolve into a decision: One of the men took the phone from behind the desk, dialed, explained the situation, and triumphantly handed me the receiver. A voice on the other end said, "Hello, what is your name?" listened to my carefully enunciated answer, and then reverted to Chinese, having exhausted its supply of English. Eventually I repeated my name over and over for the group, and they invented a phonetic spelling for the receptionist to copy onto the form.

One of the men led me to that night's cement-box room. He scooped coal into a small stove and placed a large iron kettle of water on top. Again there were plastic flip-flops and a basin aligned neatly under the bed. Horrified by the thought of wet skin in the cold, I had not even washed my face since leaving Beijing. But when the water was hot, I dumped it into the plastic container, pulled off my shoes and socks, and discovered that the warmth crept into my bones. I longed to curl my whole body into the little basin of enveloping heat, but it was not going to stay hot for long. Leave the left foot in; pull the right foot out, avoid the freezing cement floor, rub it dry; yank on a sock, a shoe; get the left foot out before the water cools.

I was tying my shoes when the receptionist walked in, followed by a stern-faced young man. They didn't always knock in China, either. He nodded at me and tapped his breast pocket. He was not in uniform, but he was asking for my passport. Stories about incessant police badgering, bribes, and closed cities jumbled back into my head. "The police will say you can't be where you are, then they'll say you can't go where you're going, then they'll say you can't go back the way you came."

My passport was strapped to my waist underneath layers of clothes. Following an ingenious tidbit of guidebook advice, I also carried an expired passport, which was what I had shown the receptionist earlier. Now I handed it to him. He couldn't read the large red "canceled" stamp. He didn't know that a U.S. passport did not come with two neat holes punched in the cover. I held my breath as he flipped curiously through the pages. He also did not know, as the police and hotel receptionists in larger cities would know, to look for a Chinese visa. He handed it back, nodded politely, and left. I was a savvy traveler, after all. I had tricked him and he had fallen for it. Just imagine if I had let him see my real passport, I thought. He would have flipped curiously through the pages, handed it back, nodded politely, and left.

Vendors were folding up for the night by the time I went in search of dinner. Someone pushed aside a heavy doorway quilt, and through the crack I saw several sets of table legs. Inside, five men sat closely around a squat coal stove. I could not seem to communicate "What do you have?" I tried several times (a rather pointless endeavor, given that I would not have understood the answer anyway), then just pointed arbitrarily to one of the series of dashes and squiggles on the chalkboard menu and joined the men near the stove.

Soon the waitress set a plate of tofu in brown sauce on one of the wooden tables lined against the walls. The feeble warmth didn't reach that far. I fetched the plate back to the stove and everyone burst out laughing. One of the men reached over and took the plate from my hands, went back to the table, and sat down to eat his dinner. My order appeared several minutes later, a plate of deep-fried breaded something, also brown. The waitress put it directly in my hands. It was good, whatever it was, but the next customer got a big plate of green beans. I was not in Mongolia any more. I would have to learn the word for "vegetables."

⋅⋅⋅

Dusk was descending rapidly over the twisting road. A tiny cluster of stone buildings huddled beneath the brown and snowy hills. I asked if there was a hotel. I did not expect there to be one. The young man hesitated, then motioned me to follow him. He led me through a small stone courtyard, corn and chili spilling yellow and red across the ground, and through a dark doorway. Everyone had said it was impossible. I was inside a rural Chinese home.

It was not a very cheery place. His family's three rooms were unforgivingly empty, undecorated boxes. The center room was a shop. Cookies and crackers, candy and shoes, cloth and canned fruit, cooking oil and hair bands were all stuffed on dim shelves beneath a single bare bulb. Of the two smaller rooms, one was for him and his four-year-old son, one was his parents'. His mother was solid, wrinkled, and silent. His father was taller, but crumpled by the shaky movements of a body that no longer easily obeyed his wishes. The young man resembled what his father had once been—quiet, curious eyes watched the world from above the even planes of his cheeks. He gave me hot water to drink. His mother brought a tiny bowl of greens and a deep bowl of rice. The food slowly radiated warmth from my tongue to the bottom of my stomach, but everyone's breath was visible on the air, and I never took off my gloves.

They live in these unheated cement boxes for months on end, I thought to myself, never truly warm except at night in their beds. I remembered my *ger,* and longed for the coziness of the ancient felt bubble, so cheerful compared to this bitter, modern cement. And somewhere, in another world, I thought, there is a carpeted living room with central heat and hot running water. It had been five months since I left Seattle, and by now that world seemed as impossible as a memory of a bygone age. Yet what is most incredible, I thought as I looked up at the four people watching me eat, is that I will one day, quite easily, step back into that other, comfortable, time and place.

Here and now, however, I had been invited into these people's home. They were feeding me. They would give me a bed for the night. Yet they were clearly disconcerted by me, sitting there unable to communicate. I too was frustrated. The door was open, but I didn't speak Chinese. I could muddle through the Seven Questions, but beyond that—how intimate can contact be through a phrasebook? We could not talk about politics or dreams. I could not tell them about my American childhood on a cul-de-sac surrounded by citrus groves. They could not tell me about living through the Great Leap Forward. They might even have had a happy memory, a funny story, from a time my books describe as chaos and starvation. I will never know.

His mother asked a question that I didn't understand. I held out the phrasebook, but she waved it away. I tried to show her that there was Chinese on the pages. She pushed it away again. I had done something wrong and did not understand what. She pointed to her son. Pointed to the book in my hand and back to her son, and suddenly I did understand. She could not read Chinese any better than I could.

I was sitting on the edge of the *kang*—a raised cement platform that took up a third of the room. The four of them stood against the wall, the little boy leaning against his grandmother. They watched me eat. The young man asked if we have rice in America. "Yes," I said, "but we don't eat it with chopsticks."

"Oh," he nodded wisely to his father, and understandingly back at me, miming, "You eat with your fingers."

Before we went to bed, his mother led me to the toilet. Across the street, behind a low stone wall, three logs lay across an open pit. We took turns. There was no traffic. There were no street lights. The canyon rose steeply on either side of us. The air was sharp. The narrow slice of sky above was full of stars. Back inside, she rolled out two mats and four heavy quilts on top of the *kang*. Her husband would spend the night with his son and grandson, and she would share her bed with me. I took off my shoes and crawled under the filthy quilts. She lay down next to me, naked, coughing the wracking cough of a lifetime of coal-heated winters.

The Seven Questions were the same as they had been in Mongolia, but in China an eighth had been added. Once they knew how old I was, where I was going, and that I wasn't married, people glanced at Greene and asked, "How much did your bicycle cost?" In Mongolia Greene had been an alien. In China she was a variation on a theme. In Mongolia she had been so foreign, so illogical that people had paid fairly little attention to her. In China she was an Arabian, a Thoroughbred, exotic to be sure, but familiar. She made sense. She belonged.

There are Mongolians who cannot ride a horse. There is probably not a two-legged Chinese over the age of four who cannot ride a bicycle. Old and black and seemingly indestructible, bicycles are as much fixtures of Chinese life as electric light switches are of an American day, invisible in their ubiquity. Everybody rides. Friends ride together—one on the seat, one standing on the pedals; one on the seat, one on the pedals, one sitting on the back rack; one on the seat, one on the pedals, one on the rack, and one more balancing on the handlebars. Families ride together—a young man pedaling, his wife sidesaddle on the rack behind him, their child on her lap. Live chickens dangle upside-down from handlebars. Pigs squeal from oblong wicker baskets tied to rear racks. Tight stacks of empty baskets totter to either side of a rider like a high-wire artist's balancing pole. Old men glide past, skinny legs motionless on the pedals, a small motor attached to their rickety cycles. Young men grab the backs of trucks, sit up, and speed effortlessly down the road. Children run errands for their parents or race with their friends, the bigger kids flying down the pavement, the littler ones, too small to reach the pedals from the seat of their father's bicycle, managing incomprehensibly to ride with their bodies in a curve from the handlebars around under the top tube to the far pedal.

No longer alone in a boundless landscape, I pedaled down roads that would once have seemed obscure and mysterious, but now felt precise and unambiguous. No longer enviously watching horses canter past, I pedaled down roads that would once have seemed inconsistent and rough, but now seemed simply *paved,* for by now any pavement was good pavement. Surrounded by the whir of bicycle tires, I pedaled through the short winter days, just one bicyclist among many.

After the sedentary month in Arshaant, I had been sorely out of shape again by the time I left Beijing. On my fancy, twenty-one-gear bicycle, I had to work hard to keep up with the riders on their battered old one-speeds. A young woman and I played leapfrog. Downhill, my heavily loaded bicycle flew past her; on the stretches of level terrain between the hills, she reappeared slowly in the corner of my eye, then sedately pedaled past; uphill, she had to walk while I shifted down, down, down, and kept pedaling. I told myself she hadn't been riding all day. I told myself she was not carrying as much weight as I was. But the young man rolling lazily along beside me, asking through the cigarette dangling from his mouth where I was from, where I was going, how much my bicycle cost, had three boxes strapped to his rear rack, each the size of a large television set.

As I dropped down out of the Taihang Mountains into the long, flat valley of the Fen River, the picturesque stone villages gave way to towns that resembled strip malls under construction. Donkey carts, horse carts, bicycles, belching coal trucks, rickety buses, and an occasional Audi 5000 filled the road. The whir of Greene's tires was drowned under horns and loudspeakers. The trucks honked "I'm here." They honked "Hello." They honked "I'm passing you, get the hell out of my way." The loudspeakers blared over the honking, sometimes a screeching pedantic voice, sometimes a Muzaked version of "Auld Lang Syne." The few private cars were almost invariably expensive new models I could not afford at home. A shining silver Jeep Cherokee flew past an old farmer bent double pulling a wooden cart of coal. The sight hit me like the collision of two worlds. But a minute later, as I pedaled past the farmer, I barely glanced at the old man. I was thinking about the Jeep, imagining being inside, clean and warm and comfortable, feet up on the dashboard, music playing.

I pedaled into Fanshi, a town that already looked like every other town, and while I settled into a cement-box room where the coal stove gave off a little more heat than the stoves in some cement-box rooms, the hotel manager sent a child running to fetch his nephew, who was the local English teacher. "Can I help you?" the nephew asked, glancing across the room at his uncle and back at me, long fingers fluttering in his lap, his book-learned English a struggle to decipher.

"Help me with what?" I thought, then realized that he meant "Is everything all right? Is there anything you need?"

There *was* something I needed. "Could you write my name in Chinese?"

I wrote it in English so he could see it. I pronounced it over and over. Together, he and his uncle construed a series of Chinese characters that he carefully inscribed on the inside cover of my phrasebook. "Eh-lika Wahm-bu-lahn," he read back to me. Close enough for hotel paperwork. The Seven Questions had already been asked and answered. Now came the eighth. "How much did your bicycle cost?"

"I don't know," I said, answering with the same lie I had learned to tell in Chinese, adding, "It was a gift from my mother." The truth made no sense. The truth was, "More than you earn in three years."

As his confidence in his English grew, the young teacher yielded to his curiosity, and the questions kept coming. "Are you rich? Do you have a car?" He translated for his uncle, who perched proudly on a stool watching the exchange like a tennis match. "What is your father's job? Why are you bicycling across China?"

Why *was* I bicycling across China?

Why was I *bicycling* across China? Because a bicycle is freedom; a bicycle is independence; a bicycle is self-sufficiency. Because traveling by bicycle takes away the option of controlling your environment, or glossing over the ugly bits. Because a bicycle lands you in places you didn't know you wanted to go, and shows you things you didn't know you wanted to see, things you cannot search out by saying, "I'll take the train here, I'll get off the bus there." The things I wanted to happen were things that only happen if you don't plan them. The things I wanted to find were things you can only find if you aren't looking for them, things, contrary to my nature, that I couldn't put on a list and check off as I went. They were the moments, images, and connections that happen in the places in between.

Why was I bicycling across *China*? Because it was on the way. Because it was between points A and Z on my map. The most clichéd of all answers was also one of the most true: I was bicycling across China because it was there. Or at least that was how it had begun. By the time I had gotten on the train in Ulaanbaatar, it had become about doing what I had said I would do, about making the idea reality. It had become about keeping the daily experience new, about not letting myself get too comfortable, about continuing to immerse myself in the cleansing, healing powers of the unknown. So now, even though the mirage of Saigon shimmered occasionally in the distance, even though the fantasy of finding Kirk in Xian hovered constantly in the back of my mind, the days—the hours and minutes—were about China, about the thrills and challenges of new words and new customs, about the tiny triumphs of learning a new way of life, about knowing how to sift the cold ashes out of the stove and add more coal after the teacher and his uncle had said good-night, about washing my feet in a plastic basin, about heading to the restaurant across the street and ordering a big plate of vegetables.

CHAPTER 8

Hell's Snow

Every centimeter of Shuanglin Monastery's walls was covered in painted clay statues. The stone halls seemed alive under the gaze of the myriad figurines. Big and little, dating mostly from the Song (960–1279) and Yuan (1280–1368) Dynasties, they stood in rows several deep, a thousand eyes peering out from a past more distant than the moon. I was 100 kilometers south of Taiyuan, where I had taken a hot shower, slept late, washed my socks, and called my father (from a sidewalk kiosk, on his calling card). The next place in larger-type squiggles and dashes in my atlas was Xian, 700 kilometers to the southwest. Outside the monastery gates, a frail mole of a man sat in his pedicab, waiting for me. He looked half my size and was probably twice my age. He had driven me here, pedaling hard for half an hour. Now he would wait, and when I was done playing tourist, he would pedal me back into Pingyao, where he had found me an hour earlier, slurping a bowl of hot, sweet breakfast soup.

The intersection in front of the hotel had been bustling like a big-city train station on the eve of a holiday weekend. The streets teemed with citizens in quilted winter clothes. Fruit vendors, pedicab drivers, and noodle-stand chefs lined the sidewalks. "Yes," I said, when the wiry old man pointed to his pedicab and asked if I wanted to go to the monastery, "after breakfast." He nodded and stayed hovering close behind me, careful not to lose his fare to another driver. The two bread twists that I had ordered to go with my soup were spinning in a wok of hot oil. I had been imagining how delicious they would taste rolled in cinnamon and sugar, telling myself that the next time I came to China, I would be sure to pack some. Now I pointed to them, to him, asking if he wanted one. His chest sinking back under curved, bony shoulders, he shook his head. I meant to be generous. I meant to be polite. But my offer was empty and absurd.

I knew that it was bad manners to leave chopsticks sticking out of a bowl, to pour your own tea, or to show the soles of your feet. I had learned that bones and other meal scraps could be tossed on the floor, but should never be put back on your plate. I had learned that to say "come here," you did not turn your palm up and crook an index finger, you turned your palm to the ground and motioned with all four fingers. But I had not yet learned that any offer, especially of food, must be turned down at least twice before it can be accepted. I should have offered again, and then again, and only after he had said no for the third time should I have believed him. Only after the third refusal would the exchange have been complete. But I hadn't learned that yet. So when he shook his head, I shrugged and turned back to my meal, leaving him standing there, waiting for me, watching me eat.

South of Pingyao I rode through coally landscapes of belching smokestacks and massive, fire-spitting chimneys, of black-faced men without hot showers to look forward to at the end of the day and women scrounging lumps of sooty fuel from the roadside. I shared a bed with two small children and their mother in a home shaken all night by straining, coal-laden trains. In the morning, my face still gray with coal dust, my eyes rimmed in a thick black that wouldn't wash off for days, I finally escaped back into quiet mountain country, and that afternoon I found myself eating another pair of bread twists.

They were cold this time, leftovers from the morning, or the day before. They inspired no fantasies of cinnamon and sugar, but they were an excuse to take a break from the biting air and the acclivitous, intermittently paved road. The hills were brown and bare. The occasional cluster of homes was brown and square, almost indistinguishable from the landscape. As I leaned Greene up against the front of a store, I looked back over my shoulder and saw no one, no sign of life, no movement. A pool table stood on a side street, near a door whose bright patchwork quilt was the only other spot of color in the motionless, sepia scene. Inside, the shop was empty except for the woman behind the counter. I bought the cold bread twists and sat down close to the hot stove.

Before I was halfway through the second twist, the pressure of the crowd had pushed my straight-backed wooden chair forward onto two legs. "Stand up," someone prodded me. There were dozens of people packed into the room, and those in the back wanted to see me, too. "Waiguo ren, waiguo ren ("Foreign person, foreign person")," I heard the explanation being yelled to the dozens of people in the street who couldn't squeeze inside. It was amazing to me that I could be so fascinating, but insta-crowds regularly materialized out of nowhere, drawn by unknowable means of communication, curiosity in their eyes and in the ricochet sounds of their chatter. It had been unnerving at first, all those eyes trained on me, but I was flattered by the attention, even though I knew it wasn't really personal, and happy to perform my role: answering questions, trying to speak comprehensible Chinese, laughing at jokes that I didn't understand.

And slowly I had learned that I could stare back, that I could examine the faces in the crowd just as they were examining me—and I was as fascinated by the villagers as the villagers were fascinated by me. Looking at them, a sea of black hair and eyes bundled in winter coats, the girls in reds and pinks, the boys in blues and browns, I had no idea who they were, or, beyond the external physical trappings of their days, how they lived. I looked and saw an unchanging dead-end routine of waking, working, and sleeping. But without language, without history, without relationships that went much deeper than the exchange of money for food, I knew that there was much I did not see.

I looked at them looking at me, the children, the grandparents, the local doctor, their chatter washing around me, the sounds increasingly familiar, the words still meaningless, and I wondered what *they* saw. Did they talk about me after I was gone, or was I fascinating only in the minutes I was live? Did they tell their friends about me? If so, what did they tell them— what I ate, what Greene looked like, what I could and couldn't say? Did a child ever decide because of me to study English, to bicycle around the world, across China? I wanted to think so. I wanted to think that somehow, in the brief moments of my visit to their world, I managed to leave an impression, or maybe the seed of an idea. I hoped that just as I was taking something with me when I left, I might also be leaving something behind.

Loudspeakers blared to life in the 7:00 A.M. darkness. I wondered briefly if the broadcast was news, poetry, or political exhortation before rolling over and burying my head under the pillow. I was in Daning, a large town in the Lülian Mountains. As the crow flies, Daning is only some twenty-five kilometers from the Yellow River, which at that latitude flows straight south, defining the eastern border of Shanxi Province. The next two days would take me south through the mountains, sharply up and down through loess canyonland, and then east across the river and into neighboring Shaanxi Province.

"You should get up," I told myself.

"No, you should stay here and explore," I answered. "You never see anything beyond your hotel room and the streets you ride in and out on."

"You should get an early start," I argued back, "you have mountains to climb today." And Kirk is probably already in Xian, the little voice in the back of my head added. I heard the door open, heard the floor girl walk in to replace my empty thermos with a new one full of hot water. I didn't stir. I was clean and comfortable in my expensive five-dollar hotel room. When I had arrived the night before, I had asked if there was hot water. "You," the floor girl had said. But when I twisted the faucets, there was only cold. I stormed down the hall.

"*Re shui* ("Hot water"),"I said.

"*You*," she said, and something about "eight."

"*Re shui mei you*,"I said in my atonal Chinese.

"*You, you*," she said again, and again something about "eight."

Eight *kuai*. Of course. There was an extra charge for hot water. Typical. Fine, whatever. And for eight *kuai* do I get "hot water now?"

She shook her head. "Now *mei you*." Even more typical. For eight *kuai* I could have hot water, but there was no hot water. I gave up, stormed back to my room, and crawled under the covers. An hour later I woke up to the sound of a gushing torrent. I rushed into the bathroom. Steam was boiling out of the bathtub. "Eight o'clock," I realized as I slipped into the blissful heat. The hot water comes on "at eight o'clock," she had said, not "for eight *kuai*."

"Climb the mountains tomorrow," I told myself now, finally getting up and heading out in search of breakfast. The sun had risen, the morning streets were busy, and several vendors were selling foods I had never seen before. I loved the simple adventure of unknown foods. If I didn't recognize it, I usually bought it. But even as I ate the fried potato patties and a bowlful of starchy white balls in sugary water, my mind was irretrievably on the road ahead, and I left Daning right after breakfast. The route climbed and fell gently above a ribbon of cold, green river, and by early afternoon I had reached Jixian, its wide, dusty streets lined with shops, restaurants, and pool tables.

It was from here on that the contour lines on the map were intimidatingly numerous and close together. Xiangning was thirty kilometers away, but I still had more than three hours before dark. I bought peanuts and tangerines, checked my compass, and asked directions. The peanut vendor pointed across the river. Directions in Chinese were always so simple, nothing but a general indication to go "that way." Double take: he was giving me detailed instructions, but they were background sounds to the pointing finger, which was all that I could understand. I followed his finger, turning left off of the main road. The pavement ended and then the rocky, gullied road reached straight for the sky. Thirty minutes and one kilometer later, I was high up on the loess plateau. Stretching to the horizon, the land was ripped open by deep, snaking canyons reminiscent of the southwestern American desert. But this was no national park. The sheer stone faces were interrupted by doors and windows. People lived inside these cliffs, building homes straight into the rock, and somehow scrounging a living from the gorgeous, inhospitable landscape: every possible tiny patch of flat land was carefully cultivated, the tidy rows just sprouting green.

The pavement reappeared, disintegrated, appeared again for a few kilometers, then disappeared completely. The road wound over little dips and sharp climbs. Pushing Greene, scrabbling for a foothold in the stones and dust, I was soon praying that each corner would be the last. But each corner revealed only one more uphill push. As the sun met the rim of jagged cliffs, a lone hunter materialized in the road, a lean brown figure with a long rifle slung over one shoulder. "Xiangning?" I asked. "Fifteen kilometers," he nodded, then melted back into the sparse forest just as the road shot up the mountain at an angle that would have been fun to ski down. By the time the road made the final climb onto flat plateau, daylight was nothing but a gray memory, with treacherous patches of ice hiding in its shadows. I could make out the shapes of a few dark buildings and one dimly lit window, but this wasn't Mongolia: I couldn't just open a door and ask to spend the night. Then the road tipped downhill.

I rode on blind faith. I rode by the dim columns of white-painted tree trunks that marked the otherwise invisible edge of the road, where the plateau plummeted a thousand feet into a black ravine. I strapped on my headlight, but a screw had come loose and it kept sagging down to light Greene's handlebars, leaving me more blind than ever. Xiangning lay somewhere in the darkness below, but I could see no sign of it. I imagined being in Europe, imagined the lights of an Alpine village sparkling invitingly out of the darkness. Here, there was nothing but a bottomless chasm of blackness. Bicycles and carts rattled uphill, knowing where they were going, knowing that there was a home waiting for them in the darkness. I continued downhill into my unknown.

Cursing, whimpering, from time to time realizing suddenly that Greene's tires were on ice, I rolled down into the night. Every bit of light or life seemed detached from reality, floating in nothingness. Bulky logging trucks grumbled uphill, their blinding headlights forcing me to stop for fear of missing a curve by a fatal six inches. More trucks snarled downhill, trying to run away from the foot jammed hard on their squealing brakes, their headlights showing me the angle of the next curve as I willed the driver to catch the flash of Greene's rear reflector. They screeched past, and I scooched my fingers up onto the handlebars as if the danger were that I might get my knuckles scraped. I tried to walk Greene, thinking that if a tire slipped over the edge I could just let go, but the slope was so steep that I could not control her weight. I straddled her, both hands clenched on the brakes, the metallic cold creeping through my gloves into my bones, right foot on a pedal for balance, left foot dragging in the road, grappling for control.

Then suddenly the city lights did sparkle out of the darkness below. Far, far, below. I had a long way to go. There was no time, no passage of time, no sensation of reality. There was nothing but curve after curve dropping slowly away into the darkness, interrupted by moments of danger as a tire slipped over a rock or another truck ground past. I knew that eventually the road would spit me out onto pavement and the terrors of the mountain would be instantly forgotten in even streets and a promise that the hot water would be on at eight o'clock. But for an endless hour, reality was only the darkness between me and the next curve, the empty space between me and the precipitous ravine. The lights twinkling below were as distant and imaginary as a picnic on the moon.

⸙

When I am back in Seattle, there will be another Seven Questions. They will be a little less predictable than the questions I encountered across Asia, but only a little. (1) Why Mongolia? (2) How many people were you with? (3) Were you ever in danger? (4) Didn't you get lonely? (5) How long did it take you? (6) How many miles did you ride? (7) "I could never do that!"

"Of course you could," I will answer, and it will not be a disingenuous response. "The only difference between me and you is that I decided to do it, that I thought up the itinerary and got on the plane. Once out there, underway, I didn't do anything you couldn't do, too." I know what people hear when I say "from Irkutsk to Saigon." I know that they try to imagine pedaling 5,000 miles, whereas for me that entirety would always remain an abstraction. The lines on the map look solid, but for me they will always be the amalgam of myriad little dots. Because when you are in the middle of it, it is never about pedaling 8,000 kilometers; it is about getting to the top of the next hill. You don't pedal from Russia to Vietnam. You pedal

sixty-two kilometers from Xiangning to Hejin, a rough, rocky ride beneath
a threatening sky.

I was still among the stunning, terraced cliffs, still climbing and dropping, dropping and climbing, the drops hardly faster than the climbs, my hands
clamped on the brakes, my eyes glued to the dust and ice of the road, when
the coal trucks began multiplying around me. I was coming, I realized, into
a village, a coal-mining village tucked into a mountain valley.

It was the most claustrophobic place I have ever been. Thick as an ashen
blizzard, coal dust swirled in the air. Like the sands of a poison-black beach,
it rose in dunes along the roadside. Like hell's snow, drifts of blackness piled
into corners. Elfin doors curved beneath neatly crafted stone arches, their
once-bright paint eaten away. From rows of pickaxes and shovels, men
turned their blackened faces and smiled, teeth flashing white through the
coal haze as thick as grimy pea soup. A red quilted jacket glimmered hopelessly in the eerie penumbral world, then turned a corner and disappeared.
Somewhere far away the sun struggled, and failed, to burn through the
perpetual dusk. A snake of heaping coal trucks crept torturously through
cramped streets. Laughing alongside, their heads not as high as the massive, churning tires, two children walked home from school, pink backpacks and light brown faces all smudged in black. With pudgy gray fingers
a little girl lifted a once-green apple to her mouth. The bite showed white
for a second before turning malignantly ashen. Had she ever eaten an apple
not gritty from the very air? Had she ever slept in clean sheets? Had she
ever seen blue sky, ever taken a breath that didn't fill her little lungs with
deadly blackness?

I couldn't breathe. I felt panic rising in my throat. I was a ten-year-old
asthmatic again, propped up on three pillows, sitting up straight with
every breath. Up on the inhale, relax back into the pillows on the exhale,
then up again, each breath loud, wheezing, and hard-fought. The air would
not go deep into my lungs, but it was enough; I knew that it was enough.
As long as I could stay in control, as long as I didn't lose the rhythm, I would
be fine. I was not scared, at home all those years ago in my bed. But here,
almost twenty years later, in some godforsaken valley in China, I found
myself at the edge of panic. I was trapped. There was no air. I wanted to
scream. I wanted to fling myself at the pedals, as hard as I could, for as long
as it would take to get out. But there was no speeding through this. There
was no room, between the massive tires of the coal trucks and the hard
walls of the cement-stone homes, to pick up any speed.

Then I glimpsed another road, winding through the valley below. I did not remember a Y, but maybe there had been one. Maybe I was never supposed to be here at all. An old man sat beside a broken cart, tools piled on the ground. *"Ni hao* ("Hello"),*"* I said, *"Ni hao."* Click. The scrawny, crumpled figure was huddled beneath a shabby, army-green coat trying to light a cigarette. I reached down and tapped him on the shoulder. His head turned, and ancient eyes met mine, staring up from the coal-smeared face of a teenage boy. "Hejin?" I asked. He nodded, an apathetic jerk of his head to say that I was on the right road, then ducked back under his coat and the lighter clicked again. The trucks continued to creep forward, nose to tail, and I crept along beside them.

It won't last. It cannot last forever. It will go away. It will be over. I knew this, just as I knew it when I was ten. All I had to do was stay calm; all I had to do was keep pedaling, slowly, rhythmically, and I would escape, and I would be able to breathe again. It lasted less than thirty minutes, the two or three kilometers through that place. It would be only the tiniest of dots in an 8,000-kilometer-long line. But while I was there, it was an eternity. And I got through it one breath, one rotation of the pedals, at a time.

———··———

I crossed the Yellow River, pedaling above massive flats of ice that drifted down the dirty brown current of a river so impressively wide that the opposite bank was lost in the haze. I was now only 200 kilometers from Xian. There were no longer radiators or coal stoves in hotel rooms—just fans on the ceilings because in the summer this was hot country. All day the landscape had reminded me of Mexico. The burnt-orange dirt looked hot and sunbaked. Big angry dogs barked at the ends of their tethers in front of small red earthen houses. People sat by the roadside, selling apples as red and orange as the earth. But their bodies did not lean back expansively in the heat; they hunched inward against the still, bitter cold. The red earth was hard with frost, and the barking dogs' breath was visible on the air. There would be one more morning of rollercoastering through loess canyons, and then it would be a flat run into the big city where I would maybe, just maybe, find a man named Kirk with whom to indulge in a few days of tourism and other activities. I fixed a cup of tea, kicked off my shoes, and sank into a comfortable armchair, feet up on the bed.

Knock. The hotel guard stood at the door. He wanted his son to meet me. When we had exhausted the limits of my Chinese, they wished me a good evening and left. I shelled a few peanuts. *Knock.* One of the floor girls and a friend walked in. She sat inches away from me, punching my shoulder to punctuate her every sentence, occasionally spitting a huge globule of saliva onto the floor as we ran through the Seven Questions. They left. I started to peel a tangerine. *Knock.* The hotel guard stood a servile step behind a policeman holding a piece of paper titled "Registration Form for Foreigner's Temporary Residence" in both English and Chinese. I served them tea. I filled out the form. I showed the officer my passport. The real one. He knew to flip through the pages until he found something he could read. He scrutinized the visa, wished me a pleasant stay, and left.

Knock. "Good evening," a thin young man in wire-rimmed glasses and a long blue coat addressed me nervously in English. Next to him stood a shorter man in an identical coat. "The town council would like to meet you. They ask us to help. We teach English in the school."

"When would they like to meet?"

"Now."

I was unwashed, smelly, and tired. I started to say no when I suddenly realized that this was the follow-up to the policeman's paperwork.

"Where?"

"Downstairs."

They led the way to a small office, where one dignified woman and a half dozen well-dressed men in their fifties and sixties had gathered. "Please sit," one of the officials addressed me via the teachers' hesitant translations. I steeled myself for the confrontation, the bribes, the orders that I could not be here or could not go where I was going. "Tea?" he asked. "Where are you from? Where are you going?" He introduced another of the men as the county chairman. "We would like to welcome you to Heyang County. Do you need anything? Do you have any problems? Can we help you with anything?"

This was it. The dreaded grilling. The brutish, threatening Chinese authority. I was having trouble keeping a straight face.

"Will you have breakfast with us?" came the next question. "You probably need to leave early. Is 7:00 A.M. all right? And after breakfast, can we take a photo together? Do you have a camera? Now will you come dance?"

Next to the hotel was a large, dimly lit hall. A mirrored disco ball hung from the ceiling. Images of misty seashores splashed across a large video screen, and high-pitched bathetic pop music bounced off the walls. Next to the dancers' neat blouses, delicate lipstick, and clean shoes, I was embarrassingly scroungy in bulky fleece and frizzy braids. Several of the officials invited me to dance, but their trodden-upon toes never survived a whole tune. Impressed by the company in which they had suddenly found themselves, respectful of their politically powerful elders, the teachers did not dance. Finally the chairman, a commanding leader, guided my clueless, amusical body so determinedly that I was actually able to follow, and to stay off his toes through an entire song. Mission accomplished, he pronounced firmly that I must be tired and sent me off to bed.

There was no message from Kirk at the backpacker-central Victory Hotel in Xian. The receptionist would not let me take Greene inside. The rooms were cement boxes, and the communal showers down the hall worked for three hours a night. The manic obsession with the deal, the bargain, the penny saved, which controlled and defined many travelers' every move, threatened to take hold of me as well. While it stemmed from a laudable desire to take a trip beyond the cushioned avenues of luxury hotels, air-conditioned buses, and English-language menus, it led to a miserly preoccupation that became just as detrimental to and distancing from the soul of a journey as locking oneself into the sterile world of a five-star tour. Eating in Beijing's finest restaurant is to experience China as legitimately as is sharing a cement *kang* and dirty quilt with a coughing, illiterate grandmother. While I too believed that the grandmother's life was a truer picture of China, for it reflected the lives of the vast majority, both were genuine pieces of the whole puzzle.

In believing that only the cheapest was authentic, budget travelers limited themselves as surely as their more indulgent counterparts. What had begun as a desire to see what a nation was "really like," how people "really lived" had warped into a goal of its own. The means had become the end. Now the cheapest bowl of noodles was a conquest to be vaunted proudly to other travelers (over more bottles of beer than most locals could afford) rather than an irrelevant side effect of having stumbled upon a locale that took one truly into the everyday life of the land. The less one spent, the better one traveled. But it was a quantitative rather than a qualitative "better." The proof was in the penny, not in the adventure.

There was no arbitrary nobility in staying at the cheapest hotel. I would not experience Xian any more profoundly by sleeping in a cement box. I could afford a little comfort. At the Jiefang Hotel, Greene fit perfectly into the elevator up to a carpeted room with a direct-dial international telephone, a thermostat, hot running water twenty-four hours a day, and MTV.

I didn't leave that room for days. I had been dirty in Mongolia, but that had been clean dirt—earth—not the gritty poison of coal, soot, and exhaust fumes. I gave my heavy fleece clothes to the hotel laundry and took everything else with me into the bathtub—gloves, stuff sacks, panniers, shoes. Round after round of steaming water turned oily, grimy black. Shampoo ran sudsless gray down my chest. Three hours later, I filled the tub one last time and lolled blissfully in the clear hot water, surrounded by the dripping of all my belongings. Then I crawled naked and warm between luxuriously clean sheets.

Maybe I would find Kirk farther south. Maybe our paths would cross in Yangshuo. But that was several weeks and more than 1,500 kilometers away. For now I was happy just to lie in bed and read, to stare at MTV and clean Greene, to stand naked in front of the mirror and stare at my body. It had been four months since my last period. I knew that women who engaged in regular, strenuous exercise often stopped menstruating. I knew that I was not pregnant. Knowledge didn't help. I was sure my stomach was bloated and swelling in a deviant, diseased way. I was sure all the bumps and lumps in my abdomen had never been there before. I felt fine, but that did not stop me from imagining a savage cancerous tumor, or an impossible baby, growing inside of me. Nevertheless, every time I considered going to a doctor, I decided that there were only two possible results: (1) it's nothing, or (2) you're dying. If it was (1), there was no need to see a doctor; if it was (2), he or she would tell me to go back to America. I didn't want to go back to America, so I chose (3), do nothing and keep worrying about it. Ignore it. Believe stubbornly that if you ignore something it will go away, that if you close your eyes, you become invisible.

As day followed day, I began to make little forays into the world, but I never stayed out long, and was always glad to be back in my room. One day, with visions of a mahogany bar, a vodka tonic, and the BBC in my head, I went in search of the Hyatt Hotel, where I had to settle for a bowl of ice cream and *USA Today* in a frilly pink café. The hotel staff wore little red elf costumes, and an endless-loop cassette in the lobby played "Silent Night," "Little Drummer Boy," and Dolly Parton singing something about a "Hard Candy Christmas." It was December 20, and I didn't want to sit in Xian through the holidays. On the road, in places that had never heard of Christmas, I wouldn't feel lonely, but surrounded by the sights and sounds of the season, I was suddenly, inevitably nostalgic for the scents and flavors of an American December 25.

Yet when I woke in the mornings, I turned up the heat and went back to bed, hiding from the light, not wanting to leave the leisure of the covers, not wanting to leave any of my haven's comforts for the cold road. I was scared that I had wimped out, scared (no matter how unwilling I was to risk being sent home by a doctor) that I didn't really want to ride any more. Only in retrospect would I recognize that for the first time in five months I was in a place where my space was mine inviolate, where I was safe in the knowledge that no one might at any minute walk through the door and sit down to watch me brush my teeth.

CHAPTER 9

"Your Bicycle from America Must Have a Passport"

I had ridden some 1,300 kilometers since leaving Beijing, pedaling south and west. Now I would veer back east across the corner of Henan Province, then turn straight south across Hubei and Hunan to Guangxi Province, through the town of Yangshuo, and on to the Vietnamese border. I had more than 2,000 kilometers to go, but Xian felt like halfway. It was the most tourist-famous city between Beijing and Guilin, and on the map it looked to me like the end of northern China and the beginning of the south. I left Xian on December 24, in air that hinted at spring. For a few hours that afternoon, I shed my Gore-Tex windbreaker for the first time in more than three months.

As the city gave way to rural quiet, the jagged eastern reaches of the Qingling Mountains loomed ahead and the road began a dogged climb into crisp evergreen forest. Intermittent clusters of stone homes interrupted the trees. Children played in the streets, spinning homemade tops with long, ungainly whips. They wrapped the bit of string or leather around the top, then with a deft flick of the wrist released the whip, sending the top spinning like a whirling dervish. An old, bowlegged woman shuffled slowly past them, her body teetering over tiny feet. Foot binding was officially outlawed in 1912, but for centuries tiny feet were considered a mark of beauty and a virtual requirement for successful marriage in the higher ranks of society, so little girls' toes were broken, bent back under the balls of their feet, and wrapped tightly to prevent further growth, leaving them forever hobblingly painful to walk on. The woman advanced slowly, pain visible in every step, until she reached a wooden chair next to another old woman, knitting needles clicking and glinting in her nimble hands, her too-small feet warming in the sun.

Life had moved outside. Families sat in their doorways eating lunch, chopstick-shovelling noodles out of big bowls. Girls bent over plastic basins, shampooing their long black hair. Laundry lay tossed over bushes to dry, as if the plants were sprouting little shirts and socks. Big black pigs wandered freely. Cats and dogs were tethered by lengths of string or chain. Yellow corn and red chili hung drying from eaves and the branches of winter-barren trees.

I spent Christmas Eve jumping around on a small square of brick floor to the music of a large boom box, wishing I could explain to the girls and boys trying to copy my feet that there was no pattern, no set sequence of steps to follow, no actual dance. A small crowd had gathered to watch me slurp a chili-filled bowl of noodles and eggs, then someone had asked if I could show them how to "dance disco." The sky outside was clear, the moon was rising, and Orion would soon be hunting low to the mountain tops. Quilted curtains no longer covered doorways against the cold, and glimpses of life in the homes across the street were visible in the rectangles of light, many punctuated by the concentric square of a flickering gray television. I was only ninety-two kilometers south of Xian, but already a world away from hot baths and MTV.

When I woke on Christmas morning, I looked around the brick-floored, wooden-ceilinged, unheated room and grinned at the bags of grain stacked to the eaves. I did not miss the Hyatt waitresses dressed as Santa's elves. I did not wish I was in Seattle with a tinseled tree and the scent of goose wafting from the oven. I was glad to be where I was, glad again to be doing what I was doing.

There were no more menacing patches of ice on the road, no more hairpin curves. The pavement was smooth, and I let Greene fly while I watched the passing scenery. The sky was a crisp, perfect blue. The northern brown was succumbing steadily to sprouting green, and the mountains were giving way to hills rounded rather than angled, sloping out into wide agricultural plains. Soon the jagged peaks were only outlines on the horizon. Stands of bamboo speckled the landscape with color. A scrawny foal towed a towering mound of hay down the road, the cart wheels barely visible beneath the massive load. Women crouched by a river brutally kneading clothes in the swirling water. Men and oxen tilled the fertile soil, pushing heavy plows through fresh furrows.

I stopped to take a picture of Greene leaning against a low red brick building with a single Chinese character painted neatly on each of its two entrances. I had finally learned to read Chinese: the character with crossed legs was female; the character whose two legs dangled loose and open was

᠆· *Greene in front of a bathroom.*

male. These were the only two characters I would ever learn to recognize, but the littlest things can have a profound effect on how at home you feel in a new country. Now, when there were two entrances to a village toilet, and when those entrances were marked, I knew where to go.

A cyclist passed in front of me as I took the photo, then stopped and stood watching me, angry at being caught in a stranger's lens. As he turned around and came back, I prepared to assure him that I had only been photographing the toilet. This was not going to be easy to explain. He waved me over to his side and dropped to a squat. He didn't *look* particularly angry, so I followed suit. In his hands he gingerly held a dirty, worn plastic bag neatly folded into a flat rectangle. I watched as he carefully unfolded the bag and pulled out first his identity papers, then an airmail envelope that he delicately placed in my hands. The return address was in Germany. His eyes were expectant as he chattered at me. I caught the word "*fanyi* ("translate")."

◟ · *Roadside dog meat vendor, Hobei Province*

I opened the envelope. Inside were a single sheet of stationery and a photo of two Chinese boys with their mother. Luckily, it was a very simple note written in English: "Many thanks and greetings to you and your family. Greetings, Jürgen Schmidt."With the help of the phrasebook, I was able to translate the message. The man nodded and pointed questioningly to the signature. "Jürgen Schmidt," I said, and looked up the word for "name."Then he pointed to the top of the page. "Lübeck, 5. Dez. 1993." I found the Chinese for "date" and "city." Had he been carrying the letter just in the hope of coming across someone to translate it? Watching him carefully wrap it up again, I wondered whether, knowing now what it said, he would continue to carry it.

Darkness now refrained from enveloping the world until six o'clock, and as long as there was light, I wanted to ride. So I rode, compulsively, into a town at four or five o'clock and on out the other side. Then daylight was gone and I was nowhere; I was still an hour away from a bed, telling myself that I was stupid and obsessed, that this was dangerous, that I wouldn't do it again. And then I did it again. But now a full moon hung luminous in the sky and the mountains were behind me, and with the spill of moonlight over a straight, paved road, night was not a scary place. Instead of danger, there was pure physical exhilaration. There was nothing but my body, working undistracted in the cocoon of darkness. It was a feeling I had not had once since leaving Irkutsk, a feeling I recognized from all those years ago on the sunny summer roads of southern France. The flying abandon of a bicycle, legs pumping, body and wheels skimming above the land, cycling for the sake of cycling, because it felt good in my body, because the drip of salty sweat, the deep, rhythmic breathing, the stretching, pushing muscles were pure and cleansing and glorious. The night was balmy and peaceful. I never wanted to stop.

The heartland of China proper, Hubei Province is known as the nation's rice bowl. The key river port for the region's cotton and grain is the city of Shashi, whose bustling, honking, flashing boulevards were replete with advertisements. I had just finished reading *Sons and Lovers,* and wanted to mail it to Agvantseren. (The selections in the Foreign Language Bookstores I hungrily visited in every big city were fairly limited. Bicycling across China, I read *Sister Carrie, Portrait of a Lady,* and *Sons and Lovers.*) I bought a pretty blue envelope, neatly copied out the Chinese character for Mongolia, and took it to the counter. The clerk pushed it back to me with an explanation I could not begin to decipher. Over my shoulder, a male voice said in English, "You must have a different envelope."

The young man was dressed in dark blue jeans and a denim jacket over a heavy brown sweater. "She says you must go to the department store to buy the correct envelope."

"Where is the department store?"

"I will mail my letter, then we will go to the department store. I can help you, yes?"

"Yes, please, thank you."

He posted his letter, clarified with the clerk what kind of envelope was required, introduced himself as Setto, and led me across the street to the department store. He asked directions to the appropriate floor, then followed the hanging placards through the dimly lit space straight to the correct counter. Life is so much easier when you are literate. It would have taken me twenty minutes of walking up and down aisles just to land on the third floor. With Setto's help, I quickly bought plain brown wrapping paper and cellophane tape. He penned "Mongolia" beneath the address, and this time the clerk was happy to accept the package.

I invited Setto to breakfast and we walked to a noodle stand on the banks of the Yangtze River. There is a distinct excitement in seeing for the first time something that has been a word, or perhaps a photo, all your life. The Mona Lisa, the Kremlin, the Yangtze. Here, some 150 kilometers south of the famed Three Gorges, the wide, slow-moving river was gray and industrial, aesthetically disappointing, but still—the Yangtze River, live. Setto was a twenty-eight-year-old civil engineering post-graduate student. After breakfast we went to meet his wife, Nan-Nan, a vivacious accountant with a ringing, infectious laugh. Nan-Nan and Setto were leaving that afternoon for a New Year's Day visit to the fishery where Setto's father worked. They invited me to join them.

We left Greene in their tiny cement home and the three of us boarded a bus out of the city. One bus led to another, and then a fifteen-minute walk down a dirt lane brought us to a low cement house beside an artificial rectangular pond. Setto's father was a tall, shaven-headed Buddhist, his mother a short, sturdy atheist. They had left the hustle and bustle of Shashi several years earlier for the quiet of a job in the country. Their home was a row of four tiny rooms, the cement walls broken by wooden doors. Wooden roof beams supported a rounded brick tile roof cracked wide enough in places to let the gray sky show through. Low chairs were scattered throughout the house, and a color television sat atop a chest of drawers. Three of the rooms had double beds; the fourth room was the kitchen. Dried fish hung on the walls. Chickens scratched in the enclosure beside the house. Setto's father cast a net into the man-made pond and caught a large silver fish. It was already cold and the temperature was sinking with the sun.

Dinner, served on a small table in the main room, consisted of eight separate plates of food: roasted peanuts, fish, chicken, spicy beans, a green leafy vegetable, hard-boiled eggs, tofu, and a second fish. Setto didn't drink. His eighteen-year-old sister Ming, who was home from school for the holiday, served her father and me little glasses of clear alcohol. She filled everybody else's bowl with rice, and we dove into the feast, chopsticks reaching, snagging, bowls held in one hand underneath the food as it traveled from dish to mouth. I loved the rice in China and was happy to devour large quantities of the fresh grain at every opportunity. I did not understand why Ming had not filled my rice bowl, but was unwilling to ask. Then, when after three toasts I refused more alcohol, Ming jumped up to fill my bowl with rice. The grain was traditionally considered filler, poor stuff to occupy the stomach, rather than a quality comestible in its own right.

Evening ablutions were performed almost ritualistically. Setto filled basins of hot water for me and Nan-Nan. First we washed our faces and hands, then he dumped the basin outside and refilled it from a steaming kettle for us to wash our feet. Clean and warm, we joined everyone else in front of the television to watch high-pitched disco-pop videos. After half an hour, Nan-Nan took off a layer of clothing and crawled under the covers of the double bed. I followed suit, and the rest of the family took the television into the other room as Nan-Nan and I drifted off to sleep, lying head to toe beneath the quilt. The next morning, as we brushed our hair and teeth, and washed our hands and faces outside in the brisk, damp air, the sun was a perfect orange circle through the pollution clinging to the horizon. That afternoon we walked along the dikes between the numerous rectangular fishing ponds and watched the fishermen return from the lake in their long, low rowboats. We sat in the wintry sun and talked. Setto's command of English made conversation easy. He said that he hated the Communists.

"Can you say that without fear?" I asked, a bit surprised.

"Yes, of course."

"What about ten years ago?"

He shook his head, "Ten years ago, only 'up your sleeve'—in a whisper."

"What are students taught about Mao today?" In Russia this question, asked about Stalin, is a logical sequitur to "What truths are now spoken that were denied a decade ago?"

"Oh, I love Mao," Setto answered, "He was a very good man."

I tried to understand. "But . . . are today's leaders not doing what he wanted?"

"No," Setto was emphatic. "They are not. Only corruption. And in 1989 they killed many, many students. They tell us what we should do, but don't do it themselves. We hate them."

Ming smacked him on the arm. "He is very bad." She grinned at me, but was clearly shocked by her older brother's brazenness.

The talk turned to movies. "American movies are all very violent," Ming observed.

"No," I said, "not all of them. It's just that those are the films we export."

"Why does your government do that?" Setto asked.

"It has nothing to do with the government," I explained. "It's about dollars. We export whatever sells."

The next morning, as I stood outside brushing my hair, clouds moved in across the pale sun and turned the sky a solid, gloomy gray. Two little crampy points were playing high under my ribs. Accustomed again to daily cycling, my muscles had quickly tightened in the days' inactivity. I lay on the ground and stretched, pulling my spine until it crackled. Probably breaking all sorts of rules about physical contact between men and women, Setto offered to massage my shoulders. Nan-Nan didn't seem to mind, and under his kneading fingers, the cramped spots quickly evaporated. His father had made one trip to fetch water in two wooden pails that hung from a pole across his straight, strong shoulders. Now it was Setto's turn. Nan-Nan and I went with him. When he stopped to catch his breath on the way back, I took the pole on my shoulders. Nan-Nan and Setto laughed as I straightened up and walked a few meters, then told me to put it down, it was too heavy. The pails were heavy, but the physical exertion was creating warmth in my body, and I went on all the way back to the house, where I set them down with a relieved thud, panting but warm.

For the first time in China, I felt that I was with people who might be friends rather than just passing acquaintances. We played blackjack and five-card draw poker, betting sunflower seeds, our laughter reflecting off the gray-brown water. Setto's father placed a small pile of coal in a wok set in a base of wood, and once it was glowing red he moved it inside, where we gathered to pass the hours around the heat. Nan-Nan wanted to know if *any* book could be published in the States. Was there Pinyin for English? Were there state-run businesses? Did I have a boyfriend? Did I plan to marry? Why not?

"Why?" I countered.

"To have children," she said.

"I don't want to have children."

"Not even one?"

"No. Do you?"

Ming giggled. Nan-Nan blushed profusely. It was like talking about sex. She nodded emphatically.

"How many?" I asked.

As recently as 1949, Mao Tse-tung had advocated population growth, maintaining that superior Communist production and distribution of wealth would support any number of people. By the mid-1950s, however, the official line had changed dramatically. Sterilization, certain types of abortions, and the import of contraceptives were legalized. Active attempts to slow population growth began in the 1970s with government campaigns for later marriage, spacing between births, and fewer children. In 1979 official policy promoting a norm of one child per family was announced. Especially in rural areas, the one-child campaign met with significant resistance and in the early 1980s, political pressure to meet family planning targets resulted in reports of forced abortions and female infanticide. Today family planning laws vary significantly from region to region, one-child policies continuing to be strictly enforced in urban areas while second births are sanctioned for most rural couples whose first child is a girl. It seemed like such an appalling choice for the government to take away from couples, yet at the same time, China's desperate need for an aggressive, adamant approach to overpopulation was inarguable.

"One," Setto answered firmly. "We will have one. Sterilization is the law after one baby." I didn't ask who would be sterilized. The IUD and female sterilization remain the most widely used methods of contraception in China, with vasectomies a distant third. Setto then informed me that in China many girls now had sex before they were married. He asked about cohabitation in America.

"Yes," I told him, "lots of couples live together without getting married."

"And you? Do you cohabit with your boyfriend?" This time it was Nan-Nan who nudged him sharply for his brazenness, however clearly curious she was to hear my answer. The truth was that there was no boyfriend, just a friendship that meandered occasionally into the sexual. But I had taken to answering that, yes, there was a boyfriend. It was so much easier, and elicited so much less confusion and sympathy, than being twenty-eight and completely single. And it was he I then pictured when I answered the rest of the questions. "No, we each have our own home." Even Setto did not quite dare ask the question I could see in his eyes: "But do you sleep together?"

That afternoon, the last of our stay, Setto, Nan-Nan, Ming, and I walked twenty minutes to a tiny huddle of a village, where Setto bought a packet of what he called "dead people's paper." His father met us halfway back from the village, and we followed him down the side of the embankment. Setto's paternal grandmother had died three years earlier. Her grave was an unmarked mound long overgrown with dry grass. Setto loosened the brittle beige pages, which symbolized the money and other offerings that had once literally accompanied the deceased beyond the grave, and set small piles of it at the foot of the bump in the ground. Then he lit a match. As each family member in turn knelt and touched his or her forehead three times to the ground, blue and orange flames flickered on the dry, cold earth, and some of the leaves caught the air and lifted up into the sky.

From Shashi I took a ferry across the Yangtze and set off south across Hubei Province. Setto had invited me to accompany him by bus up the river, from where I could cruise the Three Gorges before they were dammed. But I had again given in to the compunction to keep moving, to the absurd perception that kilometers equaled accomplishment, to the pull of an almost imaginary man. It was a decision I still regret. Sunlight glinted off little silvery fish that filled the dusty roadside markets and dangled from bicycle handlebars on their way home to the wok. Stubby palm trees waved against the sky. The click of mah-jongg tiles carried on the crisp air, audible around corners long before my eyes found the men gathered around a low table, bent intently over their game.

The road wound through fields of sugarcane. Men, women, and children worked among the stalks, cutting and bundling. Curls of thick black smoke and leaping columns of orange flame rose above the shorn acres. Stalks stood in teepee formations along the road, vendors perched beside them on little wooden stools, reminding me of fresh berry stands in Washington State. People cycled and gnawed, walked and gnawed, squatted in the dirt and gnawed, the sticky, liquid sweetness dribbling down their throats. Oddly enough for someone with a serious sweet tooth, I hate sugarcane. Like solid meringue, or nails on a chalkboard, the taste of the pure liquid sugar crawls right up my spine.

I stopped for lunch at a tiny outdoor restaurant. Faces craned from the back of the crowd, pushing forward against those in front so relentlessly that the table under my noodles was rarely on all four legs. The exotic charm and novelty of an audience had faded. I could not sit down to eat without at least a dozen people surrounding my table, and I was no longer flattered by all those eyes trained on me. It had become claustrophobic and exhausting. I had taken to talking out loud—"no, this store doesn't have what I want"—as if I were not alone, as if there were someone else beside me to distract and absorb some of the staring eyes. I had learned to eat while pedaling to avoid the stress of the crowd, but even in the time it took to buy a bag of peanuts, people would gather, watching, pointing, giggling. The daily experience had slowly become an incessant routine, its redundancy exacerbated by the frustrating limits of my Chinese.

One woman encouraged me to eat, then talked loudly into my face and expected me, with my mouth full of noodles, to answer. I had answered the same questions a million times over the past five weeks, and it was hard

 ∽· *The audience*

to remember that the scenarios that repeated themselves over and over
throughout my days were new each time around for my inquisitors. As the
table tipped and my soup sloshed toward the edge of the bowl, another
woman told jokes that elicited howls of laughter from the gathering
and wan, uncomprehending smiles from me. I no longer laughed along, and
the laughter that I didn't understand now sounded rude and aggressive
rather than curious and endearing. I no longer felt amazement at the
humanity crowding around me. I simply felt foreign: other, odd, wrong,
not belonging, and totally objectified. I felt as though I had forgotten my
lines, had never been given the script, or had woken up to find myself in
the wrong play.

Eventually I got up and made my way back to Greene, pushing through
the crowd. Another thing I had learned in China, learned quickly the first
time I had gotten on a bus in Beijing: to push. Not to nudge subtly, or turn

sideways and try to slide between people, but to put my hand on a stranger's back or shoulder and simply move the person out of my way. Greene was surrounded by a group of men curiously removing her valve caps. They had pushed and pulled at gear levers and quick-release handles. Cables sagged and stretched. The seat sat flat on the top tube. One man was busily spinning a pedal and fingering the toe clips. Someone else was squeezing the brakes and tracing the pinch of the cable.

As I put her back together, I was surrounded by a barrage of impenetrable sounds, a cacophony that I could not turn into words. I love the jigsaw puzzle of language, love making the pieces fit, making the picture whole. Language is a bridge, a connection I delight in building, yet I now found myself turning it into a barrier, a weapon. When other cyclists rode alongside me, I no longer tried to decipher their words. While they attempted to carry on a friendly conversation, all I could hear were the same sounds repeated over and over, louder and louder, so I snapped back, over and over, louder and louder, *"Bu dong, wo bu dong* ("I don't understand, I don't understand")." I hurled *"bu dong"* like a defensive rocket—"Leave me alone, I don't know what you're saying!"—mad not really at them, but at the flying sounds of which I could make no sense, at the insane frustration of not being able to communicate.

The roads now were increasingly flat and fast, busy and gray and loud, running through charmless habitation clusters indeterminably still under construction or already in decline. Dust and truck exhaust filled my mouth and eyes. The endless assault of honking, grating, blasting, squealing traffic tore at my nerves, and the language had become just more noise. My head hurt. I wanted it to be quiet. I wanted either to carry on a real conversation or not to talk at all. I wanted either companionship, to look across a dinner table into one person's eyes, or I wanted solitude, to just be left alone.

My passport, the little blue book that was my security, my immunity, the definition of my identity, was out of my control. I had been at the hotel in Changde asking for my deposit back, which the receptionist was not giving me, when a pretty middle-aged woman walked through the door, straight up to me, and said, "Passport." The theoretical advantage to using the old passport was that if push came to shove, you could walk away from it. The reality was that the people most likely to detain you would not be fooled by it. As the policewoman carefully scrutinized each page, I realized that she knew to look for a Chinese visa. The receptionist, who had clearly been told to keep me there until the police arrived, had handed my deposit back the minute the police officer arrived, and had then disappeared. Now she returned with another guest who spoke a bit of English. Having learned the Asian lesson of simply reaching out and grabbing things, I took my old passport from the officer's hands, and as the three of us walked down the hall to my room, I slipped it into a pocket and ferreted the real one out of my money belt. (The practical advantage to using the old passport was that I could keep it easily accessible, instead of having to dig under my clothes and into my money belt while everybody watched.) I served them tea and she asked to see the passport again. "Visa," she said. I handed her the passport open to the Chinese visa, as if it had been there all along. "Where are you going?" she asked.

"Guilin."

"Where have you come from?"

"Beijing and Xian."

"Where is your bicycle from?"

"America."

"Where is its passport?"

I didn't particularly like any of this—authority is always intimidating— but at some point, glancing at the man who had been pressed into service as interpreter, I realized that he, innocent bystander, was more nervous than I was, more scared of whatever power the woman wielded.

"My bicycle doesn't have a passport."

"Your bicycle from America must have a passport," she said.

"Nobody requested any documents for the bicycle when I entered China."

"You will come with me? There are some questions," she said, slipping my passport into her purse.

Greene and I followed her old black bicycle through the city traffic like a cow with a ring through its nose, my eyes glued to the purse bouncing in her wire handlebar basket. She turned through an iron gate into a large cobblestone courtyard. "Entry and Exit Formalities" read the sign on her office door. She told me to wait, and disappeared. I paced nervously between the doorsill and the austere metal desk adorned with one black-and-white photo of her in a jacket covered with medals.

I imagined all the things she could decide to do—fine me some ridiculous amount of money, put me on a train back to Beijing, take Greene away. I remembered the Town Council in Heyang Province, about whom I had had similar fears, but who had wanted nothing more than to dance, have breakfast, and take pictures together. This woman did not want to dance with me. In the grand scheme of things, I knew that I had nothing to fear—she wasn't going to throw me in jail, she couldn't brand me an enemy of the people or threaten my children's chance at higher education—but in my world of the moment, being put on a train back to Beijing would count as a disaster of major proportions.

However free I had felt to travel across China, however inconsequential the constant arrival of police to leaf through my passport had always been, China was still a land of closed cities and a dense, powerful, potentially arbitrary bureaucracy. I remembered the look on our interpreter's face at the hotel, the fear in his demeanor, the shuttering-in of his body and eyes that echoed my memories of the Soviet Union.

I remembered the outskirts of a city called Dengxian, where a half dozen young men and women in uniforms, looking more like boy and girl scouts than soldiers, had poured out of a guardhouse waving at me to stop, their leader asking, "Where are you going?" and, before I could open my mouth, feeding me the right answer, "To Xiangfan?" Xiangfan was seventy kilometers away and it was already early afternoon, but I said yes. "Yes," I said, looking him in the eyes to let him know that I understood what he was saying. "Turn right a few kilometers from here," he was saying, "do *not* try to go into Dengxian." Then they all smiled and gave me thumbs-up signs and let me through. And as curious as I was, I did *not* try to go into Dengxian.

I also remembered something I had seen just south of Xian, not long after dancing with the Heyang Town Council. On a dirt plaza below the road, a crowd stood listening to a man on a makeshift stage speak into a microphone. I stopped to watch, wondering if it was a political rally, wishing I understood Chinese. Then I saw the second man—head bowed, hands clasped behind his back as if awaiting the guillotine. "Oh, charming," I thought. "A bit of local theater, government-supported, for the people." I was reaching for my camera when I suddenly realized that it was not theater. There was no guillotine, but the public condemnation was not inconsequential entertainment. I had quickly zipped the pannier closed again, scared of suddenly finding myself embroiled in accusations of meddling or spying or worse, charges it could be difficult to counter—"No, really, I am just an innocent cyclist. I thought it was pretend."

It was not pretend. Staring out into the brittle winter sun, furious at the policewoman for interfering with my day, I reminded myself that anger was not the way to approach an official in China. I also reminded myself that, as I had learned ten years earlier in Moscow, watching an elderly couple stare at their son's photo in a foreign newspaper, this was not a game. Or, rather, it was a game with very real consequences.

The policewoman returned with a pile of Temporary Residence forms and her boss, a tall man with intelligent eyes who spoke some English. Telling myself to relax, telling myself to be polite, telling myself that this was part of the Chinese Experience—every traveler had a police-in-China tale— I cheerfully reviewed the information on the form with the senior officer, pulling out my atlas to show him where I was going as amiably as if we were chatting in a café.

"I must ask my chief," he said. "Because of 'not open area' where you must have travel permit."

"Is Changde not open?"

"Changde is open. Anhua is not open."

"I am not going to Anhua. See," again I traced my route on the map, following the roads that angled southwest rather than southeast. "Anhua is here. I want to go here, toward Lenshuijiang. Not to Anhua."

"I must ask my chief," he repeated, and left to consult with his superior. A second man had meandered in during the proceedings. Now the woman grabbed a little red book out of her desk drawer and zealously pointed out various paragraphs to him, reading them out loud to prove her points. In her rapid, vehement chatter, I could pick out only the words "American" and "bicycle." Neither of the men, however, seemed to be taking the situation as seriously as she was. Her boss returned, handed me my passport, said that his chief welcomed me to Hunan Province, and wished me a successful trip on toward Lenshuijiang. I could feel the woman's disappointed scowl as I thanked him, and hear her voice crescendo in disapproval as I walked out the door. My passport was stuffed safely deep in my pocket; Greene, it seemed, no longer needed one.

CHAPTER 10

A Tangle of Naked Limbs

I was again pedaling through the China of my imagination, following a river dammed in places to aquamarine lakes. Like etchings on ancient porcelain, fishermen in narrow wooden boats worked silently in the shadow of hills that were jagged beneath their fur of evergreens. There were no more strip malls—just lush green land and people working, everywhere people working. Human labor continued as it had for centuries. Yet at the same time, by whatever name, capitalism was taking hold. In every tiny cluster of homes, several had been converted into small businesses—stores, restaurants, hairdressers, hotels. Sometimes it seemed that every second building was a *lüguan*.

"Is there a hotel here?" I asked a ponytailed woman cooking over her streetside stove.

She nodded curiously, and did not elaborate.

"Where is the hotel?"

Now she was definitely looking at me as if I were the stupidest person on earth. "Where is the hotel?" I repeated, making a pillow of my hands, because my pronunciation still left a lot of room for misunderstanding. She lifted an index finger and pointed at the two-story cement building directly behind her. "Well, how the hell was I supposed to know?" I grumbled to myself. "It looks just like every other building on the street." She left her wok to lead me upstairs past the grand red designs painted on the front of the building, meter-high characters that no doubt declared "Hotel." It is profoundly disconcerting to be illiterate.

And then sometimes there didn't seem to be a hotel anywhere. I stopped at a Y in the road. According to my map, either road would lead to Lenshuijiang. One route looked considerably shorter than the other, but of course the number of kilometers was less relevant than all the other things I still didn't know how to ask about. I knew the word for road—"*lu*." I did not know the word for pavement. I grinned at the crowd, reached down,

patted the asphalt, and asked, *"Lu (pat-pat-pat) you mei you?"* Silence. A circle
of stares. Then a burst of ringing laughter as one man suddenly understood.
"You, you!" he nodded. *"Pu li qing you."*

"Pu li qing?" I repeated, patting the road like Helen Keller splashing her
hands in the flow of water, connecting the sounds—*pu . . . li . . . qing*—
to the prickle of asphalt on the palm of my hand, trying to remember them
for future reference.

"Pu li qing," he nodded emphatically. *"Pu li qing you."*

I had long ago learned to take even the most adamant information with
a grain of salt, not only because of all the room there was for miscommu-
nication, but because even the simplest words were open to interpretation.
I had no idea what he considered to be "paved"—or, really, what *pu li qing*
meant. But this time the road, as it wound on through a flat agricultural
valley and fields sprouting green, was, by my current standards at least, unquestionably paved. In the early afternoon, it began to climb into the surrounding hills.

The first time I stopped to ask if there was somewhere nearby to spend
the night, half a dozen people gathered around me in the dirt road—*"Pa bu
pa* ("You're not scared")?"—but no one had a bed to offer. The road kept
climbing. As far as the eye could see now—down the valley falling sharply
away into dusk, up the hills rising into long, late-afternoon shadow—
every inch of land was terraced and cultivated. Dirt pathways through the
fields connected scattered homes. I continued on, sure I would come to a
village before long. Instead, just as the light melted away, so did the pavement. A lantern bobbed in the road in front of me. *"Lüguan you mei you?"*
"Mei you," he laughed at me.

Next I approached a rectangle of light delineating the open door of a
lone house. Inside, a young boy was kneeling on the ground shaving a piece
of wood. *"Ni hao,"* I said from the doorway. He glanced up, yelped, and ran
screaming into the next room. His mother emerged immediately, yelling
frantically at me. There was more fear than anger in her face. "I'm sorry.
I'm sorry," I said in English, backing away and snatching off my helmet to
be sure she could see I was a woman, expecting her to calm down when
she heard my voice. She continued shouting and waving her arms. *"Bu dong,
bu dong,"* I stuttered, turning and scurrying back down the stone steps.

I was beginning to feel very lost and forlorn on the dark mountain road.
Finally, a few kilometers later, with my headlamp on in the black of a cloudy
night, I encountered three men repairing a tractor by flashlight. *"Lüguan you
mei you?"*

"You, you," one of them nodded, and got up to lead me down the road to a large rambling building, and in an instant the isolation of the dark road was gone. A woman crouched cooking at her wok and the television was on, broadcasting what appeared to be a British newscast dubbed into Chinese. I stared at the pictures and wondered what was going on in the world. The family brought Greene inside, then eight or ten of us gathered for dinner around a small wooden table. Later that evening, I followed a teenage girl up a wooden staircase to her room. Strips of meat dangled drying from the ceiling, but the rough wooden beams and damp brick walls in the candle-light gave the spartan space a positively merry warmth compared to the usual bleak gray of cement under an electric bulb. She poured two cups of water and we stood side by side on the outside walkway brushing our teeth. She was a hairdresser, and we decided that in the morning she would give me a much-needed trim.

The compulsion to reach Yangshuo had faded in recent days, leaving behind only the utter absurdity of chasing an acquaintance across China. I had turned a passing nothing into something that it had never been. There had been no note at the Victory because by the time he got to Xian, Kirk had forgotten all about me. But now as the girl blew out the candle and we settled head to toe together under one quilt, the warmth of another body next to mine made me want him all over again, made me want to run my hands down the skin of a bare back and slip a leg into a tangle of naked limbs.

"Don't go today," the girl and her family urged me the next morning, "go tomorrow." Fog lay low over the terraced fields that climbed the hills. An ochre brick bridge arched across a stream. There was no traffic on the dirt road. I imagined a lazy day of hiking, catching up in my journal, getting my hair cut. But it would never be that. I wouldn't be able to explain hiking. The crowd of villagers who had gathered to watch me eat breakfast would follow my every step. They would watch every word I wrote. Besides, I had a boy to catch in Yangshuo.

Unseen birds chattered from the steep, verdant hills as I continued south. Thatch roofs and red clay houses dotted the valley. Streams trickled everywhere, the drip and run and tinkle of water harmonizing with the birdsong. Monumental rock formations rose out of nowhere and disap-peared into the mist. I expected to hear the roar of a dinosaur or see, high on a hilltop, a gallant knight on a white steed. I savored the silence—no high-pitched voices, no honking, just misty green tilled and planted land behind branch fences latched with strands of grass. The calm and quiet left me ready for a meal with an audience.

In the thousand kilometers I had ridden since leaving Xian, the amount of chili in a bowl of noodle soup seemed to have increased exponentially with every rotation of the pedals. "Do you want chili?" every cook asked— a spoonful of vicious red powder held out to me with eyebrows raised. "*Yi ding dianr* ("A tiny bit")," I answered, and held the thumbnail of my right hand to my pinkie finger, a gesture akin to the American extended thumb and forefinger. The farther up the pinkie you go, the less chili you want. I like spicy food. At home I sprinkle red pepper flakes into almost anything I cook. But here, in the southern reaches of Hunan Province, I held my thumbnail to the very, very end of my pinkie and sent my voice squeaking high to emphasize "a *teeny-tiny* bit," and still the soup brought tears to my eyes.

I ate soup. I ate noodles. I ate rice. I ate dumplings and tofu and vegetables because those were the words I knew. I ate whatever the cook decided to make, no questions asked, much of it a mystery, none of it ever bad, and some of it, every once in a while, suddenly extraordinary. One day in the middle of nowhere in particular, in a nondescript cement restaurant no different from every other nondescript cement restaurant, a short, retiring woman with a haircut that bespoke no faith in her own attractive- ness led me into the kitchen to point at what I wanted. Picturing a stir-fry with a little bit of everything, I indicated all the vegetables: cabbage, tomatoes, carrots, tofu, red peppers. Within moments she had produced three dishes—carrots and peppers, tofu and cabbage, and a bowl of egg, tomato, and spinach soup. It was enough food for three people. It was also some of the best, most caringly prepared, delicately flavored food I have ever eaten.

Almost no one I met in China conformed to the western image of the shy, quiet Asian. My best friend in fifth, sixth, seventh grades, Lisa Yang, matched all the stereotypes. She was studious and meek. She understood her par- ents' Chinese at home, but I never heard her speak a word of it. She got really good grades and never spoke up in class. I was a Goody Two-shoes teacher's pet, and I was still the rowdy one. In China, women spoke at the top of their lungs, punched me in the arm to get my attention, and laughed loudly in my face.

A woman in bright white plastic rain boots was coming downhill as I was pushing Greene up a series of rocky switchbacks in the rapidly deepening dusk. She was paying no attention to me until a truck groaned past and lit my mountain bike, my panniers, and my pale western visage. Instantly she was standing inches from my face asking in a deafeningly high-pitched yell where I was going.

"Ziyuan," I named the next town on my map.

"Far," she screeched, "dangerous. Sleep at my house." Was immigration so dampening, even through the generations? I wondered, as she grabbed my arm and pulled me back down the rocky slope toward a collection of wooden houses nestled at the bottom of a hairpin curve. I could see nothing in the darkness beyond the edge of the road, but she knew where the houses were, where her friends lived, and as we walked, she called out to them, announcing what she had just found on their little stretch of mountain—an American woman on a bicycle!

As the neighbors gathered on her cement porch, I could understand her telling each newcomer the tale of finding me. I understood the part about wondering whether the figure in the dark was a man or a woman until the headlights lit up my braids. And when she got to the part about telling me that the road was dangerous, that there were bandits, I understood that too, because she grabbed at her ponytail, jerking it violently backward just as she had done to illustrate her point to me. Out of the darkness came the sounds of pigs snuffling in the straw and a river bouncing gently against boulders. As the nighttime chill crept along the valley, she and I moved inside around a dish of coal heat and nibbled sunflower seeds by the flickering light of the television before climbing into bed together.

In the morning she took me visiting. Just down the road in a dark, smoky, dirt-floored home, a tiny fire was tended by an exquisitely beautiful woman, her face in the vacillating glow that of a princess long lost in the wilderness. A stream ran beside the house, some of its water diverted into a rock pool where large fish swayed indolently against the current. The triangular courtyard was roofed in palm and wicker. Bamboo poles lay across the pool, forming a narrow, precarious bridge from which to dip in and catch the fish. A light misting and dripping filled the air, and the whole scene seemed to belong in a tropical-island oasis rather than the damp, chilly mountains.

"Do you want fish?" my host asked, tugging hard on my sleeve.

I didn't know if we were breakfast shopping or if she wanted to send me off with a fish tied to Greene's handlebars. "I like fish," I said.

"Expensive," she said. "Eight *kuai*."

"I have it," I said. Eight *kuai* seemed cheap for a whole fish. A young man balanced out across the bamboo, his bare brown toes curling adeptly around the curves of the wood, and snagged a large fish from the water. Back on dry land, he handed it to an old woman who slipped the hook end of a scale through its gills to weigh it. Then, as she looped a thick reed through its gills and out its mouth and tied it into a handle, he turned to me. "Forty-four *kuai*," he said.

It was a big fish, but forty-four *kuai* was outrageous. I thought I had misunderstood. The pronunciation here was no longer that of the north. *Ch* had sharpened into *ts,* and *sh* had slipped gradually into a more sibilant *ss.* In Beijing, "four" and "ten" had been *si* and *shi*. Here I could no longer reliably differentiate between the two. I was again dependent on finger-counting to distinguish forty-four *(si shi)* from fourteen *(shi si)*. "Shi si?" I asked, but his fingers told me that I had heard correctly: "Si shi." I made a face of great surprise. Then I wondered if fish was in fact a luxury and I shouldn't embarrass everybody by saying it was too expensive.

As I quickly undid my surprised face, I suddenly realized that eight *kuai* had been quoted as the price per *jin,* a measure of weight equal to about half a kilo. I was sure the total was absurd, but they had given me a chance to refuse (or bargain) and I had agreed to their figure. Telling myself that it was five dollars, that five dollars just didn't matter, I paid for a fish that would cost thirty in Seattle. But then the whole way home, with her arm around my waist and the fish swinging from her left hand, my host shouted out to everyone we passed, to every neighbor sitting on their porch or feeding their pigs—"si shi kuai!"—and as every new peal of laughter rolled down the road after us, I felt exponentially more used and stupid and angry. I would have been happy to treat everybody to breakfast; I was not happy to play the fool.

Yet somehow I still believed that it was not mean-spirited cheating. It was an experiment. I could imagine that someone's uncle's boss's brother-in-law's sister had once said that she had heard from a friend's cousin's brother who had been to Beijing that you could ask foreigners for ridiculously huge sums of money for the simplest things, and they were so rich that they would pay. Now they were testing the theory. In a dichotomy incomprehensible to me, her friendliness was genuine, separate from and not in conflict with the price of the fish. Or with her request for 100 *kuai* as she walked Greene and me down the road after breakfast. I gave her 10. She nodded and said good-bye. Two minutes later, she came running after me and handed back the 10 *kuai,* saying, "Bu yao ("I don't want it")."

"Okay," I was surprised. "Thank you."

"Don't go," she told me. "Stay tonight. Go tomorrow."

"No, I am going today."

She stopped and said good-bye again. I put my hand to my heart and thanked her. A few minutes later, she was running back up the hill. "One hundred *kuai,*" she said, writing with a finger on her open palm. She had gone home and her neighbors had encouraged her to try again.

I shook my head, "Ten *kuai.*"

"Eighty," she wrote on her hand.

"Ten."

"Fifty," she said.

I handed her back the ten-*kuai* note.

"Fifty," she wrote.

I may have been clueless as to the price of fish, but I knew what was reasonable for sharing a bed for the night, and ten *kuai* was more than reasonable. It must have seemed unfair that her neighbors should earn so much, and she not. I wanted to tell her to share the profit from the fish, to let her know that I understood the absurdity of that transaction, but I didn't speak enough Chinese. I continued up the mountain and she turned back home.

Up a wet and misty mountain, down a wet and misty mountain. Rough pavement grew out of the dirt and wound along a river to an unsigned fork in the road. Up again into unpopulated coniferous mountains, up and up, and then over the pass and downhill for thirty kilometers, all the way to the main road to Guilin. The next morning I sped along in a light rain. The road was flat, paved, and easy until suddenly it was torn up, cratered, and arduous. Heavy construction machinery worked the raw earth, clawing and digging until it bled thick red mud that splattered up from Greene's tires, flew sideways from passing trucks, and seemed to rain down from the very sky. By the outskirts of Guilin, I was drenched in kilos of the sticky red earth. I stopped at a sidewalk spigot, where a helpful crowd zealously threw buckets of water at me and Greene and her totally unwaterproof panniers. I reached the hotel a little less muddy and a lot wetter.

Two Europeans sat in a shadowy corner of the lobby. They got up, blond, trim, clean-cut German boys, and offered gallantly to help carry Greene upstairs. I stopped at the floor desk to get my key in exchange for a twenty-*kuai* deposit, and invited Jens and Ulf in to wash their now red and muddy hands.

"Why did you leave your key deposit in FEC?" they asked me.

"What difference does it make? I get the money back when I turn in the key."

"But why do you even have FEC?" they asked. In the towns and villages, no one had even heard of FEC, but in the bigger tourist-savvy cities, hotels had no interest in lowly RMB. I could not believe I was about to get the "you can always bargain them down to RMB if you're not a pushover tourist" speech from these clean young men.

"Don't you know there are no more FEC?" Ulf asked. "Since January first. They no longer exist. When you go to the bank to change dollars, they give you RMB."

On the flat sixty-kilometer ride to Yangshuo the next day, a new and confusing thing happened: children threw things at me—pebbles, orange peels, a dead bird. It was a preview of Vietnam's tourist-frequented Highway 1: the contempt and ridicule born of familiarity, which had not yet dwindled into the indifference of the commonplace. Curled below karst mountain-bumps, Yangshuo was Guilin's budget-traveler counterpart and one of China's prime backpacker havens. Save Berlin, I had never seen such a divided city. Three streets were lined with western-style cafés and tourist-toy stores. One short block away was the Chinese village, where a bowl of noodles cost less than a *kuai* and white faces were few and far between. I promptly ran into Jens and Ulf, who had come down the day before, and joined them for muesli and yogurt and a chocolate shake, jazz on the café tape recorder, and tablecloths on the tables.

Greg, a rock climber from Seattle, and his Russian wife, Larissa, were traveling together with Trevor, a stunningly beautiful black Englishman (and I thought the Chinese stared at *me!*) and a twenty-six-year-old worldwise Dutch woman named Barbara. Andy from Manchester had been in Yangshuo for almost two months, his dumpling body ravaged shaky from all the beer, each cigarette held in three trembling effeminate fingers as if he had never smoked before. Landis from Las Vegas was studying martial arts and spending a lot of time with twenty-one-year-old Ping, who ran the Mei-You Café, which made up for mediocre food with good music and a laid-back atmosphere conducive to extended hours of coffee and writing.

I composed Volume III of the letter home. It was wonderful to relax without an audience, to sip a bottle of beer and meander through a whole conversation rather than slurping a bowl of noodles and slamming into the linguistic dead end beyond the Seven Questions. Jens and Ulf rented bicycles and together we pedaled through the surrounding countryside, children everywhere yelling after us, "Hello, hello hello, hello." Jens and I hiked through a quiet valley. Struggling to find the words, fearing to offend, shy and young, he said that with me he had learned for the first time to like a woman "for her way, not her looks."

No one had seen Kirk, and I could no longer remember wanting so much to find him, rushing across China in search of a man I barely knew. Still, every day I glanced at the hotel register for his name. I was staying in one of a dozen cheap hotels in town; he could land at any of them. He could have come and gone. He could have decided to skip Yangshuo altogether. I'll go in the morning, I told myself every evening. But I always managed to stay for one more day. They were lazy days, filled with eating and drinking, playing cards and trading travelers' tales. Stories filtered in of a Los Angeles earthquake big enough to collapse freeways. Someone had heard that 30 people died; someone else had heard 2,000. Then one afternoon it was there, Kirk's name in the register. In the room next to mine. I knocked, but there was no answer. I taped a note to the door. I said I would be at the Mei-You.

I chose a table in the back and pretended to read, my head snapping up every time the door opened. I told myself not to expect anything. I reminded myself that we had spent all of two or three afternoons together in Beijing. The longer I waited and the more I thought about it, the more absurd it became. I hadn't even kissed the man. I had invented a relationship that didn't exist. He wouldn't even remember me. Then he walked through the door.

My first thought when I woke up beside him the next morning was that I wished I had taken more time pedaling south, wished I had cruised the Yangtze and gotten a haircut in a mountain village. But if the roiling need to find him had been assuaged in one night—if, having chased him for two months, having completely, irrationally waited a week for him to arrive in Yangshuo, I now thought idly, "I could leave today"—by the time we had had breakfast together, my hunger had turned into something else, and I didn't leave that day, either. Or the next. For four days and four nights we were together. Touching—my hand on his knee as we sipped beer at the Mei-You. Talking—not great, heart-rending, revelatory conversations, just simple, satisfying one-on-one human dialogue.

From Yangshuo, Kirk's plans would take him to Hong Kong and then on to Nepal. Should I abandon Saigon, I wondered, and go trekking instead? There was something aesthetically pleasing, like the voice-over prologue of a movie, about the idea of spontaneously abandoning my plans and running off with a man to an unexpected country. Except that I still wanted to bicycle to Saigon more than I wanted to hike the Himalayas. Even if Kirk had invited me, which he hadn't. So, soon enough, the time came for us to move on. How to say good-bye? What should this be? How much, how little? A joke, a handshake, a quick, awkward hug, and I dragged myself out onto the road, forcing myself through the kilometers, not caring about Vietnam, not caring about adventure and discovery, wanting only to turn around and pedal back to the safe, easy circle of people who could pronounce my name.

"Because I'm still in love with you, I want to see you dance again," I screamed out Neil Young's words in a desperate echo of Ping's scratchy cassette while the passing Chinese landscape stared immutably back at me, indifferent to the stranger's aching melody. Except of course I wasn't in love with Kirk. The aching longing was not about one man, it was about the ease and comfort of a little world in which I had a specific identity. It was about being a part of something, about belonging, about being two—that odd societal definition that comes with being a pair.

"Didn't you get lonely?" people ask. But on the road, or alone in cold cement rooms, I was never lonely. Bored sometimes. Tired. Frustrated. But not lonely. Loneliness was induced by other foreigners, by things western, by waitresses in stupid red elf costumes, by a man who looked and saw *me,* not just some generic, funny-looking white woman. The yearning and frustration must have turned into pure physical energy because before I knew it I was 100 kilometers and a whole world away from Yangshuo. No one spoke a word of English. Everyone was stumped by how to fill out the hotel register. In the morning there was no yogurt for breakfast, no orange juice, no toast, just a bowl of spicy noodles at a shin-high wooden table. I was back in China, and the screaming lonely ache was already gone.

The 100-kilometer days that had once been impossible were now pouring out of my legs. With 500 kilometers to go to the Vietnamese border, the pavement flew by under Greene's tires like the calendar pages in an old movie. An image, an idea, a challenge that had never been a challenge at all, just a passing comment—"if you ride fast enough, maybe I'll see you in Xian or Yangshuo"—had been fulfilled. I was no longer racing across China after a man, searching for some aesthetic resolution to a relationship that had barely existed; now I was traveling fast because the story I had told myself across 2,000 kilometers had had its ending, and there was nothing left to do but move on.

In Nanning the little hotels would not give me a room, sending me apologetically to a fancy high-rise establishment for the wealthy and foreign. Back in August when the American theater company left Vladivostok, I had agreed to call the director in January. In the meantime, he was going to try to raise the funds to return to Vladivostok and direct a show with the Russian actors. Now his voice boomed across the international line: "I got the money! We go into rehearsal in Vladivostok in April. See you there?"

"Of course. Great. See you there." I hung up and lay in the dark. I wasn't at all sure that it was great. It was now late January. What if I wanted to keep going: Saigon to Cambodia to Thailand to? . . . What if I wasn't done running? Going back to Russia meant eventually going back to the States, and then where was I going to go? As I pedaled down the kilometers of China, I did not think much about Seattle or about my failed life in the theater, which is, of course, the whole point of running away: the distance that dulls the sensations and puts things in perspective, the time that gives you room to breath and regroup. When I was riding, my desires were reduced to the simplest, most immediate little hopes: for the hill to end, for the pavement not to; for there to be a village around the next corner and fewer than thirty people around my bowl of noodles; for someone to understand my pitiable, flat Chinese, for me to hear the words in the sharp cadences of theirs. But as soon as "home" reached out to me it all came flooding back, still only slightly diluted by time and distance. I was not ready to go back.

The receptionist at the hotel in Jiucheng the next night said she had no rooms available, but told me to wait. I did not understand what for, but was willing to bet that if I hung around, I would end up with a place to sleep. Soon two men in their early twenties rolled into the courtyard. Hu and Chai were touring the country by tandem. They spirited Greene up to their room, where we sat grinning at each other and taking turns examining each others' bicycles. They were dressed almost identically in red waterproof pants and bulky blue coats. They wore the only cycling helmets I saw in China, and their heavy tandem was equipped with water bottles and Japanese parts. Chai wore a raucous tee shirt emblazoned "Testament" above a looming black-caped figure of doom, but his freckled face was that of a cherubic schoolboy, his gently serious eyes and pink lips sculpted delicately into a buttermilk complexion. Hu was taller and more garrulous, ready to dive into his classroom English, his demeanor that of an easily popular college athlete. Pinned to the front of his helmet was a red and gold Mao button.

There were three beds in the room and only two of them. "Can I sleep in the third?" I asked. The receptionist had joined us, leaning against the wall and following what she could of our half-Chinese, half-English chatter. The boys glanced at each other and nodded hesitantly, but she shook her head vehemently, and minutes later I had a room to myself.

Hu knocked on my door shortly after seven o'clock the next morning. He and Chai were curious to ride Greene, and I was curious to try the tandem, so as the hills rolled by under a heavy sky, each of them in turn dashed ahead, experimenting with Greene's gears and brakes, while I tried awkwardly to capture the rhythm of the dual pedals. When we stopped for lunch, three separate dishes plus a steaming bowl of soup were ordered by name. How wonderful, I thought, to know more words than "tofu" and "vegetables" and "rice." The fields turned greener, the air thicker, warmer, and wetter as the hours and kilometers passed. Other than lunch, we rode nonstop through the day, arriving in Pingxiang, only twenty kilometers from Vietnam, shortly after dark.

Hu asked where I wanted to spend the night.

"Someplace cheap," I said, not wanting them to assume that I was accustomed to big, fancy hotels.

"Was last night cheap?" he asked.

"Not cheap, but not too expensive."

"We cannot share a room," he said.

"Yes," I laughed, "I know. I don't understand, but I know."

It was simple, he explained, *"Ni shi waiguo ren* ("You are a foreigner")."

⌣· Early morning catch in Sam Son

BICYCLING IN VIETNAM

Time Travel Leaping

CHAPTER 11

"Hello, Hello, Hello"

In the United States, the word "Vietnam" signifies a war, not a country. Fifteen years of jungle and napalm are how we define a centuries-old land. Searching the library shelves, through row after row of books about the war, I finally spied the straightforward title *Vietnam: A History*. I pulled it off the shelf, only to see a cover photo of soldiers browsing a decimated land and the subtitle *The First Complete Account of Vietnam at War*. Vietnam—the word and the country—are inextricably bound to the years when America lost for the first time—lost a fight, lost its claim to moral righteousness, lost its innocence in a morass of lies, death, and disillusionment. Camelot's luster was dimmed, then tarnished beyond repair as the blacks and whites of the young nation's world merged indissolubly into a confusion of grays.

I was nine years old when the infamous last helicopter lifted off from the Saigon embassy roof. My father was too old to have been drafted, and I had no uncles or brothers or even family friends who went to fight. Yet one day when I was three years old, I handed my parents two little drawings on telephone notepad paper. "No More War" I titled the first one. "No More Vietnams," I named the other, as my mother taped the crayon doodles to the kitchen wall. Down the hall from the kitchen, my little sister and I slept in varnished bunk beds in a cheery room with a bright blue dollhouse, a bright yellow chest of drawers, and bright red corduroy curtains. Outside the triptych window a low, bamboo-lined stone wall separated our house from our neighbors' house. For years, lying in the dark, not yet asleep in the top bunk bed, I would stare through that curtain to the bamboo and the stone wall, and superimposed on the reality I would see an endless formation of clean marching soldiers, rifles leaning skyward against their shoulders. I supposed that they were U.S. soldiers; I was not scared that they would hurt me; but they wouldn't go away.

Now, more than twenty years later, drawn to images of empty beaches and mountain tribes, to the challenges of a land whose uniqueness had not

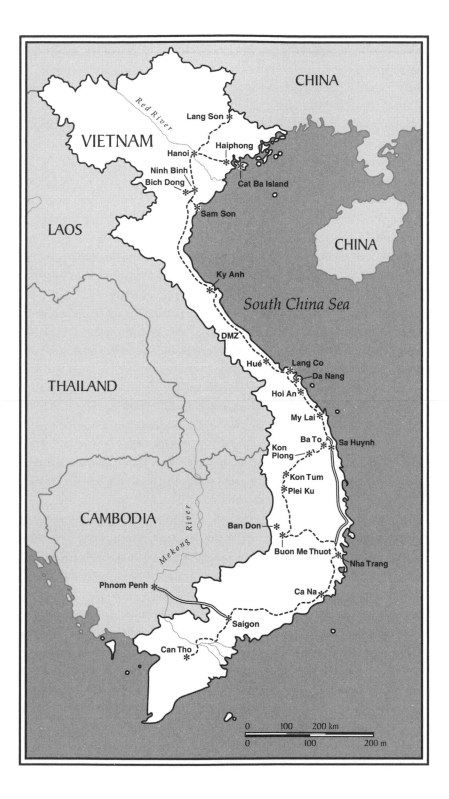

yet been smoothed and contoured for the comfort of the tourist, to a country tempting because it had been forbidden, I stood in a fine falling mist at the edge of Vietnam. And no matter how uninterested I was in doing the War Tour—the DMZ, the Cu Chi Tunnels, or Khe Sanh—no matter that I had never seen *The Deer Hunter, Apocalypse Now,* or *Platoon*—the associative images careening around in my head were overwhelmingly of mud and helicopters and bamboo cages.

Beneath the monumental arch of the Friendship Gate, Hu and Chai and I took pictures together. The arbitrary line in the landscape was an invisible sieve, turning them inexorably back into China, allowing me to pass freely into another world. I pulled off my mud-splattered Seattle tee shirt and gave it to them. Then I waved good-bye and turned Greene's tires toward Vietnam—a land where the American War was just one brief blip in a history of virtually endless struggle against foreign forces.

And once again, I began the process of learning the language and conventions of a new country. Once again, the challenge of the unknown heightened perception as I drank in every new sight and sound and smell. The air was soft and warm. Banana trees poked bunches of green fruit at the sky. Small children chased me, bare feet pattering on hot, wet pavement, reaching out to slap at Greene's panniers, little voices screaming "*Lien xo, Lien xo* ("Soviet, Soviet")." "Don't you know the Soviets are gone?" I wanted to call back, even as I realized that in their short memories, big pale strangers had all been Soviet. "And when did you ever see a Russian on a mountain bike?" I thought, laughing to myself while the real response—"*Hoa ky* ("American")!"—froze in my throat.

At the bottom of a long hill, I rolled into Lang Son. As I rode past, a tiny woman called out to me, "Hotel! Hotel!" She quoted prices in dollars and spoke an English that resembled my Chinese: fluent in the handful of phrases necessary for renting a room, at a loss beyond that one conversation.

Behind the hotel, muddy market streets teemed with diminutive people making their way from vendor to vendor on wooden planks rafting in sucking wet earth. Squares and rectangles of plastic were strung up horizontally at odd, tilting angles. Beneath their humid shade, rows of women squatted alongside wicker baskets of eggs, bananas, and rubber thongs, while all around them children set off strips of pink firecrackers that punctuated the din of the market in a blind series of smoky, lightless bangs.

I found a café, looked in my phrasebook, and ordered *ca phe sua*. A thick ribbon of sweet condensed milk swirled through the glass of dense, gritty

~· *With Hu and Chai beneath the Friendship Gate at the Chinese–Vietnamese border*

coffee. The scents and flavors of France echoed in the rich brown brew and the crisp golden ovoids of bread piled on the counter of the airy, light-blue room, but the white-suited masters of colonial rubber plantations no longer walked the streets outside. Now the most distinctive attire belonged to the ethnic Tay women, whose indigo tops and black velvety headdresses had been there long before the white suits ever came, and were still there, long after they had gone.

A gaunt and leathery old man sat down beside me and stared hard, the corners of his eyes crinkling as he formulated the foreign words, *"D'où venez-vous* ("Where are you from")*?"* The simplest question of all. I even knew the answer in Vietnamese. But suddenly I was hesitant to say the word, in any language. For what seemed to me a very long minute, I stared dumbly back at him as my mind raced through options and images and assumptions. He repeated the question carefully, his eyes asking if his pronunciation were poor and I had not understood him. Across Mongolia and China, I had always answered with a certain conceit, aware of the almost mythical aura of the word. But this was Vietnam. I answered tentatively, apologetically, *"Je suis américaine."*

"Américaine?!" His eyebrows shot up and I braced myself for the anger, the curses, the slap. His wiry, callused hand rose into the air. And as his few remaining teeth angled haphazardly into a broad grin, he reached over and patted me warmly on the shoulder, *"Bienvenue à Vietnam."*

———

There were more colors of green in Vietnam than I had ever imagined existed. Earth and sky seemed to be playing a slow-motion game of catch: Like children keeping a balloon afloat with the tips of their fingers, the earth tossed up reflections of young rice, the sky dropped them back gently on the warm mist, and the very air shimmered green. Tiny children perched astride massive water buffalo that lumbered along the fringes of rice paddies as serenely luminescent as an emerald mirage, and all across the liquid fields stretching to the adumbrate horizon, conical straw hats bobbed above brown backs bent in the perpetual planting and plucking of a life sustained from the earth. Slicing through the midst of the timeless fields of green was a tumultuous patchwork of pavement and pebbled dirt. Bicycles, pedestrians, and mopeds, tilting buses and rickety carts, all piled high and stuffed full, jostled down the noisy, narrow strip of Highway 1 toward Hanoi. Shrill, whistling, piercing horns blew through my body. Visions of low-flying planes strafing desperate fleeing masses resonated in my head.

I had entered Vietnam on February 4, 1994, four days after the U.S. embargo had been lifted. Two days later, I rode into Hanoi. The city was still plastered with magazine covers announcing the recission of the ban, but business had clearly been booming for some time. Well-stocked sections of *Teach Yourself English* primers filled the book shops, and white men in suits hurried down the streets accompanied by young female interpreters. I had expected Vietnam to be a step backward, materially, from China, but before America turned its hurt and righteous back, it had been in Vietnam in full military-cultural force for years, in immediate succession to decades of French influence; two decades of economic quarantine did not compare to China's centuries of self-imposed isolation. Also, the fact that the United States hadn't talked to Vietnam for twenty years did not mean that nobody else had. The streets were full of Toyotas from Japan, Kodak film from Singapore, and Coca-Cola from Thailand.

Vietnam felt more westernized, less insular, than China, yet at the same time more my image of bustling, sweating Asia. Bicycles and *xich lo,* the Vietnamese pedicabs, swarmed through the streets. Sidewalks and courtyards were copiously sprinkled with *com-pho* stalls, the rice and noodle stands that range in size from a dozen tables under the shade of a plastic awning to a single shin-high bench opposite a squatting cook and her pot of boiling water. The maze of narrow, colorful streets in the old city emanated the character of history rather than the blankness of gray Communist angles. There was decoration and ornamentation and architecture beneath the fresh blue sky.

The crooked, crowded lanes were humming as the city geared up for Tet, the holiday marking both the lunar new year and the coming of spring. Shopping bags bulged with ingredients for the celebrations. Plum-blossom branches, balloons, and many-colored tinseled decorations filled the streets around Hoan Kiem Lake, the numinous center of the city. According to legend, it was from these waters that the aristocratic landowner Le Loi, on his way to becoming emperor and founder of Vietnam's Le Dynasty, received the magic sword with which he later routed his nation's Chinese oppressors, ultimately forcing them to recognize Vietnamese independence in 1427. In February 1994, there were no magical swords or boating emperors to be seen in the placid lake. Instead, the circumference of the opaque jade water was traced by strolling pairs of lovers, cliques of teenage boys in neatly belted blue jeans, and pods of ponderous European tourists.

Vietnam was a country changing at the speed of technology, time-travel leaping from hand-planted rice fields to cellular telephones. Not far from the crowds streaming across a bridge to a centuries-old island pagoda, the central post office commanded the respect of modernity from behind a towering white facade. Inside, high-tech international telecommunications were efficient and effortless at a price of seven dollars per minute, while outside on the street, barefoot, torn-shirted men hauled huge loads on their bent backs and earned less than twenty dollars a month.

I sent a happy birthday fax to my mother in Southern California and collected mail from poste restante. The post office was full of foreigners collecting mail, making phone calls, and sending faxes. The whole city was full of foreigners. The French were middle-aged, traveling in minivans, charmed by the expansive friendliness of their exotic former colony. The Germans, Americans, and Australians were twentysomething budget backpackers fighting a two-tiered pricing system in a land where they could never pretend to be native. Lolling around beers in their chosen cafés, they talked of money and visa extension scams, money and train tickets, money and cheap, cheaper, cheapest hotel rooms. "Hi nice to meet you where did you come from how much did your ticket cost?" They talked about where they were going, not about where they had been. The journey was constantly being planned rather than savored.

I, too, was guilty of this, obsessed by kilometers and reaching the next dot on the map. But by choosing the bicycle, I had forced the places between the dots to become the focus of the trip. Traveling by train, cities are the point and the destination. Traveling by bicycle, cities become oases, little caesuras in the journey, respites from the road. In cities, I made contact with home and other travelers. I ran errands. I replenished my energy and eagerness.

This process of renewal was taking longer and longer as the trip continued. In a sunny little downtown room overlooking a leafy courtyard, I relaxed into hibernation. My body was exhausted, demanding recovery time. My stomach was unsettled, and I had an eye infection. Dots and globs of yellow mucus clung to the corners of my eyes, gluing my lashes shut overnight. One morning I didn't even bother getting out of bed. I lay under the mosquito net reading *The Quiet American*. It was a short book. When I finished and still didn't feel like getting up, I flipped back to page one and read it again. That afternoon, there was blood on my underwear. The immense relief—no impossible baby, no savage tumor—was almost immediately tempered by the inconvenience of menstruation. I was very glad it was there. I just wished it would go away again. Which it did. I had one period in eight months. As soon as I reached Russia, as soon as I stopped cycling, I would again be as regular as clockwork.

✎ *Boys sitting on the train tracks, between Hanoi and Haiphong*

Outside my quiet hideaway, the loud banging of firecrackers was increasing daily. Teenage boys plotted surprise attacks on each other. Children tossed them helter-skelter, laughing as the explosions startled unwary adults. At midnight on the eve of Tet, the din exploded to new proportions. Streams of white fireworks shot across Hoan Kiem Lake, and the towering tree in the hotel courtyard disappeared completely behind the smoke. The feasting would last late into the night. The festive spirit would continue for days   the city quiet, shops closed, streets empty as families gathered together at home.

One afternoon I meandered to the Hotel Metropole and sat in the plush café nibbling an almond croissant and reading the *International Herald Tribune*. In a snowy place called Norway, athletes were competing in something called the Olympic Games. Back in my hotel courtyard, I flipped Greene over. Unsure whether I should change the chain without changing the freewheel and chainwheels (of which I didn't have spares), unsure whether I knew how to install a new chain, unsure, in fact, whether I had correctly diagnosed why her gears were not shifting smoothly, I sat on the sunny paving stones with my repair book, picked out another tool I had never used, and removed the gritty old chain. It dangled a full inch longer than the shiny new one. "We are very surprised," said one of the men who had gathered

⌣· *The lagoon on Cat Ba Island*

to watch, "that a woman can do this." I grinned and shrugged my shoulders, slipping the new chain into place as if I had done it a hundred times.

⌣•

The major seaport for the Red River Delta, and Vietnam's third-largest city, Haiphong lies six flat hours east of Hanoi. A short ferry ride east of Haiphong is the mystical, pelagic world of Halong Bay. Named for a legendary creature whose thrashing plunge through the waters carved out deep rifts and valleys and left only a scattering of peaks in its wake, the Bay of the Descending Dragon is a misty archipelago of caves and silent waterways and half-seen sails where dragon tales do not seem fantastical.

Small wooden boats bobbed in the sea's undulations as the ferry tied up at the Cat Ba Island pier. The village was shuttered and quiet, most shops and restaurants still closed for Tet. The sprawling government hotel was empty, but the cozy new mini-hotel was full, its half dozen rooms home to

Swedish, Swiss, Dutch, South African, Australian, and German travelers. Sitting on the floor over dinner and beer, with the hotel's pet monkey, a baby on a chain, peering down at us with ancient, profoundly sorrowful eyes, I had to admit to myself that my disappointment at not being the only foreigner on the island was purely theoretical. In truth, it was a relief. I was scared of launching myself into this country. Intimidated, somehow.

On the brief ride from the ferry landing to the hotel, even the smallest children, many trained to hold out their hands for money, had screeched, "Hello, hello, hello," as I passed their disdainful laughter following me down the street. My temper was frazzled. I was impatient and intolerant, fighting the new world instead of receiving it, pushing it away instead of slipping inside and letting the annoyances roll by. What if I didn't want to stay until April? I wondered as I climbed the stairs to my tiny attic room. I was not drawn to explore this shrill land. I wish I had pedaled more slowly across China, I thought as I drifted off to sleep, regretting again the lost chance to cruise the Yangtze.

The next morning a group of us headed for Cat Ba National Park, founded in 1986 with a mandate to protect the flora and fauna of the island's tropical evergreen forest from the ravages of poaching, logging, and the ceaseless expansion of human habitation. The guide was less than eager to lead us into the forest. He warned us that the sodden weather would have brought out the leeches. He said he could show us one of several caves where excavations had revealed the stone tools and bones of civilizations more than 6,000 years old, but could not reduce the usual fee for a visit to both the rain forest and the cave. We knew a scam when we heard one: scare the tourists with tales of bloodsuckers and do half the work for the same price. We insisted on the hike.

For two hours he led us down muddy trails through dense, wet underbrush. I wanted to see monkeys or huge snakes, but the only wildlife we saw, curled tightly under a leaf, was one tiny, bright green serpent. Back in the guide's office, Peter from Switzerland was the first to discover a leech buried in his ankle. Whipping off shoes and socks, checking other vulnerable body parts, at least half of the expedition found the sluglike creatures in their feet and ankles. I was lucky—only one dripping spot of blood, its sucker already fallen away.

By the time we had walked back to the village, the pendulum had swung, and I honestly wanted to get away from the crowd of foreigners. I went for a walk. A narrow, muddy path wound among the houses that were squeezed between the lagoon and the hills. In dirt-floored, thatch-roofed shacks, barefoot enthusiasts sang heartily to karaoke videos playing on color television screens. Halfway down what I had just realized was a dead-end alley, an old woman, her toothless mouth dripping crimson, her lips and gums stained black with betel nut, waved me into her home. The shutterlike green wooden doors were flung open, a half dozen pairs of sandals scattered neatly in front of the entrance. I slipped off my big, awkward sneakers and followed her inside.

A low table and four beautifully carved chairs of smooth dark wood stood on the tiled floor. A toddler in a fuzzy green hat and a striped jumper gurgled in his mother's arm. Two young men in loose button-down shirts and neatly belted, fashionably baggy trousers crouched barefoot on their chairs. We sipped tea and stumbled through a phrasebook conversation. Their kitchen was a tiny fire flickering in a stone shelter across the puddled dirt lane. Lunch was served in tin pots set in baskets to keep them from scorching the wicker floor mat. Vegetable, potato, squid. We sat on the mat, bowls of rice in hand, helping ourselves out of the various dishes. As our mutual anonymity evolved into a connection between individuals, I wished I had turned east from Lang Son and followed the back roads to the coast, avoiding the ease of Hanoi and taking myself into the country. I wished I hadn't stayed so long in China. I wanted more time to explore Vietnam.

The stone islets that burst from the South China Sea to create the magical world of Halong Bay are the geographical siblings of Yangshuo's karst pinnacles. Back on the mainland, ninety-five kilometers south of Hanoi, the same rocketing, egg-shaped formations rise from an indecisive realm of mellifluous soil that parts before the advancing prows of shallow skiffs, a realm of dark waters so thick they are the liquid cousins of the earth. In Bich Dong, four kilometers inland from Highway 1, a dozen women sat floating in shallow reed and bamboo skiffs at the edge of a parking lot scattered with spotless white minivans. I bought a ticket and slipped into a low boat with a woman named Thang. Facing forward, she rowed up the waterway into a silent valley of stunning green, past people and water buffalo working knee-deep in the rice paddies, plowing, hoeing, sowing. Thang's conical hat tied under her chin with a bright pink band, and she wore an immaculate white blouse and creased blue trousers. Her skin was buttery-smooth, and a captivating astuteness shone from her round eyes.

We passed under a natural stone archway and came out into a floating market. A dozen boats butted up against each other in the ripples, and the meek oarswomen had turned into hard-selling merchants hawking embroidered tablecloths and napkins. Other women floated up through the reedy water to sell beer and Coca-Cola. French tourists, swaying in their boats, were busily buying the neat, handcrafted work. Thang shrugged resignedly at her friends as they all inquired of each other how sales were progressing: *"Di xe dap* ("She goes by bicycle")." Thang understood that I was not about to stuff a tablecloth into Greene's panniers.

"Where do you sleep?" she asked as we left the market behind and drifted on through the green, watery world of rice paddies and karst pinnacles.

"In a hotel in Ninh Binh," I said, naming the town back on Highway 1 where I had spent the previous night.

"Tonight you can sleep at my home?" She invented a way to earn some money even if I wouldn't buy a tablecloth.

"How much?"

"And you eat dinner and breakfast at my home." We passed the phrasebook back and forth.

"How much?"

"How much does the hotel cost?"

I felt badly that she hadn't earned anything from me, imagining the meager salary—if any—that the oarswomen received beyond the sale of their tablecloths. I was also eager to spend an evening in a Vietnamese home. We settled on a price, and she had something new to yell to her friends as we passed them on the way back: her tourist was going to sleep at her house!

From the parking lot, we followed a narrow path between close stone walls into a dirt courtyard. Two stone steps led up to an open porch. Inside, the one-room cement home was spare and simple, but somehow possessed of a hominess rare in utilitarian China. Two corners of the room were taken up by wide wooden beds. They were romantic beds. Movie beds. Double four-poster beds draped in mosquito netting. In the center stood a low table and four curvaceous wooden chairs. Thang introduced me to her skinny husband and her two young sons, flat-faced effervescent boys with straight-edge bangs above delicately arching eyebrows. The younger brother, his face already more studious than his grinning sibling's, wore his dark blue trousers held up by suspenders of string. Dinner was communal bowls of greens, omelet, hard-boiled eggs, and bananas, all arranged on a big silver platter around which we sat barefoot on one of the beds. Thang addressed me as "Madame." I told her to call me "Erika." She grinned and nodded, "Yes, Madame Erika."

"No, just Erika." I wanted to explain that as far as I was concerned, she wasn't working for me. I was a friend visiting her home. I wanted her to understand that in my culture, such deference was neither required nor expected. She grinned broadly and repeated, "Yes, Madame Erika." In Vietnamese, all names are prefaced with an appropriate form of address. In her culture, to call me simply "Erika" would be rude. I read that in my phrasebook, days later. All that evening, I called her simply "Thang."

After dinner, friends, neighbors, and relatives came to drink tea and talk. In one evening, I learned more Vietnamese than I had in the previous two weeks, finally mastering the Seven Questions as they were asked and answered over and over. A dozen of us were muddling through a conversation when, from across the table, one of Thang's brothers asked if I wanted to sleep with him. His hands, fingers, and eyebrows posed the question unsalaciously but unmistakably. When I shook my head, Thang tapped me on the shoulder and asked if I would prefer another of the men. "No," I shook my head, offended and bewildered. "You want a prostitute. You think all Americans are prostitutes," I began trying to piece together from the phrasebook. But the more I thought about it, the less sure I was that this accusation, even stated coherently, would be correct. Their question was straightforward. They weren't looking for a prostitute. They seemed to honestly believe that as a western woman, I would be eager to have sex with anyone, anywhere, anytime. They were, I slowly decided, candidly trying to give me what they thought I wanted. I closed the phrasebook.

Just then, I felt a hand on my left arm, fingertips stroking, tugging gently at the short, sun-bleached hair. An older woman sat curled into the chair next to me. Fascinated by pale skin and body hair, and uninhibited by any societal interdiction against touching a stranger, Chinese and Vietnamese women regularly petted my forearms. I would be slurping a bowl of noodles or asking directions when I would suddenly feel a small, soft hand exploring my body. (A strong taboo prevented the men from touching me. They asked openly if I wanted to have sex, but not once did a male hand initiate even the most innocent contact.) I had learned to respond with corresponding strokes, reaching out and running my fingertips up the women's delicate hairless limbs. They inevitably started, stared at me, and then recognition would burst into dark eyes and everyone would laugh. While more fingers reached out for my arms, giggling and tugging exploratively at the odd, hirsute skin, I asked the older woman if she had lived in the area during the war.

"Yes," she nodded.

"Did the Americans bomb here?"

"Oh, yes," she nodded emphatically, fingering the rain of bombs.

"Don't you hate me?" The question burst out of me in English.

The woman waited patiently while I pieced it together in Vietnamese. "No," she shook her head, puzzled, when she finally understood the question.

I stared at her. How could she not?

———•———

"Hello, hello, hello" reverberated in the air around me. As it ceased to be a greeting and became an attack, a one-sided game, I came to hate the word "hello." "Hello whey ah zoo fum?" they yelled from speeding mopeds, looking for a reaction, not an answer. "Hello, hello, hello," they shouted, and a hello in response elicited only hurls of laughter, or a new barrage of hellos. "Hello where are you from. Hello how old are you. Hello are you married," they called, and before I could open my mouth, they answered themselves with a chortling chorus of "yes"es. "Hello, hello, hello," men yelled, hanging out of bus doors fingering lascivious V signs (and they didn't mean "victory!") or cupping suggestive hands in bawdy reference to their own endowments. "Hello, hello, hello" as they slowed their motorbikes to point a finger at me, then back at themselves, raising their eyebrows in question, or some-times asking outright—"Hey, zoo me boom-boom?" It was tempting to yell back—"Sure, how about right here in this rice paddy?"—but I was not com-pletely sure that they wouldn't call my bluff.

Two hundred kilometers south of Hanoi, where the northern bulge of Vietnam's egg-timer shape begins to narrow into a skinny, serpentine strip of land, I turned east off Highway 1 and aimed Greene's tires toward the Pacific Ocean. Like any off-season beach town anywhere in the world, Sam Son dozed lazily in the salty coastal air. I found a guesthouse, ate a delicious dinner of fresh prawns, and went to bed expecting to be quickly lulled to sleep by the low rumble of the nearby sea. But ten minutes after I had turned out the light, the police were knocking on the door. Hating Vietnam, hat-ing all of Asia where they never leave you alone, I wrenched it open. The two men made a move to walk in, but I didn't budge. "Passport?" they asked. I nodded and shut the door to dig the passport out of my waistbelt. When I opened it again, the young officers were in the next room, looking through a Vietnamese couple's documents. The guesthouse manager was watching, her eyes wide, her hands clasped to her red cheeks. Her face stopped me in my tracks. I knew that look.

It is impossible for human beings, other perhaps than a genius (and perhaps that is the true definition of genius), to understand or interpret the world in terms other than those of their own experience and knowledge. A blind person cannot describe the difference between a blade of new grass and a eucalyptus leaf in terms of different greens, because shades of green do not exist in a colorless world. Texture, shape, and odor are the rubric within which a blind person defines and differentiates the grass and the leaf. Likewise, an American teenager on an early winter Leningrad street in 1983 may only be able to understand an old man's rebuff as rudeness, having not yet learned the rules and givens of a society in which communication with a foreigner is potential cause for serious retribution. But one of the great rewards of travel is an expanded rubric of understanding. Exposure to different cultures cannot but broaden a traveler's frame of reference, and the fear that I had not understood in an old man's eyes in 1983 I recognized immediately in a middle-aged woman's face in 1994.

It was the second time since arriving in Vietnam that I had seen signs of the web still woven. In Haiphong, on the way to Cat Ba Island, I had spent the evening with two nineteen-year-old boys eager to practice their English. Sitting in deep wicker chairs in a sidewalk café hung with a strand of little red Christmas lights, we had sipped hot chocolate and talked, while somewhere behind us Bruce Springsteen growled from a scratchy tape. The next morning, the boys had appeared at my door bearing the gift of a traditional Tet cake. I had invited them in while I finished packing Greene, then we had gone out for a late breakfast of fish soup. As we ate, they were visibly nervous about something, and finally admitted that the hotel manager had yelled at them for entering my room, a foreigner's room, a foreign woman's room. Their eyes darted constantly out to the street, as if expecting the police to materialize momentarily. I had tried to allay their fears. Since they had not told the manager their names, I reasoned, the police could not find them, but that had clearly been weak reassurance in a state where the price for misbehavior remained threateningly high.

Now the hotel manager's terrified eyes reminded me that I had to take these smooth-faced boys in uniform seriously, if not for my own sake, then for hers. I relaxed my angry shoulders and handed them my passport, shuttling helpfully through the pages to point out the Vietnamese visa. They copied down the information, thanked me politely, and sent me back to my room, but as soon as the sun rose the next morning, the manager was knocking on my door. She held out a piece of paper on which a neat hand had carefully penciled in English, "The police are here to see you. Please to come. Thank you."

Two men in uniform sat drinking tea with her husband. They offered me tea and cookies, and the younger of the two officers explained in English that the hotel had neglected to register me with the police. He said that because the officers who had inspected the hotel the previous evening spoke no English, they had been unable to ask the appropriate questions. His superior sat quietly sipping tea and nodding. They asked where I was from. They asked how I liked Vietnam. Where else had I been? Could they see my passport? Was I having any difficulties traveling in Vietnam? It took an hour to cover two minutes of real information, because the smiles and tea and cookies were ultimately more important than the facts. Where was I going next? What food did I like best in Vietnam?

Apparently properly registered now, I wandered down to the fog-shrouded beach, where the waves were constant low rollers not big enough to crash. Battered wooden boats lay like tired ghosts on the dry sand and boys played soccer without goals or sidelines other than the sea. I looked across the gray-brown, sandy water toward the invisible horizon. Somewhere out there was the west coast of America. Friends could be standing on the distant shore looking across at me, nothing between us but a bit of water. For the first time in months, my eyes could not find the landscape's extremity. I inhaled deeply, as if to pull the peace of the wide-open expanse into my body, but my senses were taut with the knowledge that at any moment a screeching, pointing, laughing crowd could materialize out of nowhere.

Did I really not like Vietnam, I wondered as I walked down the beach past a fishing boat delivering its morning catch, or was I just weary?

The sun slowly burned away the fog, and I lay in the sand and read peacefully for a whole hour before a group of boys found me. They settled in a ring around the stranger. Children of the sun and sand, they were bantam and lithe, every muscle clearly defined beneath their threadbare clothes. Their phrases of English lived in a vacuum with no real understanding. They knew a few questions, and maybe some of them were genuinely curious about how old I was or why my husband wasn't with me, but mostly they just wanted a response—to elicit sounds from my mouth. They gabbled "Yes, yes, yes," but would have done the same if I had answered that I was from Pluto. They were screeching and laughing all around me, so close and loud that at one point I literally screamed and clapped my hands over my ears, which of course only made them laugh harder. But even then I knew that they were not truly malicious. I knew that if I would take the time, make the effort, look them in the eyes and speak a little more of their language,

I could almost certainly turn myself from an alien object into a human be-ing. Unfortunately, I, wearily, wanted to read my book more than I wanted to talk to them.

The boys in Sam Son were playing, like children pulling the wings off a mosquito, toying with something so strange as to be not human. I was the most entertaining thing they had found on their beach in a while, and they were just having fun. That was not always the case. Back on Highway 1 the next day, as I sped south under a leaden sky, a boy child slapped me, the look on his face as hard and angry as the hand that left a smarting red imprint on my forearm. A teenage girl pinched my arm, twisting sharply to make it hurt. A little girl with hatred in her young eyes threw something as I passed, some-thing unquestionably intended to hit. Animosity was expressed openly only by the children, but they had to have learned it from someone. Yet because they still yelled *"Lien xo,"* because the adults still guessed *"Phap* ("French")?" I knew that, contrary to what I had feared, contrary to the expectations of the question I would constantly be asked back home—"How did they react to you being American?"—the hostility and mocking laughter were not anti-American. They were anti-foreigner, generic. I was an outsider, an alien in a society that had for its very self-preservation been forced to close ranks tightly against the alien.

Two boys saw me coming up a grade and quick as lightning strewed their empty baskets in my way. As I swerved, they grabbed at Greene's rear rack to drag me to a stop. The rage in my eyes when I whirled to face them froze the little bodies in their aggressive tracks. I was furious. I had never been hated before, and had no response other than rage. I wanted to hit them, to hurt them, to run crushingly over their baskets. Yet even as this reflexive violence welled inside me, I was appalled to see the fear in the children's frames. In the world of their short lives, it was possible, even probable, that I *would* strike back. They had no idea that I was incapable of hitting them. How they would have laughed, I thought wryly, my brief moment of sympathy swinging quickly back into cynicism, had they real-ized my impotence.

The next day, two boys on bicycles appeared pedaling alongside me, watching. Then suddenly one of them reached out and pushed at Greene's rear panniers. They were children, little boys, ten, maybe twelve years old. And there I was, retaliating, reaching out and pushing as hard as I could on their handlebars. They were good riders and did not fall, while I swerved all over the road, unbalanced by my own act. But they did stop following me. Maybe, I reflected bitterly, I'm finally speaking Vietnamese.

That evening, as I turned up the rocky hotel drive in Ky Anh, a small figure dashed into my peripheral vision, scampering up the incline behind me, chirruping, "Where are you from?"

"America," I panted, thinking, "If you touch Greene, I'm going to kill you. I don't care if I spend the rest of my life in a Vietnamese jail, I am going to kill you." The little feet pattered closer. The little hands reached out. The little fingers latched on to Greene's rack. That was it. She was a dead child. I was going to hit her. I was going to leap off my bicycle and smack a child— who, I suddenly realized, was pushing my bicycle up the hill, propelling me forward until Greene's front tire ran right into the hotel's cement porch. As my left foot landed on the ground, she was already standing in front of me, her bright little girl eyes sparkling, telling me to wait while she summoned the manager.

He showed me to a cement room with a damp quilt and thick wicker mat on each wooden bed. Bright Eyes promptly appeared outside the open, unglassed window to ask if I was hungry: *"An com?"* The Vietnamese expression *an com,* like the Chinese *chi fan,* means "to eat rice."

"Yes," I said, "soon. But first, tea." I pointed to the thermos, teapot, and container of loose leaves on the table and invited her in.

"No, no," she shook her head.

"Yes, yes, come in, sit down, have tea," I insisted.

The deep chair swallowed her tiny frame. She was thirteen but looked about nine. She was brave and she was smart. She reminded me of Bat-Ölzii back in Arshaant. She reminded me of Enkhjargal. Her chin was pointed and expressive. Her wide eyes looked straight into mine. She told me I was beautiful. I was filthy, fat, sweaty, and exhausted, my face cratered with the raw pink remains of menstrual pimples. I told her that *she* was beautiful. "No," she shook her head, "I not beautiful, you beautiful. Vietnamese not beautiful, you beautiful." She seemed to mean it, seemed to believe it, and sitting there that night, I could not imagine what might have taught the beautiful little girl to think such a thing. I would find no answer to that question for another 300 kilometers.

We had our tea, she showed me how to draw water from a well in the yard to wash my face, then Bright Eyes led me down the hill to her parents' restaurant. One of their two low-ceilinged rooms was lined with a half dozen wooden tables; in the other, the family's beds were crammed into dark, airless corners behind blackened pots hanging over an open fire. While her mother prepared dinner, I tried to explain my trip. Mongolia wasn't even listed in my phrasebook, so I settled for having begun in Beijing. Her father, a bulky man with a gentle, pock-marked face, responded that he had studied for five years in southern China. *"Ni hui suo putonghua, ma* ("Do you speak Chinese")*?"* I asked him. *"Duì,"* he nodded. After two months of linguistic frustration in China I suddenly, ridiculously, found myself thrilled by the ease of communicating in Chinese. Three weeks earlier I had felt that, beyond the Seven Questions, I could say nothing in Chinese; now I felt as if I could carry on an entire conversation. Everything is relative. Compared to ten phrases of Vietnamese, a few hundred words of Mandarin felt practically fluent.

I chattered happily; he translated for his family; and over heaping bowls of beef noodle soup, the generic metamorphosed into the specific. They looked at me and did not see an outsize, pallid alien; I looked at them and did not see shrill, contemptuous assailants. We looked, and saw each other, saw individual human beings with histories and futures, virtues and idiosyncrasies not defined by either the color of our skin or our passports. Surrounded by the warmth of the family dinner, the mocking jeers of the highway faded into the distant background.

CHAPTER 12

Mine the Need to Atone

The road played tag with the seashore, running along the coast, climbing inland over a mountain, dropping back to the sound of crashing waves. Sand dunes rose behind huddles of thatched roofs, and from beyond them came the roll of the sea. I envisaged a night in my tent on a fabulously empty beach, but in spite of the peace of the evening in Ky Anh, I knew that turning down one of those deceptively quiet lanes would instantly produce a horde of screaming, pointing, laughing children. And the sight of me setting up a tent, never mind trying to sleep in it, would be the best show since the Americans helicoptered off a Saigon roof. Even as I claimed to avoid the war, my metaphors came in its terms.

A light drizzle was falling, and while I fantasized about hot white sand and green palm fronds dancing against a blue sky background, gritty brown puddle-water spat up at me from Greene's tires. The narrow road was quiet, the landscape eerie. With every passing kilometer, it looked more like a set for a science fiction movie, like an oddball animator's oddly cratered planet. Phantom bridges were remembered only by their orphaned pilings. Unnatural concavities brimming with water warped the green earth, ponds now where the bombs once fell. Twenty-five days and a thousand kilometers after crossing the border out of China, I pedaled through the DMZ and into southern Vietnam, a region still as surely distinct from the north as the American South is different from the Pacific Northwest.

For tourists making only one stop between Saigon and Hanoi, the ancient imperial city of Hué is the stop to make. Like the lace of a gown that was once the finest in the county, Hué retains the subtle elegance of past primacy. The capital of Vietnam under the Nguyen emperors (1802–1945), Hué was devastated during the Tet Offensive of 1968, but never lost its place as the cultural and intellectual heart of central Vietnam. The women's silken *ao dais*—the flowing tunic slit up the sides and worn over loose pants— mirrored the gentle curves and currents of the Perfume River. The men with one long pinkie fingernail were in perfect harmony with the aristo-cratic echoes of the streets where they sat sipping coffee. The stores of tra-ditional herbal and faunal medicines where neatly labeled drawers and bottles reached from floor to ceiling echoed ancient learning.

I checked in to a spacious, high-ceilinged colonial room, took a hot shower, and hung up my soaking clothes, which would dry only slowly in the warm dampness. Across the courtyard in the hotel restaurant, I ran into a Dutch couple I had met in Yangshuo. While I had been pedaling south, they had flown back to Holland for his father's funeral, then returned to Asia to continue their trip. I met a doctor from Massachusetts who had bought his travel guides in the Seattle bookstore where I had worked. "They told me the owner was in Vietnam," he said. "No," I laughed, "I think she's somewhere in Africa. I'm here."

In China I had scorned the tourists whose only topic of conversation was money, whose every tale was about native cheating and triumphant traveler bargaining. In Vietnam I was appalled to hear that my own "happy" stories were simply accounts of honest prices and friendly negotiation. Over lunch with an Australian couple at a guidebook-recommended restaurant, I told the story of a young woman in an isolated restaurant who served me a bowl of soup, a tomato, and two sodas, then pulled a price of 12,000 *dong* out of the air. I did not know exactly what the soup or the tomato should cost, but every little bottle of Festi cola in Vietnam cost 1,500 *dong*. I esti-mated the soup should be 2,000 and the tomato 500. "Soup," I said, "3,000. One tomato, 1,000. Seven thousand—okay?" The young woman grinned and nodded.

When the bargaining was so friendly, so good-natured, when it was a game mutually understood, I was willing to pay more than a local. I was even happy to pay more than a local. A difference of 5,000 *dong* was a dif-ference of about fifty cents. So even if 7,000 *dong* was a few thousand more than she would have charged the subsistence rice farmer down the road, how could I really care? How could I really care about an extra twenty-five cents if those twenty-five cents might feed her child that night, when in my world they were the tax on a *grande latte*? Put in that perspective, the righ-teous argument that everyone should always pay the same price lost much of its moral persuasiveness. On the other hand, it was true that if, as the tourist population expanded, vendors, salespeople, and restaurateurs all learned that they could regularly earn twice as much from the foreigners as from their neighbors, prices risked being driven up out of the range of the locals.

As in most things, I believed that there was an acceptable middle ground. It lay in the spirit of the bargaining. It lay in being willing to pay something more, but not ridiculously much more. It lay in finding a way not to feel personally attacked or cheated every time I was charged more just because of the color of my skin. It lay in learning fair prices as quickly as possible so that I could bargain from a position of knowledge rather than just assuming in a fury that I was being drastically overcharged. It lay in understanding that the quality of the journey was not defined, in inverse proportion, to its expense. It lay in learning not to take part in the "how little did you pay?" competitions with other foreign travelers.

All of which was easy in theory, and somewhat harder in practice, because money did seem to define every interchange in Vietnam. I generally felt less welcome there as a person than as a well of cash, and I could not seem to rise above feeling hurt and angered by this objectification. In a tiny village south of Ky Anh, where I did not expect there to be a guest-house, I had stopped at a *com-pho* stand and asked anyway. *"Nha khach* ("Hotel")?" The four people in the restaurant instantly metamorphosed into twenty, pressing in close around me and Greene. *"Nha khach?"* I repeated. There was silence. Or, rather, there was a lot of chatter, but none of it was directed at me.

Then suddenly an older woman reached out from the crowd and flattened her open hand against my left breast. For all the direct questions about sex, for all the petting of arm hair and pale skin, no one had touched me like that before. *"Con gai!"* she yelled and, just before I could react, before I could slap her hand away, my brain registered what she had said and I burst out laughing instead, tugging at my braids and saying, "Yes, *con gai* ("girl")." And suddenly the whole crowd was laughing and tugging at my braids, the women all patting my breasts and shouting, *"Con gai, con gai!"* With my gender now established, one woman grabbed my wrist, nodded vigorously, and said, *"Nha khach."*

"Where?" I asked.

"Nha khach," she repeated, and waved at a double wooden bed squished into a back corner of the restaurant. I rolled Greene into the restaurant, then walked back out to the street. I wanted to go to the beach. The ocean was audible from beyond the towering wall of sand, but there was no clear path over the dunes. "Beach," I found in the phrasebook, and showed it to the women.

Nod, nod, nod. They stood still.

"Follow," I found, and pointed to myself, pointed to them.

Nod, nod, nod. The woman who had tested my gender pointed to herself, but still nobody was moving.

"*Tien,*" she said then.

I didn't know the word.

"*Tien,*" she repeated.

I held out the phrasebook. She shook her head and scrabbled inside her blouse for something, but another woman was quicker, pulling several bills from a pocket, "*Tien.*" Money. I reacted absolutely and without hesitation, "No!" and turned on my heel back into the restaurant. Confusion broke loose. "*Toi di. Di.* ("I'm going. Going")." The woman reached for my phrasebook, but I grabbed it back and zipped it furiously into a pannier. "*Tien, tien, tien,*" I snapped ferociously, hoping that the tone of my voice conveyed the screaming, "It's never about anything else!" I practically threw Greene back out onto the street and myself aboard. I hit the pedals hard, not looking back at all the astonished faces, self-righteous fury fueling my tired muscles.

But as the kilometers passed and late afternoon turned to early evening, I pictured myself—in a bulky helmet and inappropriately tight lycra pants, straddling my bicycle, asking if there was a hotel while the crowd stood there curiously debating my gender—and my outrage subsided into giggles. And as the distance between us increased, I slowly began to question my anger. I had been asking them to guide me to the beach. Why on earth would I expect that help for free? Why would I expect them to be so thrilled by my presence that they would want to shepherd my tourist activities? So that I could sit in a big-city café over a beer with other foreigners and describe how the villagers "wouldn't even let me pay them" because they were so charming, so exotic, so removed from the world (and I had found them— more points for me!), that they were generous and giving in spite of their poverty? The people of Highway 1, dirt floors and bare feet notwithstanding, were not the naïfs we wanted them to be.

Traveler bargaining, at least in the retelling, is usually self-congratulatory, prideful, and purportedly noble, argued in the name of what is right and fair. One night I would hear the Vietnamese side of the argument. In both China and Vietnam, as in many other countries, two-tiered pricing is institutionalized. Prices—especially for transportation, big-city lodging, and major tourist attractions—are officially different depending on your nationality. (It is a system that raises hackles among many western travelers, including myself, but that in looking back from a distance seems perfectly logical.) In China, the doubling or tripling of prices in out-of-the-way places, where such officially tiered pricing does not exist, had usually seemed like an experiment. In Vietnam there was often a conscious rationalization for it—not simply an interest in earning a few thousand extra *dong,* but a reasoned belief that I should pay more.

In the village of Lang Co, a fourteen-year-old waiter would present me and two Canadians with a bill charging 5,000 *dong* for a 2,000-*dong* plate of rice, 2,000 *dong* for the plate of greens that was always free, et cetera. We knew the "correct" prices, prices that were consistent all across the country as well as in every one of the many restaurants up and down that particular street. We adamantly rewrote the bill, then laid down that sum and got up to leave. The boy followed us down the street, yelling, "People in Vietnam have no job, you come here and you expect. . . . " He was not trying to cheat us. He saw that we knew exactly what he would charge his neighbor for the meal, and he believed that we should pay a higher price. And as we walked righteously away, I wondered whether he was truly wrong.

Nevertheless, not long before reaching Saigon, I would still be deeply offended when a restaurateur with whom I had spent an hour translating his menu and discussing how he could attract tourists proceeded to charge me double the standard prices for my meal. It was all of eighty cents extra, but I was obsessed by the offense for the rest of the day—hating Vietnam, hating what felt like a constant battle, me against them—until I recalled a scene that put the absurdity of it all into perspective.

In the lobby of the hotel in Hué, I watched a willowy blond German argue over her hotel bill. The receptionist wanted *dong* at 10,870 per dollar. The German insisted that that had been yesterday's bank rate, today it was 10,830. Back and forth they argued. The receptionist admitted she had not been to the bank that day, and the German said she would wait for her to go verify the new rate. The receptionist duly got on her bicycle, and returned twenty minutes later with confirmation of the lower figure. The German, triumphant in her rectitude, had spent forty-five minutes to save herself 800 *dong*—less than ten cents on a bill of twenty dollars. I wondered if she had *any* fun traveling.

Seventy kilometers south of Hué, the village of Lang Co straddles a narrow sandspit between the beautiful blues of lagoon and South China Sea, white cloud spilling over the mountain backdrop like dry ice from a stage-prop cauldron. The transition from north to south that had begun in Hué was underscored as I pedaled down Highway 1 under a flawless blue sky, the bright sun on my pale knees for the first time in six months. The charmingly ramshackle hotel in Lang Co seemed destined to be spiffed up: some day soon the little restaurant would no doubt have a well-laid terrace and a rack of picture postcards, the showers would spout hot water, and Coca-Cola umbrellas would shade the porches behind each room. But in March 1994 the porches were still bare, the water ran only cold, and the café tables tottered on uneven bricks.

The morning after I arrived, I went for a walk along the Pacific Ocean, bare feet curling in the sand. Lang Co was a tropical-island paradise. Women drew water from a well beneath the coconut palms. Happy children frolicked in the sand. The men set out at the break of dawn to reap the bounty of the sea, and returned laughing in the evening to share the riches with their families. Blink, look a little closer, and the worn faces told a righter truth about the hardships of a life in which each night's meal must be earned from a nature only slightly less capricious than the government. In the center of the village, the Catholic church rose solid and imposing above thatch-roof homes, and while a boy with eyes of cherubic peace let his little brothers tumble over him, rolling into the sand, laughing and squealing and getting up to do it all over again, I stared up at depictions of a very Caucasian Jesus and Mary and remembered a lilting little girl's voice telling me that Vietnamese could not be pretty.

A twenty-five-year-old tailor invited me into his nearby home. In a shadowy white plaster room beneath the gazes of his ancestors, whose portraits hung above a candle on the wall, he served tea and coffee on a rough wooden table piled with *Teach Yourself English* books. His father sat in a rocking chair gazing out through the vines overgrowing the window, seeing what? His long unused words of French were spoken in a voice from the past, and quiet pain pooled in eyes that had seen too much. But when his grandson pressed between his knees to watch the foreigner from a safe haven, he glanced down, and a certain peace seemed to settle behind the smoke of his pipe.

Walking back down the paradisaical beach just below the village was walking through the local toilet. Little castles of human feces littered the sand along the high-tide line. A ten-year-old boy caught sight of me and decided to teach his baby brother how to talk to tourists. He faced the toddler toward me and lifted the littler boy's tiny arm. "Hey you, pen," he called, summoning for me echoes of wet, gray mornings a decade earlier, when the urchins in Moscow still asked for ballpoint pens and bubble gum. "Hey you, pen," he instructed the baby too young still to speak much Vietnamese. "Hey you, pen. Pen, pen, pen," he yelled after me.

A little farther down the beach, a mob of children descended. Four, five, six years old, they were aggressive mites. Not gentle, not curious, they looked at me and did not see human. A boy with a wooden toy gun pointed at me and shot. I grabbed for the weapon, but I was big and awkward and he was easily too quick for me. The undercurrent of violence in the swarm swelled to the surface in their play. As if in a game of tag, they ran at me, swung, and skipped away, but it was not tagging, it was hitting. Again I wanted to retaliate, to hurt small children, to let loose a backhand against a little body, to crack a frail bone. One boy, a tiny thing I could have snapped in two, curled his baby's hands into fists, rage and hatred and defiance on his face as he boxed at me.

I crouched in the sand, bringing myself to eye level with them. They scattered briefly out of contact range, then braved their way slowly back in, pushing their friends in front of themselves. "Who taught you to hate me for the color of my skin?" I asked in words I knew they could not understand. "Who taught you to hate me for the color of my skin?" Couldn't I make them see that I was human, that I was not an alien to be tormented? It was unsettling for an upper middle-class white American girl to be on that side of racism, disturbing, especially, to see them indoctrinated so young to hate and disdain me for a body different from their own. One child pushed his friend too hard, and he collided face to face with me. They all scattered backward in fear of the blows they did not know I could never throw. I whirled up and away in my own rage and despair and silence.

By noon the sun had driven me under the shade of a café umbrella. A well-dressed middle-aged Vietnamese couple joined the group sitting at the next table. They glanced over at me. "Hello, where are you from?" the man asked in English. The greeting was standard. The accent was unusually good. He and his wife had been in Lang Co for several days. She had come to look for a particular shop, which she had found finally among the many that now fronted people's homes. Magazines hung by clothespins from a wire strung above a rickety, glass-windowed cabinet that displayed the usual assortment of pens, batteries, toothbrushes, lighters, playing cards, and other parapher-nalia. She had chatted with the elderly shop owner, unable to take her eyes off his lined face. She had told him about her life in California, asked about his life here. Finally she had no longer been able to refrain. "Don't you rec-ognize me? Me, Dad, it's me."

Thirteen years earlier, she had escaped. Now for the first time, she felt safe returning. She had not told her family that she was coming.

"What has changed the most?" I asked, looking at their stylish clothes, picturing them easily in an air-conditioned home in Southern California, trying to imagine her growing up in this village, fleeing it in a rickety boat.

"The economy," the husband, a successful Los Angeles real estate agent, responded immediately. "There is so much more here now."

The woman glanced across the table at her father, then at her little sister, a beautiful young woman sitting next to her fiancé. "She was five when I left."

Later that afternoon, as I sat reading on my porch, a lanky, disheveled blond head peered over from the neighboring balcony. He introduced himself as Dan and his girlfriend as Karin, both from Vancouver, Canada. As the sun dropped toward evening gentleness, we headed for one of the many open-air restaurants lining the street and the first of several dinners that wound their way through many bottles of beer on past the ten o'clock end of electricity.

Lazy days passed easily in Lang Co—rolling out of bed into the South China Sea for an invigorating swim before breakfast, reading or writing in the shade during the heat of the afternoon, taking long evening walks down the shore beneath Orion's bow and arrow. Immaculate white minivans pulled up the hotel drive and disgorged small groups of French tourists who walked down to the beach, snapped a few pictures, and skittered quickly back into the safety of their wheeled bubble. Two forty-year-old German men cycled up the drive with light loads and skinny tires on their shiny bikes. On a two-week holiday, they were speeding from Hanoi to Saigon at 150 kilometers per day. An American woman pulled in for lunch in a brand-new Toyota with a guide whose English was incomprehensible and who knew nothing about the places they visited. We told her to scrap her schedule and spend the night. She said wistfully that she would love to, then dutifully got back in the car and rolled off.

One night I woke to the *pop-shhhhh* of a bicycle tire deflating. "Absurd; tires don't just explode at 4:00 A.M.," I thought fuzzily as I crawled out from under the mosquito net, padded to where Greene was leaning against the wall, and pinched her rear tire between my fingers. It was completely flat. Barefoot in the dark, I suddenly imagined the gargantuan Southeast Asian insect with its colossal stinger able to puncture layers of thick rubber in a single jab. I scurried back to bed, tucked the mosquito net tightly under the mattress, and wished the pale geckoes hanging chirruping on the walls *bon appetit*.

In the morning, I remembered my silly dream about exploding tires and rubber-piercing insects, and glanced over at Greene. Her rear rim was sitting flat on the floor. There was no insect prick in the tube. The rubber at the base of the valve had simply worn and cracked and finally given. But when I settled on my porch to install the new tube, I was horrified to discover that my spares were skinny-tire tubes! The bicycle shop in Seattle had sold me the wrong size and I had been too stupid to double-check. I attempted repair with duct tape, but duct tape was not going to hold all the way to Saigon. Wondering if a skinny tube could not somehow be made to fit, I lay the slim snake of rubber inside the tire and started pumping. That I made it 8,000 kilometers across Asia on a bicycle remains a minor miracle, or sheer dumb luck. The tube looked too long and skinny, but as it filled and expanded and rounded, it turned out to be, in fact, exactly the correct size.

In many ways, southern Vietnam began not in Hué, but in Da Nang, forty kilometers south of Lang Co. "Hello-Okay-Number One," people yelled from passing vehicles as I struggled to the top of Hai Van Pass, which bounds out of the coastline and 500 meters up into the sky just south of Lang Co. It was a new phrase that would follow me over the mountain, downhill into Da Nang, and on, all the way to Saigon. In Da Nang, a city whose name resonates in American consciousness as the home of China Beach R&R, people's first guess was suddenly "American?" rather than *"Phap?"* or *"Lien xo?"* The *xich lo* drivers and Coca-Cola vendors spoke fluent, idiomatic English peppered with American slang. When asked where they had learned the language so well, the answer was inevitably a subdued, imprecise, "Before 1975." Their English was better than that of the local English teachers, but twenty years earlier they had been on the wrong side.

Unlike in Hanoi or Haiphong, there were abundant beggars in the streets. Little children carried their littler, pitiably quiet siblings and held out dirty, demanding hands. Already that much more sophisticated than the mites of Lang Co, who were still asking for a pen, in Da Nang the kids were trained to pepper every passing foreigner with "Hello you give me dollar." Men with deformed or missing limbs hobbled on crude crutches or pushed themselves along the sidewalks on rough skateboards. Ancient, leathered women reached out from under conical palm hats. Curled up in loose black pants and shirts, their chins resting on a knee, they looked like the Wicked Witch of the West, slowly melting in the sweltering humidity.

At the hotel, just as the receptionist told me there were "No single today—only double," a wispy young German walked up and also asked for a single. I glanced at him and asked if he wanted to share a room. At home, checking into a Motel 6 as I drove across the country, I would never invite a stranger to share a room. But traveling, especially in developing countries, there is an unreasoned, immediate trust and, of course, an all-consuming compunction to save those few dollars. Stefan was from Potsdam. He had studied Vietnamese at university in the days when his country's windows opened only to the east. He was happy to share a room. "All right," I told the shocked receptionist, "we'll take a double." Shaking her head, she pushed two keys across the counter and waved us away in disgust. I had just confirmed every stereotype she had about Western women's morality.

Tourists were plentiful in Da Nang, and with them came the ease of relative anonymity. Dinner at a guidebook-recommended restaurant with English menus faded into hours of repetitious tourist talk. Instead of "Hello, where are you from?" we greeted each other "Hello, going north or south?" The conversation that followed was as redundant as the Seven Questions, and I was hypocritically disdainful of these dialogues to which I was acutely drawn by the fellowship of my own kind.

A German at the next table offered me his deep-fried cuttlefish. He had not realized that cuttlefish was a type of squid. I suggested he offer it to the next beggar instead. Soon enough, one of the perpetual kids appeared out of the dark, standing in the street just behind the low restaurant wall. Gerhardt held out the plate and the little hands swept it clean in two fistfuls. *"Cam on* ("Thank you")*!"* the boy nodded sincerely and dashed off, one fist already shoveling the cuttlefish into his mouth. He was not starving, but watching him devour the food, it was clear that his begging was not a game. A child grateful for food quickly defeats cynicism. Seconds later another urchin materialized, pointing to his friend, barely visible again at the edge of light, and asking if there was any left for him. Gerhardt apologetically showed him the empty plate. Eyes darting warily, the child pointed to his bowl of crispy dried noodles. Gerhardt held it out just as the waiter appeared. The child whisked the bowl empty with a grateful nod and was gone into the night just ahead of the waiter's slap.

I stayed in Da Nang long enough to pick up mail, have a broken pannier zipper replaced, and extend my visa until mid-April. Then I headed another thirty kilometers south to the charming riverine town of Hoi An. Karin and Dan were just sitting down to a pineapple pancake breakfast when I arrived. After breakfast, the three of us wandered through Hoi An's enchanting streets. In the seventeenth and eighteenth centuries, then still known as Faifo, Hoi An was a major international port, home to merchant communities from Japan, China, Portugal, and the Netherlands. The town escaped serious damage during the American War and today reposes like a gentleman past his prime but happy in retirement.

At the market I ordered a lightweight top and a pair of loose pants more suited to the intense humidity than heavy cotton tee shirts and blue jeans, and more appropriate than shorts. Hot and sticky in the motionless air, we sank into wide wooden chairs and drank *nuoc chanh da,* rolling the cold glasses of iced lemonade across our sweaty legs and foreheads.

That night I spied another travel bicycle in the hotel courtyard, and went in search of its person. A blond Jesus-haired Swiss-German, he had cycled 17,000 kilometers from Switzerland to Turkey to Egypt, from Pakistan to India, from Malaysia to Vietnam, and was now aiming north to Russia, then back toward Switzerland. I suddenly felt like a schoolmarm on a day trip.

Karin and Dan and I rented mopeds and rode out to My Son, the intellectual and religious center of the Champa Kingdom for more than 700 years. A kingdom of seafaring merchants, the Cham civilization began developing in what is now central Vietnam as early as the first century A.D. Heavily influenced by their maritime contacts with India, they eventually adopted much of the Hindu religion as well as the Indian alphabet. The last five kilometers of the road to My Son were extremely rough, and I could barely control the heavy moped as it heaved over the ruts and stones. Its noise and weight and oily stench made me love Greene all over again. The road was still impassable to a minivan, so although intensive restoration work was under way, My Son retained the feel of a newly discovered jungle ruin.

The crumbling, overgrown temples and towers exuded stronger memories of their ancient life and worship than the more manicured complexes I knew from other countries. We followed footpaths through the long grasses and imagined for ourselves the walls and roofs that were now gone or tumbling apart, tried to imagine the lives that had once been lived among them. Before arriving in My Son, I had not known that there had once been a significant Indian influence here in the far eastern reaches of Asia. I had never heard of the Chams or their kingdom. I did not know that a millennium ago, there had been a full-blown culture in this place, a nation battling with the emergent Vietnamese culture to the north, to whom they would not succumb until late in the fifteenth century. All I knew was that the Viet Cong had hidden in the area, and the Americans had blown it to bits.

I almost didn't go to My Lai. Ninety kilometers south of Hoi An, twelve kilometers east of Highway 1, near the shores of the Pacific, four hamlets cluster together in the shady green landscape. Here, on the afternoon of March 16, 1968, American troops plunged into an orgy of rape, torture, and slaughter that left behind scores upon hundreds of Vietnamese corpses. I wasn't doing the War Tour, I told myself as I pedaled south, I didn't have to go. If I didn't stop I could catch up with Karin and Dan in Sa Huynh that night. We could have dinner and a beer and go swimming at sunrise. The official tributes at My Lai, I was sure, would be cold, overblown socialist realism and grossly simplistic propaganda, none of it touching the simple truths of individual terror and anguish. I did not want to go. Yet something compelled me to turn east off the highway.

A manicured alleyway lined with small, delicate statuary led to a weighty white monument depicting the dead, the wounded, and the morally triumphant. One woman cradles a crumpled grandfather, another huddles face down over a fallen body, and above them a mother, her infant's body drooping over one arm, raises a defiant, clenched fist at the sky. I had not felt so self-consciously and ashamedly American since the day I first crossed the border. What self-indulgent, prying, voyeuristic, dramatizing right did I have to come here and gawk?

Heels clicked on the flagstone behind me. A woman in her midforties, dressed in a neat red blazer and white blouse, greeted me in English. She showed me where to leave Greene and told me to take my time wandering the grounds before coming inside to visit the museum.

A gentle breeze wafted through the trees. The grass was long and bright green, the tranquil glen an excruciatingly serene contrast to the echoes of chaos and gunfire. The site was perfectly understated, prompting the imagination toward a reality that could not be grasped. Only the foundations of burned houses bore testimony to the senseless atrocities of one afternoon. In front of each foundation was an unadorned granite marker mutely inscribed with the names and ages of the family murdered in that home:

Do Thi Hiep	55 years old
Nguyen Thi Tuong	25 years old
Do Cu Bay	10 years old
Do Cu	4 years old
Pham Cu	1 year old

The amorphous sense of duty that had compelled me to turn off the highway had been powerful, but, oddly, not directly about the war. What it was about I would grasp only years later, walking the dog down a steep

Seattle street, past the neat flower gardens and pretty brick homes, trying to figure out how to write about that afternoon at My Lai.

My father's father took his family from Germany to Holland in 1936. Within a few years they fled again, eventually reaching the United States. Growing up in Southern California, my Germanness and my Jewishness were inextricably intertwined. The part of me that was German was the part of me that was Jewish; the part of me that was Jewish was German. The perception that German and Jewish were by definition polar opposites always troubled me. I could not accept the assumption that what was Jewish had to hate and fear what was German, nor that what was German necessarily wanted to kill what was Jewish.

My skills in French and Russian long ago surpassed my German vocabulary, but it is still only the language learned as a kindergartner in Munich that feels like a mother tongue. (Only the word *Jude* sends shivers up my spine.) I look German, my name is German, my accent in German a mishmash of regional dialects, but not necessarily foreign. I am at home in Germany. Except when I visit Dachau. At Dachau I am Jewish. Not American, and not German—those people wanted me dead. (The conflict that I want to deny does exist.)

At the same time, whenever I encountered guilt for the Holocaust among my teenage and twentysomething German peers, I was perplexed. I did not understand their shame for acts committed decades before their births. It was not, after all, their fault. Why then, standing alone in the fresh green grass of My Lai, did I feel so guilty? I was not yet three years old in March 1968. Why, staring into the ditch where Americans then younger than I was now had indiscriminately dumped and slaughtered more than 100 unarmed villagers did I feel that the shame was mine, the responsibility mine, mine the need to atone?

The woman in the red blazer found me again and showed me to the museum, where the subtlety did slip away into screeching propagandistic captions under grainy blowups of viciously graphic black-and-white photographs. She asked if I would sign the guestbook, then left me alone with a pen and the pages of comments. Many were from other young Americans reflecting the same nebulous shame I was experiencing, many from grateful and apologetic U.S. veterans. Yet the most frequent theme in the book did not refer to the war in Vietnam. The phrase that recurred over and over on the pages at My Lai, often inscribed with no additional comment, was "Never Again." In Dachau I am Jewish. At My Lai I was American.

CHAPTER 13

Tigers and Fireflies

I had always disdained tourists who claimed to hate a whole country. I disdained them for not having taken the time to explore, not having made the effort to find the truth beneath an unfriendly or abrasive surface. Dan said he swung back and forth between loving Vietnam and hating it, which made sense. But I had not loved Vietnam for more than a few scattered moments, and that was not enough. It was an odd, unpleasant sensation, hating a country, a people; traveling and hoping not for contact, but for quiet and solitude, hoping just to be left alone.

After arriving in Sa Huynh, seventy quick, flat kilometers south of My Lai, I had strolled down the beach from the hotel to the village, where flowered courtyards opened onto a maze of picturesque, sun-drenched sandy lanes. The children had materialized immediately. Mocking, poking, throwing things, the urchin mobs of Vietnam dehumanized me in ways I had never imagined. I did not have to stay another month, I thought as I fled back to the hotel, a run-down concrete resort where Karin and Dan were the only other guests. I could ride straight down the coast to Saigon and escape. Hundred-kilometer days were short by now; I could be there in a week. Except that I couldn't. I had wimped out, pedaling down Highway 1. What was the point of a bicycle if I just cruised the highway? I was slipping tangentially across the country, bouncing off its shell. I dreaded the thought of going "out there," as Karin put it over a dinner of fresh snapper that night, but I also knew that the country I had seen, the people I thought I disliked, were the country and the people of the highway. I needed to go inland.

Highway 1 was a healthy red ribbon on my map. Two ample orange routes wound from the coast up into the central highlands—one from Qui Nhon to Plei Ku and one from Ninh Hoa to Buon Me Thuot. An equally robust orange road connected the three highland cities running north from Buon Me Thuot through Plei Ku to Kon Tum, where it came to an abrupt end, attached to the coast by nothing but a dubious thread. This was the route I chose—an empty white line on the map from Duc Lam southwest to Kon Tum. The next morning I forced myself out onto the highway, backtracking north from Sa Huynh into a headwind. I had long since ceased believing in the existence of tailwinds. I imagined fierce, roly-poly Wind Gods with eyes of red and bodies of black laughing at the hapless foreign cyclist struggling into their western headwind, eastern headwind, southern headwind, northern headwind.

At thirty-three kilometers I found the turnoff, took a deep breath, told myself it would only be a few days, and swung off the pavement. Hamlets of palm-roofed mud homes dotted lush, green, suddenly silent hills. It was quiet. For the first time in forever, it was quiet. Scattered raindrops were falling as I rode into Ba To at three o'clock. I decided to stop. I was not here to compulsively tick off kilometers. I would stay and explore the village. A passing cyclist directed me into a government compound whose one-story buildings ringed three sides of a large courtyard.

It took almost two hours, an English teacher who barely spoke English, a policeman, and many, many cups of tea to check in. While the various officials took turns looking through my passport, I sat and answered the others' questions, all the while uncomfortably conscious of my tight cycling shorts and massive white legs. Every once in a while one of the men got up to chase off the crowd of children who had gathered at the edge of the porch, but they drifted back almost immediately, gone only as long as a wave sucked down the beach, and back as inevitably as the next breaker rolling up the sand. Eventually the men showed me to a room, where I quickly changed into my new pants and thongs, then set out to visit Ba To. Within an hour, I had locked myself back inside, prisoner of ten-year-olds.

Crashing through the market on my heels, the children left a lane of broken merchandise and knocked-over piles in their wake. Trailing their comet of destruction behind me, I somehow managed to purchase soap, bananas, and peanut brittle before a man appeared at my side and inquired gently where I was from. He was my height, but skinny, and so self-effacing that he seemed barely to exist, standing there beside me, a pool of stillness in the midst of the chaotic riot. He was a mirage of a person, a ghost, someone who had learned to disappear. His English was excellent. Under the screams of the swarming kids, I could not hear what it was he had done before 1975.

We left the market, and the children followed us out onto the main road. They were unrelenting, stepping adeptly on the backs of my thongs, taunting us with lewd gestures, pushing us into each other, then running between us like football players driving through the opposing line. Only a few of them were truly unbearable, and several, especially two girls in white straw hats, were genuinely eager to practice English. But by now I hated them all. They were wild critters, unfettered and out of control. Like worrying little animals, they attacked the outsize intruder, and no one reprimanded them. A returned exile who had not yet been granted full status in society, the ghost of a man beside me bore the mites' tyranny in silence.

He invited me to accompany him home for a glass of wine, but before we could turn down a nearby side street, several men abruptly called him aside. After a brief conversation, he waded back through the sea of children and, with his eyes averted into the middle distance somewhere, said, "Good-bye, maybe we see each other tonight, maybe I will come to hotel, nice to meet you." I glanced over his shoulder at the watching men and back at him, but there was nothing in his eyes. He had already disappeared. "Okay," I said, and he was gone down a side street and I never saw him again.

_____•

I had hoped to be on the road by 6:00 A.M. to escape the monster-children, but at 7:30 I was still sitting in the office surrounded by a dozen officials and one very nervous English teacher. He was describing the road to Kon Tum. "Very dangerous. Wild animals. Tigers. No houses. Montagnards with knives."

"That's why I want to leave early, to get to Kon Tum today," I stated ludicrously. Even on a good dirt road, I could not cover the 130 kilometers they said it was to Kon Tum, and 7:30 was hardly early to men who had been up since 5:00 A.M.

"When we go to Kon Tum, we go to Highway 1, then we go Highway 19 by Plei Ku," he told me.

"I will be very careful," I said pointlessly.

I was worried they would flat-out decree that I could not go. I was half-hoping they would flat-out decree that I could not go, forcing me back to the bland safety of the highway.

"You to make up your mind," he finally enunciated carefully, wiping his brow in nervous concentration, meaning, "I guess you've made up your mind."

"Yes," I said.

"Good luck," he shook his head in farewell.

I waved good-bye and pedaled off into a different country. It was wet and quiet. Every few kilometers, a stream crossed the road. Before long, a low house appeared in a cleared patch of green. I heard voices chattering,

"Tieng Duc, tieng Duc ("German, German")." A single man sorted himself out of the dozen people gathered near the split-bamboo fence. Glancing back uncertainly like a teenager pushed by his buddies to ask a girl to dance, he planted himself in the middle of the road, took a deep breath, and pronounced the words, *"Pause, bitte.* (Break, please")." I smiled and stopped. He squatted in the road, a look of intense concentration on his face. His friends giggled in the background.

"Wohin gehst du ("Where are you going")*?"* he produced to a new round of giggles. At least they laughed at each other, too.

"Nach Kon Tum ("To Kon tum")."

He was stuck again, searching for words. *"Mittagessen, bitte* ("Lunch, please")."

"Gerne ("Gladly")." I accepted the invitation, rolled Greene through the gate, pulled on pants over my shorts, and replaced my unwieldy shoes and socks with thongs. We squatted in the yard around a large ceramic jug nestled inside a wicker basket and sipped at home-brewed rice wine through long bamboo straws. Dung was thirty-six and had worked in East Germany for two years. A silvery watchband swung loosely below the turned-up cuff of a spotless white shirt. Full red lips and the stylish cut of his thick black hair gave him an air of gentle androgyny.

"Do you have a camera?" he asked.

"Yes, but it's broken." My batteries had died the minute I turned off Highway 1.

"Do you have film? I have a camera, but no film." He showed me an East German point-and-shoot into which I slipped two AA batteries and a roll of film.

People with features more angularly Indian than roundly East Asian gathered in the yard. They stood quietly watching—smiling and welcoming, not jeering. Cigarettes dangled from the men's fingers. One barefoot woman who stood barely as tall as my shoulder wore an orange shirt that no longer covered her protruding, pregnant belly. She and two other women in straight, knee-length black skirts laughed with a mixture of pleasure and incredulity when I pointed the camera at them. A girl no more than ten years old posed close to them, a black skirt and two necklaces her only clothing, a baby clinging to her bare back. An infant slept in a cloth sling knotted over his father's shoulder. The man's thickly veined hands clasped the child gently to his skinny body. Deep furrows dug through his forehead above sunken eyes, and the left side of his upper lip distended darkly with an untreated abscess.

A middle-aged woman, her hair combed into a neat bun, her light-blue shirt and black pants fresh and clean, was overseeing the cooking in the backyard. Several younger women rinsed dishes in red plastic basins while another tended the stove, a hollowed-out mud mound into which she pushed short bits of wood to keep the fire smoldering. Inside the one-room home, a candle glowed on an altar decorated with bananas, flowers, and bundles of joss sticks. Fried spring rolls, vegetables, fat, ground meat with blood, endless quantities of rice, and more homemade alcohol were being laid out on a blanket spread on the floor. Dung explained that the feast was in celebration of his son's second birthday. The kids romping outside were barefoot, dressed in filthy, oversized tee shirts or tangled shorts. The baby in Dung's lap wore a pristine white top spattered with Latin letters, a pair of bright yellow shorts that fit him perfectly, and a new pair of tennis shoes.

We gathered around the edges of the blanket, passing bowls, clicking chopsticks, raising toasts to friendship and the child's future. Someone had a tiny leopard-spotted kitten which they called *meo* ("cat"), although it resembled no domestic cat I had ever seen. They tried unsuccessfully to feed it small bits of overripe banana, but it just went on mewling plaintively in the palm of my hand. A man with distant, joyful eyes that seemed to live in a reality different from everyone else's spent the hours happily repeating my age and itinerary: "Twenty-eight-years old. Kon Tum—Plei Ku—Buon Me Thuot—Saigon." Each time I smiled back affirmatively, his crooked grin spread even wider, baring empty gums on top and an uneven collection of metal on the bottom as he nodded with vigorous pleasure at the successful communication. Eventually a dish of sweet, glutinous black rice brought the lavish repast to an end.

There was a gentleness in the eyes, a softness in the curiosity, an inclusive generosity in the laughter that took me in, not as an exotic oddity but as a fellow human being. The hellos were greetings, not barked grenades. The questions were questions, not mocking arrows. The afternoon reminded me of the long-ago evening in Tosontsengel. The poor, the oppressed and rejected, welcome and give and share so much more readily than those of us who have more, I thought as I took out a Seattle postcard and thanked them for "my best day in Vietnam." Riding north on Highway 1, I had already been fantasizing about the beaches at Nha Trang, where I expected to meet the coast again, 350 kilometers south of Sa Huynh. Now, as I headed back into the wet, green landscape, I was thinking that I didn't ever have to return to the highway. I could stay inland all the way to Saigon.

A wide river wound through the verdant mountain valley in a land-scape reminiscent of the Pacific Northwest, except that in the Pacific North-west the bridge would have been more than naked stone pillars. I heaved Greene onto one shoulder and balanced across the stony riverbed. Shades of Mongolia, except that now she was light enough to carry, and in the sweat-ing Vietnamese heat I did not bother to take off my shoes and socks. The road waved on over the hills past two low, thatch-roof buildings. Through the empty window-holes, I could see a blackboard propped on a chair and the figures of children in haphazard rows, three at each rough wooden table. No books, no paper, no pens.

I stopped to check my compass. North. I was supposed to be going southwest. And the map did not show the road to Kon Tum crossing a river. The scruffy children in tattered shirts, shorts, and bare feet were by now bunched outside the schoolhouse staring at me. A ponytailed woman and rangy man walked down to the road. "Yes, yes," the man confirmed in a deep, torn voice, "this is the way to Kon Tum." The children were quiet, laughing gently but not mocking, watching curiously but not attacking, their school day ended by my arrival. It was three o'clock. I was only twenty kilometers from Ba To. But reveling in the newfound friendly country, I accepted their invitation to spend the night.

Huong, the young woman with the ponytail, was twenty-four years old and shared the dirt-floored house next to the schoolhouse with her deaf-mute mother and an infant daughter who had been born at home only a month before. A few blackened pots hung from the wall above a tiny fire. Skinny branches stuck out between the three rocks that supported a heating kettle. As the ends burned, the branches were pushed farther in. In the second, larger and darker room, the baby's hammock stretched above a bed, and a large bag of rice slumped in the corner on the uneven earthen floor.

Huong's mother became my interpreter. When I struggled to under-stand what the others were asking, she tapped me on the shoulder and her mime was as comprehensible as perfect English. To ask if I had children, she swooshed both hands from her stomach down and out. The answer, Karin and Dan and I had agreed, was not "no," but "not yet." I had also given up admitting that I was not married. I had learned to say, "My husband doesn't like to travel by bicycle. He has to work. He will fly to Vietnam and meet me in Saigon." Suddenly I could not remember the word for "to fly." I mimed airplane, and Torn-Voice, who had not said so much as "hello" in English, immediately announced "helicopter." Huong's mother nodded, and mimed many machines flying overhead, mimed falling bombs, mimed the loss of her hearing. Torn-Voice pointed to her and said, "Vietnamese," then pointed to himself and said, "Montagnard."

With the term "montagnard," meaning simply "mountain-person," the French had lumped together the many distinct ethnic tribes of the Vietnamese highlands. In accession to the foreigners' limited vernacular, knowing that the colonists would not or could not learn to differentiate among them, the highlanders had learned to use the word themselves.

Then one of several women lingering at the doorway watching our conversation thumped herself on the chest and called out proudly, "Hré!" Although the Hré language was written down only in this century, the tribe's history dates back into the last millennium. Subjugated by the Cham in the eleventh century, the Hré spent much of their subsequent history caught between the appetites of the Cham, the Vietnamese, and the French, all the while struggling to maintain their own identity. Today they remain one of the most numerous tribes in the Vietnamese highlands. Traditionally animistic, believing that good and evil spirits inhabit both people and the natural world, the Hré are a primarily agricultural civilization, cultivating a wide variety of crops including tobacco, coconuts, manioc, and hemp in addition to their ancient staple, rice. The woman proudly proclaiming her heritage from the doorway wore a long skirt and a heavy, beaded necklace unlike anything I had seen along the coast.

Dinner for four adults that night consisted of two herring-sized fish, one tomato, and a huge pot of rice. Torn-Voice left after dinner, and Huong's mother made up the wide kitchen bench for me. For herself she strung a hammock across the room. Then she barred the wooden door shut, slicing her hand like a blade across her throat to explain that there were dangerous bandits out there, then carefully showing me how to unbar it in case I had to go out in the middle of the night—a single-handed swoosh between her legs.

When we got up the next morning, it was not actually raining, but the cloudy sky seemed to be considering its options. "The road twists up, up, up a mountain," Huong's mother explained, then repeated her cautions of the night before, slicing her hand across her throat to warn me of the vicious people ahead. Then, in fingers clearer than words, she added, "If the road is too hard, come back to us for the night."

Around the edge of a silent green valley, the mountains suddenly reared up like a green wall. Greene's gears were slipping again. Several teeth on the second chainwheel ring had worn down to ineffective bumps and did not match the grip of the new chain. The road was rocky, muddy, and steeper by the minute. We had left the river behind. I hiked, pushing her slowly into the thickening jungle, sweat dripping salty on my lips. I had not reset my odometer since leaving the highway. It read 57.6. My watch said 9:10 A.M. In the hour since leaving Huong's, I had gone three kilometers. The earth was red and gummy. The leaves were thick, flat, dripping platters. The walls of green trickled and chirped, clicked and twittered. It was like nowhere I had ever been before. Around a corner a small group of sinewy, dark-skinned men were laboriously felling huge trees. Their ink-black eyes watched me silently as I passed. A band of laborers worked their way down the mountain—two women bearing heavy loads on their backs, a half dozen men in ragged shorts and tattered shirts carrying nothing. "Where are you going?" one of the men asked.

"Kon Tum."

They nodded passively. I made no sense to them. But at least I seemed to be on the right road.

I looked down again. My watch still said 9:10 A.M. The odometer still said 57.6. The watch had stopped working; the odometer had not: time was passing, but the kilometers were not. The road was a dark tunnel through flora so deep and green that it was almost black, but by early afternoon it flattened out somewhat and I was able to ride several hundred meters at a time before a soaking muddy stretch had to be walked. It was a world in which seven or eight kilometers per hour felt like flying.

A white-water river tumbled down a gorge, bounding over red rock. Two hefty teenagers, a boom box in a bag slung across one of their shoulders, were resting beside a stream. A pop-music tape rasped loudly on dying batteries. I stopped to splash water on my face and neck, then we set off together, one of them gallantly pushing Greene up the next hill. The red mud was giving way to swirls of soggy, crunchy leaves that we kicked through like the drifts of childhood autumns. The jungle canopy was now allowing a few rays of sun to filter through.

A young Montagnard woman and her grandfather appeared in the road ahead of us. The sprightly old man, eyes sparkling with welcome, asked for my address. He would never write me a letter, but all across Vietnam, people collected addresses like autographs. Reaching into his pocket for a bit of paper, he dislodged a gleaming blade that fell to the ground and lay shining in the damp leaves. So it was true: the Montagnards did carry knives. He gave a shy, elfin laugh, then whisked the knife back into his pocket with an embarrassed shrug and a brilliant grin. I wrote my address on the bit of paper. He clasped my hand warmly and wished me well.

In Ba To they had said that Kon Tum was 130 kilometers away. At the birthday party lunch they had said it was between 150 and 200 kilometers. Torn-Voice had estimated that Kon Plong, the one town between the highway and Kon Tum, was only 15 kilometers away. A small valley opened up to one side of the road. The boys stopped and pointed across silent terraced rice paddies to the smudge of a village where they lived. They said Kon Plong was 60 kilometers away.

Not long after I said good-bye to the boys, the jungle suddenly ended and I found myself at the top of a pine-trimmed hill looking out over a tilled valley of fecund red basaltic soil. The road dropped down to a stream where a little hut stood surrounded by burnt-out campfires. Inside were three wide platform-beds and the smell of smoke. It was five-thirty, the roof was tight, and the beds were safely above the ground. On the other hand (trusting Torn-Voice's estimate more than the boys'), Kon Plong had to be somewhere just around the corner. I had no food left except a few of the dinky bananas I had bought in Ba To and a package of freeze-dried neapolitan ice cream that a friend had jokingly sent to me in Hanoi. I pushed on.

But Kon Plong did not appear around the next corner. Or the one after that. I was berating myself for passing up the shelter, grateful at least that I was out of the jungle, when the road dipped around a curve back into densely arbored forest. I knew nothing about jungle-camping. Having not used my tent since leaving Mongolia, I had sold it to Karin and Dan. Now I wished for it back—not so much for the roof, in spite of a mist so heavy that it was really a light drizzle, but for the floor. Too many things creep and crawl in the jungle. Back where there had been trucks to run over them, squished snake bodies had curled frequently across the road, and while I had grown up catching and playing with gopher snakes, I did not much want to share my sleeping bag with an unknown Vietnamese jungle serpent. I had some vague idea that sleeping on the jungle floor was a bad idea and wished I had a hammock, although at the moment both were moot points: thick undergrowth covered every inch of the hills.

Two figures appeared like ghosts ahead of me, a wizened couple with large baskets on their backs, he carrying their wood-cutting tools, she a transistor radio. Chattering softly in a language that was not Vietnamese, they watched me pedal past. At the next curve, I looked back and they were gone, melted soundlessly into the green tangle. That jungle lane felt more desolate than any space I had encountered in Mongolia. There were dwellings tucked deep into the leafy denseness where people could believably exist unseen, unknown, and unknowing of the world beyond the next valley.

Then, with the speed that increases as the equator approaches, the sun was gone and night was rushing down. The glowing tip of a cigarette sparked out of the deep twilight ahead of me. My stomach flip-flopped. I froze in my tracks and searched the dusk. There was no movement in the empty shadows. Another cigarette flashed farther down the road, then my eyes snapped toward a third burst of light, hanging in the air above my head. Fireflies. It wasn't ghosts. I was not going crazy. It was fireflies. But my stomach did not calm down. What had I gotten myself into? Were there unexploded bombs in these mountains? "I know I should have stayed in the rice-field shelter. I've learned my lesson. Please let me find a place for the night," I whispered to whatever spirits might be lurking nearby. Or I could just keep walking, I thought. It was wet, but not cold. I could just keep going.

But in the murky white moonlight of a misty jungle night, the spirits promptly presented me with a clear patch of grass scattered with long bare branches. Indulging in some fantasy about snakes not crawling over sticks, I dragged them into a rectangle. I opened my pocket knife and stuck it into the ground. The finger-long blade was not particularly sharp, and I had no idea what, exactly, I thought I might want to stab with it, but it seemed like one of those wise preparedness things that some experienced adventurer in a book would do. As I spread my mat and sleeping bag inside the rectangle of sticks, the Ba To English teacher's warning echoed in my head. At the time I had dismissed it as silly, but now I began to wonder. Were there tigers here?

It's funny about tigers. In broad daylight it sounds like a grand adventure to meet one in the jungle, but stranded in the moonlight facing a night in your sleeping bag on a patch of jungle grass, the fact that you don't really believe that there are tigers in the area is superseded by the notion that there could be just one or two, and you start to think that maybe they are not as cuddly as you had imagined and that your bicycle pump cum weapon would be scarce deterrent to a big cat looking for a midnight snack. Nevertheless I laid the pump on the ground next to the knife, all ready to beat the attacking beast around the head after having frozen it in the surprise glare of my feeble headlamp. At every sound I snapped on the little light to scan the milky darkness, but the beam just bounced back off the fog. I clicked it off and lay in the warm drizzle, the night above me punctuated by the unpredictable blink of fireflies. I closed my eyes and was amazed, the next time I opened them, to find the sun filtering through the mist. And no snakes in my sleeping bag.

⚓

I was sure I would find Kon Plong around the corner. But corner followed corner and no town appeared. A set of long-abandoned buildings crouched in a disappearing clearing. Houses balanced high on stilts along the base of a steep hill. Pine trees grew green out of the red earth. Large swaths of hillside bore the scars of centuries of slash-and-burn agriculture. The governmental push of recent years to turn the highland tribes toward sedentary farming was slowing the ancient practice, but had not yet brought it to a halt. A dark young peasant walking behind his water buffalo stared silently as I passed. Had he ever been to Hanoi? To Kon Tum? To the coast? We were not 100 kilometers from the sea. Had he ever seen it? Had he gone to school? Did he speak Vietnamese?

I ate the last of my bananas and continued to climb. The jungle was fading into dry plateau. I was moving slowly, needing food. A little stream crossed the road and I stopped to filter water and eat the freeze-dried ice-cream that no longer seemed like such a joke. A man in a reed hat and a girl in a calf-length straight black skirt passed me as I crouched beside the trickle of water. Their faces and woven clothing looked more Andean than Vietnamese. They slowed briefly, wordlessly, watching me, then continued solemnly on their way. They looked as if they could walk forever.

The whole previous day I had covered all of sixteen kilometers, but now the road was growing steadily broader and smoother, and when the first road marker I had seen since leaving Highway 1 said "Kon Tum 57 km," I felt as if I were already there. "Hey, hey, hey," a man sitting beneath a tree called out a few hours later, "Hello-Okay-Number One." I was back in the world. Late that afternoon I rolled along a wide, flat road down a mountain and into Kon Plong. Like a movie set for a western frontier town, or maybe even like the real thing, wooden plank houses stood a level above the street, wooden ramps climbing up to their front porches. I found a café and ordered *ca phe sua da* (iced coffee with milk). Several children snuck up to peer over my shoulder at my book and report back to their friends what they had seen. After a while, a man in his early thirties approached and introduced himself as Minh. He was a veterinarian, and spoke some English. I asked if there was a hotel in town. He shook his head, but added tentatively that I could sleep at his home. I hesitated, considering pushing straight on to Kon Tum.

"Are you fear?" Minh asked gently, wanting to know if I was scared to sleep in his home.

He was shy and completely unthreatening, and although I did have doubts about the propriety of sleeping in a house without another woman (his wife, he had said, was away in Kon Tum), I told him honestly that I was not afraid. I followed him down the street. His two small children peered around corners watching me as I hung up my wet sleeping bag, washed quickly in the backyard, and changed into a dry tee shirt. Minh and a friend prepared a little omelet and a pile of greens for dinner. A bottle of homemade herb alcohol stood open on the table.

People came to visit. Someone invited me to sing karaoke. Someone else wanted to take me on a moped tour of Kon Plong. A policeman came, glanced through my passport, and asked if I would visit his home and meet his wife. I declined all the invitations, wanting only to sit and read my book and go to bed early. Minh's cement-floored home was partitioned into several small rooms. In the back, the kitchen opened onto the yard. In the front, the living room looked out onto the street through barred windows with heavy shutters but no glass; in between, another small room was just big enough to hold the home's one bed, which the kids and I shared for the night while Minh slept on a hard, slatted bench in the front room, with no mosquito netting.

Over breakfast in the predawn light, he invited me to stay for a day or two. I shook my head and said I was leaving. I could feel his disappointment, yet when he repeated his gentle invitation, I heard myself snap angrily, "I *said* I'm leaving." I went to load Greene, and Minh sat down at his table with a pen and a single sheet of paper and began writing something.

Greene had taken me into parts of Asia inaccessible to tours and guidebooks, but the merit of travel is not in the simple seeing. It is in the time spent savoring and absorbing, it is in flowing with the unexpected adventure or invitation rather than trying to force the hours and days into the straight line of reaching a destination. This demands a great openness, an ability to live in the moment and to relinquish control over the minutes of one's day. To cope with the endless sensory intake, to respond unfettered by the assumptions and givens of one's western upbringing, requires a deep well of energy. And mine was gone.

The four days since leaving Highway 1 would remain my most vivid memories of two and a half months in Vietnam. The gentleness and smiles of the highlands had redeemed my cynicism about the grasping, slapping hands of the coast. But now I was tired. Gut-tired. Tired into my bones, into my very soul. Emotionally, mentally worn out. Minh's invitation to stay, his friend's invitation to a night of karaoke, the policeman's invitation to meet his wife were all invitations into precisely the Vietnam I had been looking for when I left the highway. They were the moments in between, the moments that make up the line on the map. I had found them, and I had no energy left to appreciate them. I was road-weary, and that weariness was expressing itself as unreasonable, frustrated impatience. In the moment that I snapped at Minh, I knew my trip was over.

When Greene was packed and I had carried her down to the street, Minh came out and handed me an envelope. Inside was the letter he had been writing. Two weeks later, a translator whose office was a battered wooden table in the middle of a busy Saigon sidewalk turned it into English for me.

> *Dear Ereka,*
>
> *If only we could speak your language it would have been easier for us to make ourselves understood. What a pity! Anyhow, knowing you're going to leave here and keep your tour going on, we are made bold to write these few words to say that we have been deeply impressed by your courtesy and sympathy; and we don't know what else to say than wish you "Bon Voyage" and good luck!*
>
> *We also avail of this opportunity to express to you our feelings. As you may have known that mostly Vietnameses are sort of "guest-loving people"; however like other human beings, among us there are a lot of persons who don't care how to behave themselves in good manner. We really hope you wouldn't mind this truth. You're not only a foreign tourist but a pretty woman. We should respect you and warmly welcome your presence among us.*
>
> *Good bye. May happiness be with everybody. Perhaps will we be able to meet again each other sometime in the future?*
>
> > *Best regards,*
> > *Nguyen Xuan Minh*

CHAPTER 14

The End

The road beyond Kon Plong wound through hot, dry plateau, vast and open under a wide cerulean sky. The jungle's wet, dense green was a memory of long ago. Sweat ran in rivulets down my back and dripped stinging into my eyes. Barefoot people with thick jet-black hair padded along the road, puffs of red dust exploding between their toes. My throat was drier than my three empty water bottles when Greene's tires bumped over a sharp gray line in the red earth and rolled onto pavement four kilometers north of Kon Tum.

The downtown market was a cornucopia of fruit and friendly-faced vendors. The cafés were full of men staring silently at karaoke videos smearing across a television screen. I sipped iced coffee to the strains of Karen Carpenter singing "I'm on Top of the World," and imagined stuffing Greene into a box and heading back to Russia—and for the first time found myself looking forward to it. Out of the corner of my eye I saw a man pass the café, do a double take, and stop. Chunkily built and probably in his mid-forties, he came in and sat down across from me. "How long have you been in Kon Tum?" A Kentucky drawl accented his excellent English, and his tone was oddly accusatory.

"Since yesterday."

"No," he shook his head. "I have been in Plei Ku for two days, visiting all the tourist hotels to invite travelers to come stay in our new Kon Tum Mini-Hotel. You were not there."

"That's right, I wasn't; I came from Duc Lam."

"From Duc Lam?" he laughed incredulously. "No, it is not possible, there is no road."

Two days later I rode south straight through Plei Ku, barely even glancing down the intersection where the highway plunged back toward the coast, and soon I was out of the city and back in the baking clarity of the plateau, pedaling down the hours, breathing the clean, dry heat deep into my lungs.

Two days after that, I left Greene in a hotel room in Buon Me Thuot and boarded a small bus for Ban Don, a village famed for its elephant hunters. A matrilineal tribe, the Mnong of Ban Don capture and domesticate the region's wild elephants. Crouched in the aisle of the bus, two young women seemed to sleep when they were not silently vomiting onto the floor. I dozed off too, and woke to the sound of laughter as several hands on my shoulder kept me from tipping off the seat into the aisle. Arriving in Ban Don, I realized I did not really know what I was looking for. Elephants, I guessed. But first, I was thirsty. I stepped into a restaurant and ordered an iced lemonade and lunch. The police arrived before the food. The skinny gray-brown officer wore a gray-green uniform and appeared with two young male interpreters in tow.

"There is elephant festival today. You pay five dollar."

An elephant walked down the street outside.

"Where is the festival?"

"Tomorrow. You stay here in ethnic minority people home. Two dollar."

"I have to go back to Buon Me Thuot today. I just want to visit the village."

"You must pay."

"But the festival is tomorrow."

"The festival is tonight at six o'clock and tomorrow."

"But it's only two o'clock and I just want to walk around the village. I will leave before six."

"You must pay."

"Just to walk around your village?"

"Yes. Five dollar."

I could have been patient. I could have kept smiling. I wasn't in the mood. "This is very bad," I said.

"Yes," agreed one of the young men placatingly, "it is the city council." More elephants walked by. The men pointed at them and mimed that I should take pictures.

"I can't," I snapped, "you will make me pay." I was now dangerously close to the point of no return. In the game of face, open anger is an irrevocable dead end. "Must I really go back to Buon Me Thuot?"

The policeman smiled a toothy, crooked smile and nodded.

"Is there a bus?"

"No bus."

"I must walk?" This was a stupid question. I knew perfectly well that I could hitch a ride, now or in several hours, but reasoned that they didn't

⌣· *Along the road out of Ban Don*

know I knew, and would not be willing to watch me *walk* off down the road.

"No," he said, "You can hire a car."

"You think all tourists are rich. I'm not. I travel by bicycle." We *are* all rich, of course, but sometimes Greene was my trump card.

He shrugged his shoulders, "No bus."

I stormed outside. Across the street, a crooked wooden sign was lettered in English: "Welcome to Ban Don." Pointing bitterly to the sign, I turned to the interpreter who had followed me. "No one is welcome here." I stopped. I thought I was being a savvy traveler. In fact, I was being an idiot. I wanted to visit the village. And for that matter an elephant festival, whatever that might be, could be fascinating, and what was five dollars?

I took a deep breath and determined to try again from square one. It was too late. The policeman smiled his broad smile, his eyes looking right through me, and said, "You can go home now." Who's bluffing, I wondered, he or I? Will I really walk away? Will he really let me go? I strode off down the dusty road. He didn't stop me. I didn't turn back. Mountains rose purple-black in the distance. Thatch-roof houses of dry brown grass rose out of the baking earth on stilts. Sweat dribbled down my back. A sluggish river cut through the parched red landscape. I peered enviously from the bridge at the people splashing in the water, bathing and washing clothes. Teenage girls in long uneven skirts and loose shirts, with baskets on their backs and babies in their arms, smiled shyly at me and darted away. The late after-noon sun stretched into thick liquid rays and everything glowed, bathed in the viscous broth of light. I trudged on.

⁓•

Two days later I was back on the shores of the Pacific Ocean. I rode into Nha Trang under a bright moon hanging low in a crystal-clear sky, and was on the beach before eight o'clock the next morning. Where Europeans take off their clothes and seek the sun, Vietnamese cover up in long sleeves and seek the shade. They prize light skin for the same reasons we prize a deep tan. Just as their paleness proves them above toil in the fields, our tans prove us wealthy enough to leisure on tennis courts and Caribbean beaches rather than labor in cramped fluorescent offices and noisy factories. A woman covered from wrist to ankle under the broad brim of her hat appeared at the foot of the towel where I lay in my bathing suit.

"Massage?" she asked.

"No, thank you."

"Massage. Very cheap." Her fingers ran down my calf, hinting at the muscles they could loosen.

"No, thank. . . . " I have often claimed that one day, when I am fabu-lously wealthy, I will hire a masseuse who will always be there, like a shadow, ready to knead pleasure into tense and knotted muscles. The previous day I had cycled for thirteen hours, dropping down from the highlands back through the twittering jungle to sea level, and now, in an automatic reac-tion to say no to all vendors, I was turning down an incredibly cheap massage on the beach. I rolled over. She knew what she was doing, releasing the strain of 183 kilometers into the heat and sand.

Afterward, I stretched my newly loose and invigorated muscles in the cool, clear salt water, diving through the waves and floating beyond them. From wandering vendors' baskets, I bought fresh fruit, sweet little breads, and *The Pelican Brief*. As the temperature climbed, I moved to the shade of an umbrella, where I sipped fresh coconut milk and read my book. When the milk was gone, the teenage waitress deftly split the coconut open with one swoop of her machete and handed me a spoon for the viscous young meat.

Ever since pedaling into Kon Tum, I had been eagerly imagining my triumphant arrival in Saigon, the attainment of a goal that had long been noth-ing more than an idea, the realization of an idea that had once been nothing more than a fantasy, a finger traced down a map. But the morning I woke up in Ca Na, 130 kilometers south of Nha Trang and only two days from Saigon, two days from the end of an eight-month, 8,000-kilometer-long journey, I was suddenly hesitant for it to be over.

I opened my eyes to an orange world. The sky above the distant mountains was an incandescent sunrise color that I would have laughed at on a postcard. I rolled over, and twenty minutes later it was daylight as if there had never been a night. For two days I lazed on my balcony or floated out into the crystal-clear water while wealthy women from Saigon dipped fully clothed into the shallows. They splashed and played in the rippling swells, then waded laughing back into the hot, dry sun, where their light clothes dried as quickly as their skin. I walked down the beach, a strip of sand that narrowed to a spit with lagoon on one side, ocean on the other, and the village across the channel between the two. But my body flinched with memories of the Lang Co and Ba To child mobs, and I let the channel stop me. I sat in the hot sand and watched boys in perfectly round basket-boats ferry people across the 100 meters of current.

Seven thousand eight hundred kilometers down; 200 to go.

South from Ca Na, the road ran through dry desert country. Sweat evaporated so quickly that I wasn't even damp as I pedaled into the hot headwind. A lonely complex of three restaurants sprang like an oasis beside the desolate road. These were not *com-pho* stands with two low tables and the family's beds in the kitchen. The tables and chairs were tall; the menu was in English; the entrance was decorated with flower beds and painted windmills. I ordered lemonade. The waiter brought me a can of Schweppes.

"No," I repeated, *"Nuoc chanh da."*

Puzzled, he brought me half a glass of lemon juice.

"Ice," I said, *"da,* like it's served everywhere."

Skeptically, he brought me a second glass, full of ice. I imagined the number of times he had served deliciously refreshing glasses of *nuoc chanh da,* only to have them sent back or left untouched by foreigners scared of the unfiltered water. As a minivanload of French tourists filed in and filled two large tables next to me, I wondered again, as I had more than once over the past eight months, whether the West was not sanitizing itself beyond survivability. The waiter brought the fish I had ordered, a plate of rice, and a fork. I asked for chopsticks and a bowl. I asked for the plate of raw, leafy greens and *nuoc mam* (fermented fish sauce) that are an inherent part of every meal and that I saw on the table of the Vietnamese patrons behind me. Just as I was finally ready to dig in, a Frenchman approached, pointed to the greens and warned, "You know, it's recommended not to eat that."

⌣· *A man and his dog in the Mekong Delta.*

I pedaled into Saigon on the afternoon of April 3, 1994. It was a city as redolent of American influence as Hanoi still was of the French. Billboards shouted out brand-name products. Young women wore chic jeans. Mopeds were quickly eclipsing the bicycle, raising the volume of life one more notch. It was a rambunctious, reckless city looking to the future. Where Hanoi was elegant, Saigon was energetic. Where Hanoi was genteel, Saigon reached out and grabbed you. Where Hanoi acknowledged the foreigner with reserved indifference, Saigon slapped you heartily on the back and expected you to laugh along. Where Hanoi's leafy suburban avenues sheltered Ho Chi Minh's patrician mausoleum, Saigon's teeming commercial thoroughfares led to the War Crimes Museum. Tee shirts, stamp collections, and helicopters made of Coca-Cola cans filled the tables of downtown sidewalk vendors. Mangoes, papayas, and countless bolts of bright weightless material crammed the market stalls alongside ballpoint pens, tennis shoes, and cigarette lighters. "Photocopy," "Coffee," "Conference Hall"—advertisements beckoned in English above women crouching on the sidewalk next to pots of clams and hard-boiled eggs.

I rode south to the Mekong Delta, but my trip was over, my energy gone, and I didn't stay long. It was a world where land was a mere interstice in the quintessence of water. Myriad boats plied the liquid green thoroughfares. Shallow skiffs ferried passengers from bank to bank, the oarsmen standing in the rear. Large boats served as floating stores, their shelves crammed with cigarettes and crackers. Boats of every size were nomadic homes for entire families. Dry-land homes lined the canals like suburban cul-de-sacs, boats bobbing at their rickety landings like cars parked in cracked driveways. Houses stood on stilts, laundry drying from their porch railings, altars sheltering in three-sided thatch huts open toward the water. Toilets were a hole in the wooden floor above the same current in which people fished and bathed and washed their vegetables.

On a brilliant rowboat tour into the watery byways, fruit was plucked right off the trees and plopped still warm into my mouth. I had no idea that there were so many fruits I had never known there were. Slimy yellow bubble-gum-flavored fruit slithered from my fingers into my mouth. Hollow pink fruit crunched sweetly between my teeth. Mounds of ripe green bananas threatened to sink whole boats under their weight. The oarswoman asked when I was returning to Saigon.

"Maybe tomorrow, maybe the next day. I have a bicycle, I can go whenever I want."

"A bicycle?" she shook her head. "Can Tho to Saigon by bicycle? It is 150 kilometers. It is too far."

The sun settled in a rich glow toward the horizon. A single skiff sliced rhythmically through the final undulating ribbon of sunset and disappeared back into the shadows of watery night. Sitting on my balcony in the soft April air, the pressing heat of day having left behind only the tingling of burned-beneath-the-tan skin, I watched the market wind down, and realized that barefoot brown children and women in conical hats no longer seemed exotic.

Back in Saigon, I meandered into the Municipal Theater across the traffic circle from Graham Greene's Hotel Continental. Two men were playing badminton on an empty stage. I sat in a back row staring into the light beyond the proscenium arch. I could not believe it was over. Soon Hong Kong, then Beijing, and finally Vladivostok, by plane and by train. Russia was as close to home as I could imagine: a place where I would look like everybody else, where I would be literate, where I would get up in the morning knowing that I would sleep in the same bed again that night, rather than pointing my tires down an unknown road toward a hallucinatory destination. I looked forward to the purposeful work of a rehearsal room, and knew already how I would miss the daily mystery around the next corner.

I wandered back into the sun. Children played on streets whizzing with traffic. Children sold fruit, lottery tickets, and postcards—children who spoke tourist English, but couldn't write their own names in Vietnamese. Children begged pathetically, then disdainfully refused food. Children begged with dignity and graciously accepted food. Children in neat white shirts, red neckerchiefs, and dark blue pants balanced leather bookbags on their handlebars, two or three to a bicycle, skinny legs pedaling, laughing— children growing up in a country finally not at war with anyone, or even with itself. I sat in a sidewalk café sipping an avocado shake, unable quite to believe where I was, or how I had gotten there. An eleven-year-old street vendor slipped into the chair beside me. He didn't talk me into buying a postcard, but he did convince me to let him take my bicycle for a ride. Stretched flat along Greene's top tube to reach the handlebars, his toes barely reaching one pedal at a time, he piloted her proudly and adeptly through the crowds.

Appendix: Metric Conversions

1 kilometer	0.6 mile
2 kilometers	1.2 miles
3 kilometers	1.9 miles
4 kilometers	2.5 miles
5 kilometers	3.1 miles
6 kilometers	3.7 miles
7 kilometers	4.3 miles
8 kilometers	5.0 miles
9 kilometers	5.6 miles
10 kilometers	6.2 miles
20 kilometers	12.4 miles
30 kilometers	18.6 miles
40 kilometers	24.9 miles
50 kilometers	31.0 miles
60 kilometers	37.3 miles
70 kilometers	43.5 miles
80 kilometers	49.7 miles
90 kilometers	56.0 miles
100 kilometers	62.0 miles
200 kilometers	124.3 miles
300 kilometers	186.4 miles
400 kilometers	248.6 miles
500 kilometers	310.7 miles
600 kilometers	372.8 miles
700 kilometers	434.9 miles
800 kilometers	497.1 miles
900 kilometers	559.3 miles
1,000 kilometers	621.4 miles
2,000 kilometers	1,242.8 miles
3,000 kilometers	1,864.2 miles
4,000 kilometers	2,485.6 miles
5,000 kilometers	3,107.0 miles
6,000 kilometers	3,728.4 miles
7,000 kilometers	4,349.8 miles
8,000 kilometers	4,971.2 miles
9,000 kilometers	5,592.6 miles
10,000 kilometers	6,214.0 miles
1 kilogram	2.2 pounds
1 centimeter	0.39 inch (5 cm = 2 inches)
1 meter	39.0 inches

Bibliography

Bawden, C. R. The Modern History of Mongolia. *New York: Routledge, Chapman & Hall, 1989.*

Conly, Shanti R., and Sharon L. Camp. China's Family Planning Program: Challenging the Myths. *Washington, DC: Population Crisis Committee, 1992.*

Major, John S. The Land and People of Mongolia. *New York: Harper & Row, 1990.*

Mole, Robert L. The Montagnards of South Vietnam, A Study of Nine Tribes. *Rutland, Vt., and Tokyo, Japan: Charles E. Tuttle Company, 1970.*

Népote, Jacques, and Xavier Guillaume. Vietnam. *Hong Kong: Odyssey Publications, 1999.*

Worden, Robert L., and Andrea Matles Savada, eds. Mongolia: A Country Study. *Washington, D.C.: Library of Congress Federal Research Division, 1991.*

Wu, Jingrong, ed. The Pinyin Chinese–English Dictionary. *Beijing and Hong Kong: The Commercial Press, Ltd., and New York: John Wiley and Sons, Inc., 1979.*

About the Author

Erika Warmbrunn now lives in New York City. Her translation of Chekhov's *The Seagull* was produced off-off-Broadway in 1999. On Broadway she has written and performed the live simultaneous translations for the Sovremennik Theater of Moscow's productions of *The Cherry Orchard, Three Sisters,* and *Into the Whirlwind*. As a stagehand she has worked on the Tony Award—winning productions of *Titanic, Cabaret,* and *Beauty and the Beast*. She misses her bicycle, Greene, who is still in Seattle.

THE MOUNTAINEERS, founded in 1906, is a nonprofit outdoor activity and conservation club, whose mission is "to explore, study, preserve, and enjoy the natural beauty of the outdoors. . . . " Based in Seattle, Washington, the club is now the third-largest such organization in the United States, with 15,000 members and five branches throughout Washington State.

The Mountaineers sponsors both classes and year-round outdoor activities in the Pacific Northwest, which include hiking, mountain climbing, ski-touring, snowshoeing, bicycling, camping, kayaking and canoeing, nature study, sailing, and adventure travel. The club's conservation division supports environmental causes through educational activities, sponsoring legislation, and presenting informational programs. All club activities are led by skilled, experienced volunteers, who are dedicated to promoting safe and responsible enjoyment and preservation of the outdoors.

If you would like to participate in these organized outdoor activities or the club's programs, consider a membership in The Mountaineers. For information and an application, write or call The Mountaineers, Club Headquarters, 300 Third Avenue West, Seattle, WA 98119; 206-284-6310.

The Mountaineers Books, an active, nonprofit publishing program of the club, produces guidebooks, instructional texts, historical works, natural history guides, and works on environmental conservation. All books produced by The Mountaineers Books fulfill the club's mission.

Send or call for our catalog of more than 450 outdoor titles:

The Mountaineers Books
1001 SW Klickitat Way, Suite 201
Seattle, WA 98134
800-553-4453
mbooks@mountaineers.org
www.mountaineersbooks.org

The Mountaineers Books is proud to be a corporate sponsor of Leave No Trace, whose mission is to promote and inspire responsible outdoor recreation through education, research, and partnerships. The Leave No Trace program is focused specifically on human-powered (non-motorized) recreation.

Leave No Trace strives to educate visitors about the nature of their recreational impacts, as well as offer techniques to prevent and minimize such impacts. Leave No Trace is best understood as an educational and ethical program, not as a set of rules and regulations. For more information, visit *www.LNT.org* or call 800-332-4100.

Other titles you may enjoy from The Mountaineers Books:

MILES FROM NOWHERE, A Round-the-World Bicycle Adventure, Barbara Savage
Funny, honest, poignant account of the Savages' 2-year, 23,000-mile, 25-country tour, filled with stories of their encounters with other cultures and the challenges they faced on their trip.

ESCAPE ROUTES, Further Adventure Writings of David Roberts, David Roberts
Collection of 21 compelling and insightful essays reflecting the adventures and challenges of David Roberts' life. From river-rafting in Ethiopia to climbing the Eiger, Roberts adventures span the globe.

ON TOP OF THE WORLD: Five Women Explorers in Tibet, Luree Miller
At the peak of the Victorian period, when women were bound by cumbersome clothing and strict Victorian morals, the five women profiled in this book burst forth to claim the adventurous life.

THE TOTEM POLE: And a Whole New Adventure, Paul Pritchard
The award-winning firsthand chronicle of Paul Pritchard's physical and emotional battle to recovery after a life-threatening head injury.

CHINA BY BIKE™: Taiwan, Hong Kong, China's East Coast, Roger Grigsby
Features six extended tours through northeastern, east-central, and southeastern China, and three through Taiwan and Hong Kong.

ADVENTURE TREKKING: A Handbook for Independent Travelers, Robert Strauss
First-hand advice on trekking, featuring overviews of the primary trekking regions of the world and the best treks in these locations.

FOOTPRINTS ON THE PEAKS: Mountaineering in China, Zhou Zheng and Liu Zhenkel
The first detailed, comprehensive history of mountaineering in China. Narrates many past and contemporary climbing triumphs and tragedies.

TREKKING IN NEPAL: A Traveler's Guide, 7th Edition, Stephen Bezruchka, M.D.
A recently updated and expanded guide to Nepal's most rewarding trekking routes, covering 21 major areas over all types of terrain, plus alternative and side trips.

BICYCLING COAST TO COAST: A Complete Route Guide— Virginia to Oregon, Donna Lynn Ikenberry
Based on Adventure Cycling Association's "Transamerica Bicycle Route," the tour is broken into 77 day trips running through ten states.

BICYCLING THE PACIFIC COAST: A Complete Route Guide, Canada to Mexico, 3rd Edition, Tom Kirkendall & Vicki Spring
The most detailed and professional guidebook for the 1,816.5-mile route —broken up into 35 day trips averaging 53 miles per day, with options to shorten and lengthen.

CYCLING THE GREAT DIVIDE: From Canada to Mexico on America's Premier Long-Distance Mountain Bike Route, Michael McCoy
The only guide to America's first long-distance, off-pavement bike route features information on segments or through-rides, including thorough route descriptions, maps, and more.